A NEW STRUCTURE
FOR NATIONAL
SECURITY POLICY
PLANNING

Significant Issues Series

Timely books presenting current CSIS research and analysis of interest to the academic, business, government, and policy communities.
Managing editor: Roberta L. Howard

～

The Center for Strategic and International Studies (CSIS), established in 1962, is a private, tax-exempt institution focusing on international public policy issues. Its research is nonpartisan and nonproprietary.

CSIS is dedicated to policy analysis and impact. It seeks to inform and shape selected policy decisions in government and the private sector to meet the increasingly complex and difficult global challenges that leaders will confront in the next century. It achieves this mission in three ways: by generating strategic analysis that is anticipatory and interdisciplinary; by convening policymakers and other influential parties to assess key issues; and by building structures for policy action.

CSIS does not take specific public policy positions. Accordingly, all views, positions, and conclusions expressed in this publication should be understood to be solely those of the authors.

The CSIS Press

Center for Strategic & International Studies
1800 K Street, NW
Washington, DC   20006
Telephone: (202) 887-0200
Fax: (202) 775-3199
E-mail: books@csis.org
Web site: http://www.csis.org/

A NEW STRUCTURE FOR NATIONAL SECURITY POLICY PLANNING

STEPHEN A. CAMBONE

WITH CONTRIBUTIONS BY

PATRICK J. GARRITY AND ALISTAIR J. K. SHEPHERD

THE CSIS PRESS

Center for Strategic
and International Studies
Washington, D.C.

Significant Issues Series, Volume XX, Number 3
© 1998 by The Center for Strategic and International Studies
Washington, DC 20006
Printed on recycled paper in the United States of America

00   99   98   3   2   1

Library of Congress Cataloging-in-Publication Data

Cambone, Stephen A.
  A new structure for national security policy planning / Stephen A.
Cambone.
      p.   cm. — (Significant issues series : ISSN 0736–7136, v. 20, no. 3)
  Includes index.
  ISBN 0-89206-345-9
  1. National security—United States—Decision making.   2. United
States—Defenses—Decision making.   3. Administrative agencies—United
States—Reorganization.   I. Title.   II. Series.
UA23.C2325   1998
355'.033073—dc21   98-37026
                                                                        CIP

ISSN 0736-7136

Cover design by Robert L. Wiser
  Archetype Press, Washington, D.C.

Contents

Preface

SINCE THE END OF THE COLD WAR there have been increasing calls for a new national security act, one that recognizes and is able to function effectively within a dramatically changed international security environment. The National Security Act of 1947 (NSA '47), the current grand design of U.S. national security, is now more than 50 years old. The key government departments and agencies that compose the national security structure, including the Department of Defense (DOD), the Joint Chiefs of Staff (JCS), the National Security Council (NSC), and the Central Intelligence Agency (CIA), are legacies of the act. NSA '47 responded to an international security environment dominated by a single, overarching threat and superbly marshaled the forces and energies necessary to confront it.

The security challenges the United States now faces have changed significantly and will likely continue to change. It is important that we now ask what, if any, institutional changes should be implemented to ensure that the United States is properly prepared for the twenty-first century. This book develops an intellectual and operational framework for national security policy planning. It is intended to serve as a practical guide to changes that can be made today as well as to foster further debate.

Fundamental alterations should not occur in advance of the consideration of several questions crucial to the understanding of national security requirements in the years ahead.

- What should be the focus of national security policy?

- How can the effectiveness of the national security organization be increased?

- What tools must be given to national leaders to maximize their abilities to formulate and execute national security policy?

- How can national security policy be brought back to the forefront of public interest?

Findings

The continuing grand debate on the organization of the national security structure has failed to develop a clear consensus on the answers to the preceding questions. It is possible, however, to identify two divergent schools of thought that have emerged within the foreign policy establishment. The assumptions that each brings to the debate are instructive as the United States seeks to reorganize capabilities.

The *issues* school focuses on global problems that impede the achievement of a fair international system based on the improvement of the quality of life of the world's population. Resolving these issues, its advocates maintain, will address the most obvious sources of human conflict and suffering.

The *interests* school sees national security from the perspective of national interests, with a focus on the minimization of risks to the United States as a sovereign state in the international system.

Recommendations

The reforms proposed are essentially an appeal to leadership, creating through a more agile and accountable organization the ability as well as the political and institutional imperative for the president to take the lead in forging a public consensus on security affairs.

The report's first major recommendation is the creation of a new institutional structure for U.S. national security: the National Security Directorate (NSD). The NSD would be charged with developing, planning, and executing policies and operations as assigned and directed by the president as NSD director. The NSD would be an organization within the Office of the President and would consist of five directorates: Crisis Management, Regional Affairs, Home Defense Affairs, Finance and Trade, and Science and Technology. This structure is designed to be flexible enough to accommodate either the interests perspective or the issues perspective and to address a variety of threats. It also would provide the president with a line-management capacity with respect to the highest executive priorities, which the president would assign to the directorates. The structure, having no bureaucratic life of its own, would operate only by direction of the president. Each directorate would be headed by a cabinet secretary in the capacity of a principal member of the NSD (PNSD). The PNSD would "chop" from the cabinet departments the personnel and resources needed to perform the assigned role and execute the mission.

The second major recommendation is to replace the position of national security adviser—the president's principal counsel on national security affairs. The national security adviser would become the deputy director of the NSD (DDNSD), a formal cabinet-level position. The choice of DDNSD would belong to the president, who may choose the vice president for that position. If the president chooses someone else, that candidate, like the PNSDs and the cabinet secretaries, would be subject to confirmation by the Senate, thereby preserving Congress's check on the executive branch. The confirmation process is meant to impose on the president, via the positions the nominees present, the obligation to articulate clearly and publicly the nature and object of presidential security policy. The nation's security policy would then be entrusted to a chain of command fully accountable constitutionally, in other words, accountable to the American people.

The third major recommendation is the establishment of a joint career path that would create a cadre of senior civil servants who could operate across department lines in both department as well as directorate capacities. The NSD directorates would thus have a joint staff, drawn from departments and agencies throughout the government, responsible for the development and execution of policy. This jointness would operate much like the system used by the JCS. No staff member could rise to the level of assistant secretary or deputy secretary without having served in more than one directorate.

Finally, the advisory role of the NSC would be replaced by a council of advisers. It would be composed of the director of central intelligence (DCI), the chairman of the Joint Chiefs of Staff (CJCS), and the PNSDs and would be convened whenever the president wanted its corporate advice; but it would have no executive functions. The DCI and CJCS would retain their independent positions as advisers to the president. The president also would have an invigorated cabinet under the direction of a secretary of the cabinet who would provide subcommittees to conduct the ordinary business of government that required the attention of the president. The NSD thus would be freed from the day-to-day management of affairs.

Acknowledgments

THIS REPORT could not have been completed without the assistance of a number of people. Of great help were the members of the project's steering committee: Dr. David M. Abshire, Dr. Zbigniew Brzezinski, Dr. Fred C. Iklé, Dr. Douglas M. Johnston Jr., Ambassador Max Kampelman, General Edward C. Meyer, USA (Ret.), Dr. Anthony A. Smith, Dr. Don M. Snider, and Dr. Harlan K. Ullman. An early working group primarily consisted of Mr. Larry DiRita, Dr. Daniel Gouré, Dr. Janne E. Nolan, Mr. Gardner Peckham, Mr. Will Tobey, and Mr. Peter Wilson. Helpful comments on the draft also were received from Mr. Gary Schmitt, Dr. Harold Brown, Dr. Paula Dobriansky, Dr. Carnes Lord, and Mr. David Ochmanek. Thanks also go to Dr. Marin Strmecki and the Smith Richardson Foundation for providing the funding for this study. Finally, this report depended on the efforts of CSIS Political-Military Studies staff members Mr. Christopher Szara, Ms. Lesley Young, Mr. Alistair J. K. Shepherd, Mr. John Kreul, and Mr. Joseph Cyrulik.

1

Introduction

THIS DISCUSSION AND THE RECOMMENDATIONS are the results of a study of the need to revise the National Security Act of 1947 (as amended) to reflect the changing nature of U.S. foreign and defense requirements and the changing character of the tools for meeting those requirements.

The premise of the study was that as the United States approached the end of the first post–Cold War decade it would be possible to identify an emerging consensus on both the requirements and the tools of foreign and defense policy. Although today the United States is approaching its national security with less urgency than during the post–World War II period, the seven or eight years that have gone by since the fall of the Berlin Wall and the collapse of the Union of Soviet Socialist Republics (USSR) should have been sufficient for a new consensus to have emerged and for new structures to be recommended.

Closer inspection reveals that a consensus has not yet emerged on these areas. Although there is agreement that what Americans did and how they did it in the past might be changed, little agreement has emerged on what to do and how to do it today, and much less in the future. Because this finding would render an effort to make dramatic changes in the structure and function of the national security apparatus highly contentious without necessarily accomplishing any meaningful objectives, the study has been refocused. Instead of a consensus, the discussion assumes that

- there are five general areas of interest or concern to be addressed by policymakers in the future,

- each area has been fundamentally affected by the changes that have occurred in the strategic environment, and

- each area will need to be addressed through the integration of government resources in a way that provides for both longer-term policy planning and near-real-time management of high-value operations.

The book therefore takes an organization and process approach to the question of revising the National Security Act of 1947 (NSA '47). That is, the proposed reforms do not rely on an agreement about what to do; instead they rely on a way of organizing the national security apparatus so that the interests or concerns that the president, Congress, and American people deem important in time, or that powers hostile to the U.S. challenge over time, can be addressed in a manner that preserves the accountability of the branches of government to each other and to the American people. As a result, no recommendation is made for a major overhaul of the National Security Act of 1947 (NSA '47).

In place of major structural changes to the security apparatus, the accountability and flexibility of national leaders to formulate and execute national security policy should be enhanced. At the current point in the post–Cold War era, this is judged a more compelling approach because the "what" of security policy may remain undefined or a matter of dispute for some time to come. Absent an ideologically driven threat to the nation's legitimacy and very existence, the political, economic, and military power and potential of the nation make it possible for quite different concepts of security to be proposed and, as the record of the past years suggests, acted on simultaneously by the government. The relatively benign security environment of recent years has made it possible for what James Madison in *The Federalist* called "the number of interests and sects"[1] to play themselves out. This is not a bad thing. As Madison pointed out, that very multiplicity—by which he meant not many separate factions populated by discrete constituencies but a desire by individual citizens to pursue multiple interests—both prevented the rise of illegitimate authority (one insufficiently representative of citizens' multiple interests) and assisted the development of a truly public policy (based on the self-interest of citizens, rightly understood).

As messy, time consuming, and inconstant as such democratic politics might be, Madison correctly warned that it was better than its alternative: a balkanized policy in which faction opposed faction and no basis for agreement existed. It seems, however, that on the matter of national security policy and strategy Americans may be confronting a balkanization of opinion. On one side we find those who argue that there are compelling issues of human rights, environmental degradation, resource scarcity, and so forth that ought to form the basis of the nation's security policy. On the other side are those who argue that the end of the Cold War did not alter the nature of man or of nations and states and, therefore, it is the nation's interests—defined in terms of military threats and access to labor, capital, and resources—that ought to animate policy. The argument between these factions has been raging for nearly a decade, with no resolution in sight.

The result is an unsurprising lack of consensus on security policy. In addressing this predicament, *The Federalist* advised that government could continue to function, and the debilitating effects of factionalism could be reduced, if the system of government was designed in a way that government officials would come to understand their roles less in terms of the faction to which they belonged than in terms of the obligations of their offices. *The Federalist* was addressing constitutional officers and offices, but the advice is equally valid for the organization of the administration of the government and especially so in the case of national security policy.

In no field is the good of the nation as a whole so evidently paramount as it is to those who hold high office in the country's foreign and defense establishments. And in none is the accountability to the citizenry more crucial. The Office of the President, and the positions of the president's relevant cabinet officers, are in possession of the necessary constitutional power to conduct the nation's security affairs. Officials in these posts have the obligation to use those offices to lead the citizens to see their interests less in terms of singular functional affiliations and more in the multiplicity of interests shared with fellow citizens.

This does not mean that national leaders should avoid debate—even rancorous debate—in favor of compromise. To the contrary, the nation's history suggests that precisely the opposite is called for in times of factional dispute. A public opinion divided against itself cannot provide the support leaders require to make prudential—which is to say, controversial—day-to-day policy decisions. Nor, when called upon, is a divided public likely to be able to render with clear mind and conscience the most solemn of judgments its sovereign capacity imposes on it—whether to wage war or to pursue peace.

The proposed reforms are intended to foster changes within the Office of the President would create the political necessity and the institutional imperative for a president to take the lead in transforming opinion on security affairs from its current balkanized state to one approaching a consensus. After this is achieved, the question of a major overhaul of the NSA '47 might be more easily and purposefully accomplished.

Chapter 1 lays out the positions of the two factions dominating the national security debate in the United States. Here they are identified as the *issues* faction and the *interests* faction. The positions are treated in both conceptual and practical terms. This discussion ends with a reflection on President Clinton's effort to address these two factions, not for the purpose of critiquing his handling of them or his security policy as a whole but to demonstrate the hold each has on U.S. national security policy.

The discussion then moves to the orientation of national security policy. It opens with a brief review of the Cold War for the purpose of establishing the unique character of that struggle in U.S. history. In support of this suggestion, the section continues with a an overview of U.S. security policy before World War II. That review concludes that, although security policy in the past had a number of different specific objectives, its hallmark had been a reliance on the moral authority, economic might, and prudential application of military power for its success. This conclusion serves as the springboard for a discussion of organizing to meet future challenges to U.S. security.

Before it turns to the suggested organization for the future, Chapter 4 reviews U.S. security policy organizations in the past. The review emphasizes the remarkable authority that the president has exercised in the formation and execution of policy. Preserving presidential authority in a new era and providing the president with flexibility to meet what are known will be difficult challenges presented in as yet unknown contingencies animate the proposed organization within the Office of the President.

Chapters 5, 6, and 7 present a proposed organization. That proposal calls for five directorates: crisis management, regional affairs, home defense affairs, finance and trade, and science and technology. Each directorate would be headed by a cabinet secretary who would be dual-hatted for the purpose, and each secretary would have a joint staff drawn from departments and agencies throughout the government. Each directorate would be responsible for the development of policy and the execution of operations critical to the implementation of that policy. The president would be the director of the proposed National Security Directorate (NSD), and its day-to-day operations would be directed by a deputy director who, like the cabinet secretaries, would be subject to Senate confirmation. To complement the NSD, the cabinet would be organized to provide subcommittees, to meet at the deputies level under the direction of a chief of staff, and to conduct the ordinary business of government that requires the attention of the president. The director of central intelligence (DCI) and the chairman of the Joint Chiefs of Staff (CJCS) would retain their independent positions as advisers to the president and, in addition, would sit with the five directorate heads as the president's Council of Advisers on those occasions the president wished to consider its corporate advice.

This organization would not invest the president with new powers, but it would strengthen presidential control over the planning and execution of security policy. The confirmable status of the principals and the statutory limits on staff assure opportunity for congressional oversight. The Council of Advisers would provide a forum for adjudication among the principals and the subcommittees of the cabinet as well as a mechanism for oversight of the administration of government. This combination provides the president a means of restoring energy to the administration of national security affairs while it assures presidential sensitivity to domestic requirements while meeting newly developing foreign circumstances. That is, the Council of Advisers identifies the president as accountable for the conduct of the nation's security affairs and provides the means for that presidential accountability vis-à-vis the

American people, the Congress, and the administration. Chapter 8 presents a critique of the reform, the implications of making the changes put forward in the critique, and a brief description of two alternative organizations.

Four separate appendixes provide additional background information. Appendix A, in a discussion of future challenges to U.S. security, offers an extended discussion of positions taken by the issues faction and the interests faction. Appendix B presents the evolution of the structure of U.S. national security decisionmaking. Appendix C contains the text of several presidential directives regarding national security organization. Appendix D is the National Security Act of 1947.

Chapters 2–9 endeavor to follow the guidance of *The Federalist.* Chapters 2–4 seek to understand the sources of faction in national security policy thinking, transitioning to a discussion of the way past presidents have acted and organized themselves for that purpose. Chapters 5–9 place responsibility for overcoming the factional differences in the body politic and for setting the national security agenda in the Office of the President. The proposed organization gives the chief executive the means to carry off that agenda while it guards against crisis and the advent of unexpected or premeditated threats to the public interest. Subordinates are entrusted with the authority and responsibility to accomplish their tasks. The supporting structure of the government is subtly altered to enhance the sense of responsibility felt by members of the staff of the various organizations. In this way the obligations and responsibilities associated with actually providing for the common good are meant to serve as a medium through which the officers of government judge the relative merits of the policy prescriptions offered by the two factions. Made accountable to all the people in their multiplicity of factions, the officers of government—if they wish to be and to be seen as successful—are obliged to bridge the differences that separate the two national security factions.

Note

1. James Madison [Publius, pseud.], No. 51, in *The Federalist* (New York, 1788).

2

The Factionalized State of National Security Thinking

THE ORIGIN OF THE FACTIONALIZATION of national security policy in the United States is a story deserving of its own study. What is of interest here is the documentation of the state of that factionalization. This is needed to establish two points: first, that at least two broad views of U.S. national security are currently contending for ascendancy in policymaking;[1] and second, that the likelihood is small that a consensus on which the national security organization might be remodeled will emerge out of these broad views.

Two Broad Views of National Security

No taxonomy of views is ever entirely satisfactory. Categories of analysis are often arbitrary. And, depending on context, the views of individuals or groups that can be categorized in one way might as easily have been categorized in another way.[2]

Nevertheless, categories are useful for ease of analysis and, with the foregoing disclaimer in mind, this study will suggest that contemporary views on national security can be grouped in two categories. The first is the view of national security animated by *issues*. The second is the view animated by *interests*. This is not to say that those in the first category do not see a national interest in dealing with the issues whose resolution they identify as critical to the nation or that those in the second do not list a set of issues that must be considered if the national interest is to be realized or protected. Rather, the terms are meant to reflect the point of departure or conceptual basis for the thinking represented in each category.

Issues-Based View

Those who concentrate on issues usually focus on the need to address problems that impede the achievement of an international system characterized by the international community's concern for the improvement of the world population's quality of life. If these issues are resolved, they contend, the most obvious sources of human conflict and suffering will have been addressed, the world as a whole made a more peaceful place, and individuals made more secure.

Most who hold this view do not believe in world government or abolition of the nation-state. Hence, proponents of the issues-based view still recognize that states, even as they work to resolve the issues that bedevil them, have particular or peculiar interests that can lead to conflict. That said, this faction's formulation of the issues inevitably requires greater and greater dependence on the international community for issue resolution and, therefore, the subordination of each state's particular and peculiar interests to the will of the international community. This implies, ultimately, a willingness to surrender a measure of national sovereignty, as that expression has been traditionally understood by the post-Westphalian nation-state.[3] In particular, it is argued that an individual nation's claims to legitimacy and differentiation, and therefore to the exercise of power within the international community, need to be interpreted through international law and norms, which have become increasingly less concerned with governing civilized conduct among nations and more concerned with protecting the rights of individuals against the power of the state.[4]

This discussion of the conceptual basis of the issues-based approach is essential for understanding the agenda of those who embrace its advance and the policy prescriptions they advocate. For the sake of convenience the agenda might be grouped as follows:

- *Sociopolitical issues:* religion, ethnicity, population growth and migration, transnational crime, human rights and humanitarian concerns;

- *Economic issues:* economic sources of conflict, including access to resources, environmental degradation, global markets, and capital flows;

- *Military–strategic issues:* weapons of mass destruction (WMD) proliferation, conventional arms races, rogue states, terrorism.

The issues grouped in each category are classified as threats or risks primarily because of their potential for upsetting the operation of the norms of international community. Hence, although religious association is recognized as a right, activities associated with it must be regulated by the international community to assure that they do not become disruptive of others' rights, religious or otherwise. A clean environment is not as much a necessity as a right belonging to all—the "global commons"—because pollution in one place can affect others elsewhere, and all eventually, and therefore production of goods and services can be regulated accordingly. Rogue states pose a danger to the international community—and are subject to intervention by it—not only because they possess WMD but because they are by definition unreconciled to the new international norms.

These sharp characterizations are not meant to create caricatures of the issues or those who promote them. On the contrary, they are meant to show the radical departure in international affairs they represent and the revolutionary impact they would have on national security policy if they were embraced. This is evident from a cursory examination of the way an issues-based agenda item might be analyzed and the prescriptions for policy that analysis would put forward.

The analysis of an issue ordinarily includes the description of the problem(s) in a particular state or region in terms of international norms, a demonstration of how the problem gives rise to conflict(s)—in progress or in prospect—with those norms or with other actors, a case for the global character of the problem(s) with respect to either cause or effect, and a prescription for action, usually multilateral or global in character—to ameliorate the cause and/or effect of the problem(s).

The policy response and actions called for can fall into two broad sets. One set addresses the problem directly through multilateral political, economic, or military interventions to restore order, lay a base for sustainable development, defuse a crisis, or protect the interventionists, whether they are public (government) or private (nongovernmental organization [NGO]) actors.[5] A second set is intended to address the underlying sources of concern and ordinarily entails convening international conventions to endorse a course of action or to create international norms and law. This is meant to reduce the rate at which the same problem might recur or to prevent new problems from emerging.

The composition of the solution sets will differ depending on the issue. Population and migration issues might be addressed through a multilateral military intervention under United Nations (UN) auspices, as in the case of Haiti, to stem the immediate problem. Simultaneous efforts would be taken via international agreements and institutions to provide economic aid to restore the economy. In the background, the world community would be urged to adopt and apply measures to control population growth, empower women and minorities, and provide for sustainable economic development, perhaps through international microgrants. To the extent that migration might be the result of natural environmental factors, there might be increased calls for enforcement and strengthening of the provisions of the Rio Treaty to cut carbon emissions (as at the Kyoto meeting in late 1997) or to halt the deterioration of the ozone layer.

The particulars associated with addressing the issues of nuclear proliferation would be different, but the approach roughly similar. International agreements would be sought to control the spread of nuclear weapons and regulate international nuclear industries. These would be supplemented with agreements limiting or banning other WMD. Proposals would be drafted to place the weapons in decreased states of readiness to be monitored by international inspectors. Agreements would be reached to permit international inspectors unimpeded access to suspect sites, irrespective of national laws. Reservations would be made for direct action against proliferators if they threatened the well-being of the international community.

This discussion is hardly meant to be comprehensive. It is meant only to be suggestive of the underlying concepts and approaches associated with an issues-based view of national security for the purpose of contrast with an interests-based view of national security.

Interests-Based View

Those who view security from the perspective of national interests are usually less concerned with the normative or legal authority of the international community. They are more interested in the construction of an international system in which the risks to the United States as a sovereign state can be managed in ways that result in an overall reduction in risk to the territory or people of the United States or at least that do not themselves contribute to an increase in risk. Proponents of this view believe that once the integrity and safety of the nation are secured, the United States, because of its inherent strength and power, could and in all probability would contribute to the development and maintenance of norms of behavior among states congenial to the principles and values that rest at the heart of the U.S. political system.[6]

But a lack of success in furthering these norms of behavior and, for some, even a lack of effort do not raise a question about the legitimacy of the American political system. The view of those with this perspective is that citizens exist in a nation and derive their political and civil rights from their sovereign status. International law reflects not the universal application of agreed norms irrespective of, or to enhance the quality of, national laws as much as it reflects the agreed code of conduct among civilized nations engaged with each other in international relations. Hence, national sovereignty remains of paramount concern. Although it may be delegated under specific conditions—to the UN Security Council, for example—it can never be alienated.

The stark differences between the two factions are apparent from the following categorization of interests-based concerns, which was provided by a group that rated interests in light of their relation to "the ability of the U.S. government to safeguard and enhance the well-being of Americans in a free and secure nation."[7]

- *Vital interests:* (strictly necessary...); these include preventing, deterring, and reducing the threat of a WMD attack on the United States, the rise of a hostile hegemon in Europe, and an unstable international economic and financial system;

- *Extremely important interests:* (if compromised would severely prejudice but not strictly imperil...); these include preventing, deterring, and reducing the threat of WMD use anywhere; preventing, deterring, and reducing regional WMD proliferation; encouraging peaceful dispute resolution; maintaining a technological edge in military capability; suppressing, containing, and combating terrorism;

- *Important interests:* (if compromised, they would have major negative consequences for...); these include discouraging massive human rights violations, promoting pluralism, promoting a reasonable international environmental agenda, reducing U.S. illegal alien and drug problems;

- *Less important interests:* (intrinsically desirable but that have no major effect on...); these include balancing trade deficits, preserving the territorial integrity or particular political constitution of other states, creating or maintaining democratic governance in other states.

The analysis of national interests by those holding this view frequently includes a review of the interests of other states as they might affect the U.S. interest; an assessment of the relative capability of the United States and other states to promote or defend that interest; consideration of the need for unilateral action by the United States—or by a multinational organization with the United States in the lead—in defense of that interest (with action defined in political, economic, or military terms, as appropriate); and maintenance of a web of bilateral and multilateral relationships designed to provide the United States the greatest flexibility in managing the risks it faces.

The approaches to securing these interests will vary depending on their rank. For vital interests, by definition almost no action or expense is ruled out. Throughout the Cold War the United States made it plain that were its vital interests in Europe or elsewhere threatened by hostile actions of the USSR, the United States was prepared to accept the consequences of war up to the level of global nuclear war. Nonetheless, the United States was willing to engage in arms control negotiations with the USSR and to agree on limiting nuclear arsenals. But this willingness was related to advancing the U.S. capacity to deliver on its deterrent promises and thereby reduce the risk of war; it was not motivated by an aversion to nuclear deterrence per se. Hence, in pursuit of Strategic Arms Limitation Talks or the modernization of its strategic offensive forces in the mid-1980s, the United States was relatively insensitive to the demands of other states—some allies, others not—that it adopt policies aimed at reducing the risk to those states should nuclear war occur. These demands included reducing U.S. force structure, agreeing to no-first-use pledges, and adopting nuclear disarmament as a guiding principle of policy.

For lower-level interests such as environmental concerns, proponents of this view would agree to international conventions only when they had been sufficiently hedged to provide the United States with the ability to protect its higher-order interest in maintaining the health and stability of the world's leading economy. Absent that health and stability, they argue, not only would Americans suffer but the engine of prosperity on which global progress depends would be throttled. This would lead to not only a global decline in living standards but also a reversion abroad to economic systems and political practices better left in the past. This determination to defend the national interest might be cited by some as the reason the Rio Treaty has not made a substantial dent in carbon emissions. That said, an interests-based view is not blind to the importance of managing environmental resources in ways that are beneficial to the nation and, by extension, to others. Hence, there was a commitment to the Rio Treaty, the Law of the Sea convention, and domestic efforts to curb pollution of land, air, and water.

No Common Ground?

The ascendancy of international norms and law as the source of rights for individuals and the conformity of their governments to those norms (if not the detailed application of international law) are of critical importance to the saliency of the issues-based approach to security. The story of this ascendancy is worthy, too, of its own extended treatment but is beyond the scope of this study. What is noteworthy here is that the appeal to these norms in particular has the effect of transferring obligations of nations from protecting and advancing the peculiar and singular rights and interests of their own citizens and to imposing on states the responsibility of enforcing these norms in the name of the international community or international civil society. In the context of the U.S. political tradition, the appeal to these norms—for example, in the position taken by the secretary of state at the July 1997 Asia-Pacific Economic Cooperation (APEC)–ASEAN Regional Forum (ARF) meeting with respect to the coup d'état of Hun Sen earlier that month in Cambodia— appears entirely consistent with the nation's commitment to those truths it holds to be "self-evident, that all men are created equal."

But the appearance is deceptive. Until quite recently the prevailing opinion in the United States was that the natural rights of man were the basis of the claim of citizens to be the sovereign authority with respect to their own government. That is, the basis of legitimacy for government and the justice accorded to law was based on the consent of the governed in the constitution and enforcement of the law. Within the U.S. tradition the defense of the nation and, by extension, its interests amounted to a defense of the natural rights of Americans and, by extension, the right of others to the selfsame claim of legitimacy, to found their regimes, and to operate their governments.[8] The consequence of this view is that sovereignty is the sine qua non of justice because the former is the expression of the right of consent by individual citizens in the creation and operation of the constitutional order charged with assuring the latter.

The notions that the rights enjoyed by Americans because they were Americans ought to be enjoyed by people everywhere and that the United States had an obligation to help those people attain and practice good government based on those rights gained currency at the turn of the century, gathered momentum during the middle stages of the Cold War, and burst forth in the enthusiasm surrounding the fall of the Berlin Wall.[9] As that evolution progressed, the concept of natural rights and the constitutional principles associated with them slowly but inexorably migrated from the principle of legitimacy for sovereign nations to a set of agreed norms that governs the state's administration of the affairs of those members of the international civil community who reside within its boundaries.

In contrast with the issues-based approach, the interests-based approach tends to emphasize the sovereignty of the state and the individual rights of citizens. Proponents of the Interests view fall easily into the older tradition of U.S. foreign policy epitomized by John Quincy Adams, who once declared that Americans are friends to liberty everywhere but obligated to defend only their own. This is often cited as a form of parochialism tending to isolationism and chauvinism. And so it can easily become. But Adams had a rather different thought in mind, born of his association with the nation's founders: the first concern in contemplating foreign adventures was not the good to be done abroad but the effect of the adventure at home and whether the peculiar and exceptional blessings of liberty enjoyed by Americans would be put at risk. The risk he worried most about was not defeat abroad; it was whether the policies required and consequences of the adventure would undermine the faith of the people at home. The point is made when the context—a debate on enlarging the Union—of Adams's oft-quoted sentiment is recalled. Adams worried that expansion would reinforce the hold slavery had on the nation by allowing for the creation of new slave states.

For those who today stand in opposition to an issues-based approach, the concern is not slavery but the status of the nation's sovereignty within the international community. It has its expression in opposition to such policy proposals as placing U.S. forces under UN command, or accepting the rulings of the International Court of Justice as binding in criminal cases, or permitting the inspection of U.S. private property by personnel empowered by international treaty without regard for the Fourth Amendment rights of U.S. citizens. For some who take this view there are undoubtedly elements of parochialism, isolationism, and political opportunism. But for most (who were once known as internationalists) the question turns not on an unwillingness to cooperate with others in the international system but on whether the United States does so with the aim of protecting its citizens at home or promoting the development of an international society. They repose no faith in the latter for the simple reason that it exists by definition independent of the sovereign authority of the American people. They continue to place their faith in the notion that a U.S. security policy rooted in the principles of the U.S. political tradition will not be hostile to the efforts of others to build a decent way of life for themselves and, on the whole, will drive Americans to be favorably disposed to assist them in the effort, which includes the waging of war.

Like Adams, who did not oppose expansion in principle but only how it was done, interests-based proponents do not oppose international cooperation or the participation of the United States in the likes of multinational and multilateral organizations. The key is the terms on which that participation is based.[10] In the U.S. political tradition sovereignty is not alienable although authority to act without consulting the sovereign authority may be delegated for specific purposes. Likewise, those who take an interests-based view are prepared to empower the organs of the UN, NATO, and even some NGOs to operate autonomously within a specified area of activity but no more. This demand that sovereignty be reserved to the state is directly in opposition to the conceptual basis of the issues-based faction. That is, international relations are conducted by states, not peoples; the objective of security policy is the promotion of U.S. interest, not the development of international community.

Practical Consequences of Conceptual Difference

The conceptual differences that separate the two factions are not rooted entirely in theories about rights and sovereignty, law and justice. The substantial changes that have occurred in the international environment, the changing character of the domestic and international economy, and the concerns of citizens in many countries whose increased wealth permits them to give attention to others' quality of life have led to a reassessment of security policy in the United States, among its allies, and even among some of its erstwhile adversaries. But even among practical men and women there is little agreement to be found on what to do in response to these evident changes.

The difficulty of coming to grips with the contemporary security environment was expressed by Henry Kissinger in two interventions he made at a 1991 conference that examined the new world order:

> So, we are living in two worlds. The more traditional one which needs a new definition of equilibrium which takes into adequate account the lower importance of weapons, conventional or nuclear. The other, a world that takes into account the genuinely universal problems—environment, population, development—I suppose those are genuinely universal problems. The challenge to our society seems to me to be to run these two world orders side by side and not to neglect the fact that there is a need for some new concept of equilibrium....
>
> I believe that as in all revolutionary situations the old coexists with the new. One of the problems is that the old, the traditional concept of balance of power is also in a massive change.... But for this we have tools of understanding. Then there are the problems which are truly global as mentioned earlier (the nexus of population explosion, the global warming, the deterioration of the environment, the energy question). Once you recognize them as problems, they can only be dealt with on a global basis with a number of caveats.... There are two new orders emerging; a new old order and a new order. The problem with the new order is fairly well exemplified by somebody like myself—I can be tremendously impressed by what I heard and I can feel something ought to be done, but I don't have any precise idea of what to do.[11]

Kissinger's comments highlight two reasons why practitioners as well as theorists have difficulty reaching consensus on the content and direction of national security strategy. Taking them in reverse order, the reasons are that proponents of an issues-based approach have not yet provided a "tool set" that is obviously appropriate to resolving the issues they identify. The second is a lingering doubt, at least among the interests faction, about the global character of the issues that have been identified.

The development of a tool set is hampered by the sheer magnitude of the issues brought forward for resolution. Famine, migration, drought, pollution, overpopulation, and disease, for example, have been the lot of mankind from time immemorial. Few solutions for them have been found in the past and the presumption that they can or will be found in the present or future is difficult to affirm. But even in cases where the specific problem is sufficiently contained to attempt a meaningful effort to ameliorate it, the size and complexity of the task immediately raises questions of return on investment. And in cases where investments are made, the returns more often than not prove to be less than hoped for.

Hence, the issues faction has a difficult task in persuading the nation to embrace its agenda with enthusiasm and provide the requisite effort—peacekeeping forces for Somalia, strict legislation in conformity with international agreements on pollution control, foreign aid for reconstruction in Bosnia, and so forth. It may be fair to say that because the tools have not been provided, the issues faction has not had a reasonable opportunity to develop both the policy successes and public support it deserves. But it is equally the case that the public campaign to develop policies and support—waged by proponents in opposition to an interests-based approach—has contributed to the confusion in the public mind over what the actual interests of the nation are.

The argument over tools, however, may not be as critical as the still unproved case that the issues being presented are global in character, threatening to U.S. citizens, and of a nature that demands a reorientation of U.S. concepts about both national security and the strategy for resolving them. Kissinger's aside—"I suppose those are genuinely universal problems"—captures this problem. Those wishing to make the case face two challenges: to prove, first, that the issues they put forward have the global consequences they adduce and, second, that only global responses are adequate to address those consequences.

With respect to the first challenge, the issues faction continues to defend its own overly alarmist public presentations of the issues and the often weak historical and even weaker scientific bases for its claims. Paul and Anne Ehrlich have advised that proponents of an issues-based agenda need to present their concerns in a manner more likely to receive public support.[12] The historical and scientific bases for the claims of the issues faction have proved susceptible to criticism in public debate. Although this criticism has not proved fatal to the arguments of the adherents of the issues-based faction, it has left them in the uncomfortable position of defending themselves rather than in the far more preferable position of setting the nation's security agenda.[13]

Although there is a debate over both the magnitude and the immediacy of the new security threats to the nation's well-being, the more daunting challenge for the issues faction is persuading the public at large that addressing these new threats requires a subordination of the nation's sovereignty to multinational organizations like the UN or its accredited agencies and organizations or, in cases where military action is contemplated or undertaken, to collective security organizations. The reasons offered by the issues faction for subordinating sovereignty run from the practical—no single state possesses the resources to do what is in its own interests and those of others in a given crisis—to the highly political/legal/theoretical— the use of force except for direct self-defense is legitimate only if undertaken in accordance with, or under a mandate provided by, the UN in the name of the international community. On this latter point some will argue that even unilateral or collective self-defense can be suspect if its conduct complicates or impedes the functioning of an agency like the UN:

> When the collective security system is functioning smoothly under Chapter VII of the [UN] Charter, a unilateral or even multilateral exercise of the right of self-defense would disrupt procedural steps being taken in the Security Council to resolve the crisis, and such action would contradict the purpose of collective security. That purpose is for the right of collective self-defense to be executed through the Security Council until, we would argue, that body reaches deadlock and can no longer responsibly manage the crisis.[14]

Those who have held this view on the use of force—either in terms of constraining its use or mandating its use on behalf of the international community—have found little support for it in the course of the nation's painful experiences in Somalia, Haiti, and Bosnia and in U.S. reluctance to involve itself in Algeria, Rwanda, and Zaire. Indeed, so spirited was the response against the issues faction's underlying concepts on the use of force that Congress sought legislation prohibiting U.S. forces from serving under foreign commanders in the belief that this would prevent U.S. forces from being assigned to peacekeeping and peace-enforcement operations. This was intended not only to protect U.S. forces from dangers over which they had no control but also to end or severely curtail such operations once the international community came to understand that U.S. forces would not be at its disposal.

The issues faction has had greater success with the more practical kind of multilateral efforts such as humanitarian relief operations; the development of conventions aimed at improving the environment, slowing population growth, defending the rights of women and children, and outlawing nuclear proliferation; and the development, stockpiling, and use of chemical weapons. Even so, that success has been measured more in terms of a general agreement that such issues should be addressed than in the means or measures that should be used. Significant domestic resistance to new Environmental Protection Agency regulations, use of federal funds for family planning by international agencies, granting of asylum to women subjected to tribal rites, nuclear disarmament, and intrusive monitoring and inspections regimes continues to persist.

If the issues faction has a difficult time persuading the public of the necessity of acting on the problems it has identified, the interests faction has an equally difficult time persuading the public that the threats posed to the nation warrant the policies and tools they recommend. With the defeat of the USSR in the Cold War and with the capabilities of China undeveloped and its intentions as yet unknown, the state-oriented interests faction has not persuaded the public that one state, or several, with the means and dedication to do the United States grievous harm actually exists. Abroad it is easier for the public to point to potential trouble spots and state actors—for example, Taiwan, Iran, and Syria—but these do not strike U.S. citizens as critical threats to U.S. interests of the sort that require the adoption of the policies advanced by the interests faction.

Calls for the United States to adopt policies of benevolent global hegemony, equilibrium, or selective engagement have so far failed to win wide support. Proposals to extend the Bush-era policy approach of competent management of the nation's affairs excite the public today no more than they did when these proposals were actual policy. The reasons for the lack of interest in interests-based policies are not settled. Two, nevertheless, seem to stand out. The first is the cost of such policies. The second is almost a paradox: The interest the public most ardently seeks to advance is its own, at home.

The cost of maintaining a military equal to the tasks identified by the interests faction exceeds what is currently being appropriated to the military. This is not because the interests faction seeks to be excessively active in the use of the military. For the most part this faction believes that the power of U.S. forces is adequate for deterring reasonable states from challenging U.S. interests and that the United States should avoid using the military to deliver social services to "failed states." The object of the military is to wage war, not to conduct peace operations, the most ardent members of the interests faction argue.

Maintaining a first-class force in an age of technological revolution is expensive. The immediate sources of the high cost of the military are that the military must act in concert with the Weinberger-Powell doctrine of overwhelming force while it maintains a worldwide presence staffed with an all-volunteer force that is expected to sustain only very low casualties when that force is engaged. It is especially expensive when allies are thought to be unable or unwilling to share the burdens of preserving peace and deterring and fighting war.

But war against whom? If the reasonable are deterred and the unfortunate are outside the scope of interest, for what is the military maintained? In response to this question the interests faction confronts the same difficulty as the issues faction—that the real threats lie in the future.

The interests faction identifies as future threats a resurgent Russia, a rising China, an ambitious India, or a smaller state able to pose an asymmetric threat to U.S. forces. But critics contend that these threats, like the risks raised by the issues faction, are not inevitable. Wise policy, it is said, can reduce the probability of such threats; and if they cannot be obviated, wise policy can reduce their magnitude. Most telling, however, is the argument that even if such wise policy is not forthcoming, the magnitude of the effort required to pose a credible threat to the United States amounts to an unmistakable strategic warning. This warning, in turn, would allow plenty of time for the United States to respond.

In addition to its lack of clarity about who it sees challenging U.S. interests in a way that would lead to war, the interests faction has also had difficulty convincing the public that the same policy instruments used during the Cold War to bring down the nation's enemy will not suffice to prevent the rise of new enemies. Deterrence, arms control, forward presence, and free trade are still hallmarks of U.S. policy and are on the whole supported by the issues faction. Although it is true the issues faction would reorient these elements of policy to provide smaller forces, address the residual stocks of weapons, rely on bases instead of permanent deployments, and include provisions for worker's rights, issues proponents argue this reorientation is dictated by the new environment and is not an abandonment of U.S. interests. In reply, the interests faction finds itself trying—without much success—to overcome the characterization of its opposition to the details of these policies as its support for large offensive nuclear stockpiles, the deployment of hundreds of thousands of U.S. military personnel in lieu of local forces, and the continuation of foreign sweatshops that exploit the labor of children and women.

The unhappy rhetorical position of the interests faction can be explained, in part, by the lack of consensus even within its own ranks on the priority of interests to be addressed and the means most appropriate to the stated ends. That said, its failure to excite the public is due less to the interests faction's rhetorical failing than to the second reason offered above—the absorption of the public in its own affairs. Now, after its sacrifice for victory in the Cold War and without a clear, present danger to its well-being, the public seems to have turned to repairing its domestic circumstances. Worries about poor schools and schooling, deteriorating roads and bridges, crime, drugs, and jobs seem to dominate the public mind. This does not represent isolationism. The McGovern-like calls of Representative Richard Gephardt (D-Mo.) and the demand for self-alienation by Pat Buchanan have found little resonance in the public. What the public seems to want most is a restoration of its confidence in the country: good management of the nation's economy, security in the streets, a reasonable expectation of employment, and a relatively comfortable retirement.

This is a tall order indeed. And the government, Congress and executive alike, has committed itself to filling it. The politics of the 1990s suggests that it has been a full-time preoccupation. The public threw itself into the effort immediately following the fall of the Berlin Wall, refusing to pause for even a small celebration of its Cold War victory. President George Bush was dismissed, ending 12 years of Republican administration. Two years later the Congress was taken over by a Republican majority for the first time in more than 40 years. In 1996 President Clinton was reelected, the first Democratic president since Roosevelt to be elected to more than one term. And despite Clinton's historic achievement, the Republicans held the Congress in 1996, itself a historic achievement. At the same time the public withstood a downsizing of industrial and corporate jobs, a recession, tax increases, slow economic growth, and a nearly imperceptible rise in disposable income. In return it demanded a more vigorous attack on the trade and budget deficits and a low inflation rate.

Without ascribing cause and effect to the result, the country stands on the verge of the new decade with an economy growing at a moderate rate, low inflation, a budget-deficit reduction under way (and a surplus promised), and trade deficits that seem less compelling. Whether this is a temporary condition, as some would argue, is of some importance to the interests faction. If it is temporary and the economy falters, the likelihood of the public redirecting its attention to foreign and defense policy—assuming no radical change in the international environment—is small. If it is not a temporary condition, at least the resources—if not the public's willingness to appropriate them—for an interests-based approach to policy will be available.

The same would seem to be true for the issues faction—prosperity at home would make resources available for activity abroad. But, like the interests faction, it too faces the difficulty of persuading public opinion. For both factions, then, the challenge remains to persuade opinion; but, barring catastrophe for the nation abroad, their efforts are unlikely to result in a deep consensus on security policy.

President Clinton has attempted to meld the concerns of the issues and interests factions into a national security policy that would command majority support, if not serve as the basis for a national consensus. From the beginning he has made it clear that his administration would take an issues-based approach when such an approach was called for. In his inaugural address the president cited the will of the international community as a new standard of conduct for the United States and, by extension, for other states. In his policies of muscular multilateralism, engagement and enlargement, and cooperative threat reduction; in his decision to create an under secretary of state for global affairs; in his insistence that the State Department take on environmental issues as a key element of its approach to other nations; in his determination to favor multilateral and multinational approaches to problem solving; and in reserving the right to act unilaterally "only when we must," the president has done more than any individual to embed the issues-based approach in U.S. security policy.[15] So insistent has he been on this point that his foreign policy has been characterized by a leading foreign affairs expert as "international social work."[16]

Nevertheless, the president has not been able to move too far from an interests-based approach to security policy. There is no better illustration of this point than the speech by President Clinton announcing his decision to commit U.S. forces to Bosnia under the peace implementation forces (IFOR). The introductory arguments and concluding phrases appealed to the issues faction, highlighting the humanitarian nature of the problem, the need to meet the security challenges of the breakup of Yugoslavia, and the importance of the United States assuming its position in the multinational effort. But at bottom most opinion was persuaded by the president's simple observation that what was at stake was the viability of the NATO alliance and continued peace—the traditional kind—among the states of central Europe. This appeal to a classic interest of the United States was complemented in the Dayton Accords process by what can only be described as a demonstration of a sense of realpolitik that would make even the most ardent member of the interests faction blush.

The same approach was on display during consideration of NATO enlargement. Casting the policy in issues terms—peace and prosperity, political reform, and so forth—when the time came to decide which states would be extended invitations and the terms on which the ratification debate in the U.S. Senate was to be conducted, the president chose a policy more obviously associated with the interests faction than the issues faction.

The same approach can be discerned in the administration's dealings with Russia and China. Reform and the promotion of democracy have been at the core of the administration's issues-based approach to Moscow; but at Helsinki the administration claimed (to the chagrin of issues faction leaders) to have secured the U.S. interest in seeing European security develop along lines managed, as during the Cold War, by the United States. Engaging China, not containing it, is the watchword of administration policy in Asia. This engagement policy is intended to promote reform, human rights, Chinese participation in multilateral efforts to improve the environment, and so on. Yet the president made clear in his decision on Most-Favored-Nation status for China that, however important these issues might be, engagement is better accomplished by subordinating those issues to an engagement policy dedicated to supporting the classic interests of trade and regional stability.

Whether one views the security policy of the president as a new departure unique to the post–Cold War era or, less dramatically, as an effort to best meld different approaches to sustain the support of the divergent factions or, more critically, as an ad hoc approach that makes use of whatever argument serves the moment probably depends on one's own politics and political affiliations. For the purposes of this effort, however, the point to be taken is that these three possibilities fairly well represent the range of choice open to policymakers. Aside from the detailed content of any particular policy, a lack of consensus drives policymakers to find either unique solutions to problems and concerns or solutions that will gain support from the majority. In the latter case that support can be persistent or episodic, depending on the seriousness of the problems and the domestic political circumstances, including, most important, the confidence of the public in the president's capabilities. If the aim is development of a new and unique policy course, the security apparatus of the nation might need adjusting, for no other reason than reducing institutional opposition to change. If, instead, what is taking place is a slow melding of views, what might be needed is an apparatus that is decidedly less oriented to a classic interests-based approach to policy and better able to incorporate new approaches to both emerging and persistent problems. If the nation is to support only an ad hoc approach, change may be needed as well as a way of making the apparatus more flexible.

Thus as America approaches the end of the decade it is confronted with the reality of two factions, with apparently coincidental agenda points, unable to agree on an overarching concept for, or definition of, the nation's security. As a result, they have had little success on agreeing on the ways and means to address common points. And they certainly have not been able to reach agreement on priorities for policy attention and, perhaps of equal or greater importance, programmatic funding. The public today finds itself as bemused as was Kissinger in the early 1990s and, like him, "tremendously impressed by what I heard and I can feel something ought to be done, but [without] any precise idea of what to do."[17]

This prospect brings full circle the subject of organizing for national security. How should the national security apparatus be organized to address affairs—whether issues or interests—that the public finds peripheral to its concerns? The government, after all, has obligations to "provide for the common defense" and "promote the general welfare" of the people. How can it best accomplish these goals when no consensus exists on what defense to provide or welfare to promote?

Notes

1. Appendix A contains an extended discussion of the positions that have been taken by the two factions.

2. In addition to the works cited in the following footnotes, these sources, among others, were consulted: Ken Booth and Steve Smith, eds., *International Relations Theory Today* (University Park: Pennsylvania State University Press, 1995); Chester A. Crocker and Fen Osler Hampson, eds., *Managing Global Chaos: Sources of and Responses to International Conflict* (Washington, D.C.: U.S. Institute of Peace, 1996); George J. Demko and William B. Wood, eds., *Reordering the World: Geopolitical Perspectives on the 21st Century* (Boulder, Colo.: Westview Press, 1994); Kim R. Holmes and

Thomas G. Moore, eds., *Restoring American Leadership: A U.S. Foreign and Defense Policy Blueprint* (Washington, D.C.: Heritage Foundation, 1996); Torbjörn L. Jnutsen, *A History of International Relations Theory* (Manchester: Manchester University Press, 1993); Douglas Johnston, ed., *Foreign Policy into the 21st Century: The U.S. Leadership Challenge* (Washington, D.C.: Center for Strategic and International Studies, 1996); Jeane Kirkpatrick et al., *Security and Insecurity: A Critique of Clinton Policy at Mid-Term* (Washington, D.C.: Empower America, 1994); David A. Lake and Donald Rothchild, *Ethnic Fears and Global Engagement: The International Spread and Management of Ethnic Conflict,* Policy Paper no. 20 (San Diego, Calif.: University of California, Institute on Global Conflict and Cooperation, January 1996); Janne E. Nolan, ed., *Global Engagement: Cooperation and Security in the 21st Century* (Washington, D.C.: The Brookings Institution, 1994); Paul R. Viotti and Mark V. Kauppi, eds., *International Relations Theory: Realism, Pluralism, Globalism,* 2nd ed. (New York: Macmillan Publishing Co., 1993).

3. The classic expression of this view can be found in Boutros Boutros Ghali, *Agenda for Peace* (New York: United Nations, 1992). A more fully developed argument on the subordination of sovereignty can be found in Morton H. Halperin and David J. Scheffer, *Self-determination in the New World Order* (Washington, D.C.: Carnegie Endowment, 1992).

4. Lori Fisler Damrosch and Rein Müllerson, "The Role of International Law in the Contemporary World," and Jonathan I. Charney and Gennady M. Danilenko, "Consent and the Creation of International Law," both in *Beyond Confrontation: International Law for the Post–Cold War Era,* ed. Lori Fisler Damrosch, Gennady M. Danilenko, and Rein Müllerson (Boulder, Colo.: Westview Press, 1995).

5. Lori Fisler Damrosch, ed., *Enforcing Restraint: Collective Intervention in Internal Conflicts* (New York: Council on Foreign Relations, 1993) provides a number of case studies, for example, Somalia and Cambodia, as well as discussion of the broader conceptual and legal rationale.

6. Richard L. Kugler, *Towards a Dangerous World: U.S. National Security Strategy for the Coming Turbulence* (Santa Monica,Calif.: RAND, 1995) develops his argument for security strategy with this notion in mind.

7. The following is drawn from *America's National Interests* (Washington, D.C.: Commission on America's National Interests, July 1996). The Commission was chaired by Robert Ellsworth, Andrew Goodpaster, and Rita Hauser.

8. This is not to say that every defense of the nation's interests has been honorable: witness Lincoln's denunciation of the war with Mexico. But the fact that interest and principle are inextricably linked has been at the heart of the debates about the objectives and morality of U.S. foreign policy since the founding of the Republic. A noteworthy account of the development of thinking in the United States on the aims of its security policy and its theoreti-

cal and moral foundations is presented by Walter A. McDougall, *Promised Land, Crusader State: The American Encounter with the World since 1776* (Boston: Houghton Mifflin, 1997); see also Matthew Spaulding and Patrick J. Garrity, *A Sacred Union of Citizens: George Washington's Farewell Address and the American Character* (New York: Rowman & Littlefield, 1996).

9. This history can be quickly summarized by recalling three expressions by U.S. leaders.

When asked why he was conducting military operations against Mexico and what his policy with respect to that country was, Woodrow Wilson, who would go on to promulgate the Fourteen Points, declared, "I am going to teach the South American republics to elect good men." Note that he did not restrict his teaching to Mexico only.

In his inaugural address President Kennedy declared the issues for which our forebears fought were still "at issue around the globe...." Because we are the "heirs" of our own revolution, he proclaimed, "Let the word go forth"—but *not,* as most recall, that "we shall pay any price, bear any burden...to assure the survival and the success of liberty"—but as a consequence of a far grander claim: that the United States was "unwilling to...permit the slow undoing of those human rights to which this nation has always been committed, and to which we are committed today at home and around the world." Thus, in a phrase, the president took under the protective mantle of the United States all who were committed to "those human rights" in fact or in prospect. The inevitable consequence was that we should engage them to teach what those rights are and how they are to be practiced.

In the post–Cold War era President Clinton is fond of saying that the "democracies" won the Cold War. His inability to distinguish the victory of the democracies—the United States, France, the United Kingdom, Germany, Japan, and so forth—from the idea of democracy is telling. It suggests that the idea of democracy now possesses a power and, by extension, a legitimacy independent of the citizens who have established separate constitutions to bestow on them and on their posterity theblessing of liberty. Hence, when the president spoke at his inaugural of the "will of the international community," it was not an abstraction but, in his view, a normative reality to which the United States and all other states would need to conform. In presenting this view the president is careful to characterize the era of the "global village" to which these norms apply in terms evocative of American rhetoric in the Wilson–Kennedy tradition. In an October 1995 speech he put it this way: "The common good at home is simply not separate from our efforts to advance the common good around the world. They must be one and the same if we are to be truly secure in the world of the twenty-first century." This view completes the logical progression begun by Wilson, who would "teach" others, and Kennedy, who would protect them. Clinton would render all equally secure so that everyone, particularly Americans, could be secure.

10. The notion of the terms of participation is clearly expressed, for example, in the reservations proclaimed by the Senate in U.S. participation in the UN, the North Atlantic Treaty Organization (NATO) and the Chemical Weapons Convention. In each case the reservations were made to protect the right of Americans to decide issues of war and peace (the UN and NATO) and to safeguard the constitutional rights of U.S. citizens.

11. Hans d'Orville, ed., *The Search for Global Order* (New York: United Nations, InterAction Council, 1993), 135, 143. Comments reported here were included by d'Orville in the volume even though they were made at an earlier session of the group—at Prague in 1991.

12. Paul R. and Anne H. Ehrlich, *Betrayal of Science and Reason* (Washington D.C.: Island Press, 1996).

13. For three examples of the debate over the severity of new security threats put forward by the issues faction, see "Environmental Scarcity and Violent Conflict: A Debate," in *Report of the Environmental Change and Security Project* (Washington, D.C.: Woodrow Wilson Center, Spring 1996); David A. Lake and Donald Rothchild, "Containing Fear: The Origins and Management of Ethnic Conflict," *International Security* 21, no. 2 (Fall 1996); and Ross Gelbspan, "Hot Air, Cold Truth: Why Do We Pay Attention to Greenhouse Skeptics?" *Washington Post,* May 25, 1997, p. C1.

14. In a monograph outlining a concept called "cooperative security," the idea was put this way: "…the concept of cooperative security…must begin with the central principle that the only legitimate purpose of national military forces is the defense of national territory or the participation in multinational forces that enforce UN sanctions or maintain peace." Ashton B. Carter, William J. Perry, and John D. Steinbruner, *A New Concept of Cooperative Security* (Washington, D.C.: The Brookings Institution, 1992), 11. This monograph was part of a larger project aimed at developing in some detail the theme of cooperative security. The results of the project can be found in Janne Nolan, ed., *Global Engagement: Cooperation and Security in the 21st Century* (Washington, D.C.: The Brookings Institution, 1994).

15. The President's gloss on the issues-based approach to security policy can be found in *A National Security Strategy of Engagement and Enlargement* (Washington, D.C.: The White House, February 1995). The first paragraph of the preface states:

> The end of the Cold War fundamentally changed America's security imperatives. The central security challenge of the past half century— the threat of communist expansion—is gone. The dangers we face today are more diverse. Ethnic conflict is spreading and rogue states pose a serious danger to regional stability in many corners of the globe. The proliferation of weapons of mass destruction represents a major challenge to our security. Large scale environmental degrada-

tion, exacerbated by rapid population growth, threatens to undermine political stability in many countries and regions.

16. Michael Mandelbaum, "Foreign Policy as Social Work," *Foreign Affairs* (January/February 1996). Mandelbaum was an adviser to the Clinton campaign in 1992.

17. d'Orville, *Search for Global Order,* 135, 143.

3

Orienting Security Policy

THE DISAGREEMENT between the issues and interests factions on
both the underlying concepts guiding security policy and the
specific priorities of policy is a source of frustration for contemporary students and practitioners of foreign and defense policy. Those
who would urge an issues-based approach lament the loss of opportunity to make a fresh start—a radical departure—in security affairs. Those who would urge an interests-based approach find few
developments or events that require the studied and serious engagement of the power of the United States.

But these laments may in their own way be prisoners of the peculiar experience of the United States during the Cold War. The period of a little more than 40 years, ending in 1990, when the USSR
posed an ideological and physical threat to the idea and existence of
the United States was not only unique in U.S. history but also in the
era of modern nation-states. The uniqueness was not the physical
threat posed by the USSR although the medium of the threat—
nuclear weapons carried by intercontinental missiles and bombers
—certainly was new. The threat of nuclear attack remains today, but
it is not at the core of and it does not dominate U.S. security policy
thinking.

The unique aspect of the Cold War was the enmity of the USSR
toward the idea of the United States. Communism, like the democratic republicanism of the United States, presents itself as a universal form of regime that has as its purpose the protection and advancement of the rights of its citizens. These ideologies differ in
many fundamental ways, but key to the evolution and progress of
the Cold War was that the U.S. regime began with the natural rights
of men who, in an act of sovereignty with respect to those rights,
delegated to government certain obligations and responsibilities
while they reserved to themselves the right to alter or abolish the

government if it should become destructive of citizens' rights. Revolution was a recognized activity but not an essential one in the American scheme. Nor was it necessary for all regimes to be of the same kind for either the legitimacy of the U.S. regime to be recognized or its safety to be assured. The power of reason affirmed the regime's legitimacy; its inherent strength and prudent policies were to be relied on for its safety.

For the Communist regime in its Leninist and, therefore, Russian version to come into being, it was theorized that revolution was needed to overcome the forces of history that had locked labor into a subservient relationship with capital. Given both the weight of history and the strength of capital, this revolution would not be a singular event but a continuous effort and, until the effort succeeded, it was essential that citizens remain under discipline administered by the Communist Party. But it was not enough for communism to triumph in one state; if its triumph was not universal, capital would restore itself and crush the revolution.

This ideological drive to international revolution was the unique threat posed by the USSR to the United States. As the most powerful state in the world and one explicitly committed to the principles that gave rise to capitalism, the United States was an enemy of the USSR. The United States could not avoid Soviet enmity; its mere existence stood as an alternative form of regime that beckoned others to adopt its capitalist ways, increasing the number and power of the enemies of labor. It is ironic that it was the Marxist–Leninist rulers of the USSR who understood with a clarity that slowly diminished in the United States during the Cold War that it was the *idea* of the United States that undermined Soviet legitimacy, the security of the Soviet regime (though not the territory of the state), and the promises of the revolution the USSR was leading.

Hence the struggle between the United States and the USSR was one of epic proportions when viewed in ideological terms. Ideological coexistence was not a real option; grudging respect for the power of one by the other might have produced détente but never normal relations. A struggle of this kind, a Cold War in which the depth of ideological enmity was matched by the unimaginable levels of destruction that could be inflicted in the event of conflict, had been unknown to the United States. Now, and for the time being, it is known no more.

That the abrupt end to that struggle should cause disorientation is hardly surprising. But an acknowledgment that it was a unique phase of U.S. history might help restore an orientation based on Americans' more typical concerns and approaches toward security. A consultation of the past is intended not as an argument that the end of the twentieth century has brought us back to the nineteenth or the beginnings of the twentieth. It is intended instead to suggest that the rationale for U.S. security policy has traditionally been rooted less in the requirements imposed on the United States from the outside than in the internal U.S. estimate of what has been needed to preserve, protect, and defend the virtues of the nation and its citizens from foreign influence and power. With that objective secured, it was historically a debate about whether and how the United States would make initiatives with respect to the ordinary business of the world. This luxury of choice was made possible by the inherent strength of the nation, prudent policies designed to capitalize on that strength in the context of evolving international events, and the fact that no nation viewed the very existence of the United States as sufficient cause to make war on it.

These conditions seem to prevail once more. But before a discussion of the organization of the national security apparatus to meet contemporary circumstances, it is worth a brief review of U.S. security policy history to help restore the orientation of security policy.

The Cold War orientation of U.S. national security policy, and the organization that reflected it, was a new phenomenon in U.S. history.[1] It was brought on by the "total war" experience of World War II and the ideological conflict of the Cold War that, in turn, were reinforced by the immediacy of the threat posed by nuclear weapons.

Before World War I, the United States had no armed forces to speak of. In the 100 years preceding World War I, the United States was engaged primarily in the consolidation of the U.S. regime on the North American continent. This effort animated policy toward Mexico and Spain, England and Russia. For the latter two, North America was a matter of imperial policy on the periphery of the continent and they ended the contest with the United States by the mid-1860s. For England, this was a process begun with the Webster-Ashburton Treaty of 1842 and ended with the Dominion Act and the settlement in 1872 of claims around the *Alabama* affair. For Russia, it ended with the sale of Alaska in 1867. Both powers appreciated the demonstration of U.S. potential during the Civil War.

With respect to Mexico, the primary political and territorial issues were settled in the 1860s when Maximilian was run out; but true political détente was not achieved until the eve of World War I. (It might be argued that normal relations are yet to be established.) Of the European powers only Spain was finally, in 1898, overcome through war; but that war comes as close to being an accident as any—made possible by poor political leadership in the United States and incredibly obtuse policies in Spain. But, on almost any scale, war with Spain was a trifling affair and hardly set the stage for the emergence of the United States as a world military power.

The late nineteenth century surge in naval activity was meant to coincide with, and underscore, the increased global perspective of the United States as the industrial revolution took hold. During the industrial revolution, the U.S. economy moved from a more or less self-sufficient one that was engaged in trade to supplement domestic production to one driven by industrial production and international trade. Before the end of the nineteenth century, the United States was relying on trade for both hard currency and manufactured goods. Tariff laws and other trade regulations were the core of both its foreign policy and its domestic economic policy. It is worth noting that, until the income tax was put in place, the federal government relied for its revenues primarily on tariffs and excise duties. The influx of immigrant labor and investment from abroad, coupled with increased trade with the Orient and the building of the railroads and telegraph systems after the Civil War, fueled an industrial explosion. The economic crises of the 1870s and 1890s reflected the shift in the base of the U.S. economy from its domestic roots to the international market. From the close of the Civil War to the beginning of World War I, U.S. vital interests were hardly challenged as the entire world, as then constituted, turned its attention to industrialization and trade.

It is not a coincidence that that same period marked the U.S. coming of age on the diplomatic scene. It was a peculiarly American debut for, apart from continuing entanglements in the Caribbean and Central America that were driven by a combination of ideology, lingering foreign policy concerns, and trade and economics, the United States relied for its international position on the inherent strength of its geographical, political, and economic position and attributes. The international system was policed by the United Kingdom; its normative character, however, was increasingly defined by the United States as a consequence of growing U.S. economic strength and moral attitudes played out against a backdrop of liberalizing trends in Europe. In 1872, the United States participated in its first international conference, called by the King of Belgium to address issues related to the Congo. Trade interests led to deeper involvement in Pacific affairs, which would include the absorption of the Sandwich Islands, insistence on and participation in an open-door policy in China, and the mediation of the Russo-Japanese war. Each of these was reflective of the type of influence the United States could wield as an interested actor: powerful in economic and normative terms but in military terms (primarily naval at the time) not a direct threat to other major powers although competent to represent the limited range of U.S. interests.

The character of U.S. security policy as it had evolved from the mid-nineteenth century is well represented in President Wilson's approach to the war in Europe during 1914–1916. Wilson appreciated the potential leverage neutrality afforded the United States vis-à-vis Britain and France on the one side and Germany on the other. The United States was a source of munitions, food, and cash for each of the combatants. In addition, it was a potential source of military power that each side was intent on denying to the other. Given these circumstances it was not hard for Wilson to choose a policy of neutrality, particularly in light of the lack of enthusiasm for war among the U.S. public. But to this neutrality he brought his own variety of normative authority. Seeing the war as a product of the politics that the United States had abandoned and certain that the adoption of U.S. standards (at least as he chose to present them) was a sure way to prevent such wars in the future, Wilson played on the threat of abandoning neutrality to gain the acquiescence of the belligerents to his formulations for an armistice and peace.

In the end, circumstances Wilson could not avoid overcame his aim to remain out of the war and broker a peace as a noncombatant. But that his overarching normative concepts remained intact is well known and frequently cited as the source of his personal failure and, ultimately, the failure of the League of Nations. How much praise or criticism Wilson deserves, and whether "Wilsonism" in 1916–1920 or since was an apt reflection of the nation's moral sense, is not a matter of concern here. The point is that the conduct of the United States before and even after its entry into the First World War was not prompted by a direct and apocalyptic threat to the nation. Nor did the belligerents pose an ideological threat to the nation. Wilson chose his approach to neutrality in the hope of bringing U.S. principles into international relations; there is little evidence he or anyone else believed that U.S. domestic institutions would be transformed by the victory of one side or the other on terms different from those he was offering. But even if Wilson so believed, his fellow countrymen did not, as the fate of the League in the U.S. Senate demonstrated.

But if Wilsonism was rejected in 1920, much of the attitude that went with it persisted. That is, the combination of a reliance on high-mindedness, economic leverage (to be sought or protected), and the maintenance of military power sufficient to defend the other two animated the Washington and London naval conferences, the conclusion of the Kellogg-Briand Pact, and even the efforts to soften the economic impact of the Versailles Treaty. The same could be said of the refusal to recognize the USSR. The operation of these three elements of security policy was not always a success, as the sorry story of relations with Japan and the attitude of the United States toward Japan's operations in China attest.

This is not to suggest that there was not another approach to security policy advanced within the United States. The Progressivism of Teddy Roosevelt, revisionism of Mahan, and jingoism of Hearst did fuel efforts to push the United States into the world arena. Roosevelt's disgust with Wilson's neutrality, however, is remarkable because it illustrates an alternative policy course, not a fundamental difference in appreciation for the sources of U.S.

power or the role of the United States in world affairs. Roosevelt differed with Wilson less over the purposes of U.S. policy than its objective and the lack of manliness displayed by Wilson in its conduct.[2] Thus, at bottom, the World War I experience did not immediately change the approach of the United States to security affairs. Its policies continued to be rooted in economic and commercial relations, developed against the backdrop of American "exceptionalism." It is true the United States took a larger hand in European economic affairs, but this was driven by a desire to sustain an equilibrium so that a resort to military solutions would not be sought. In its way it was not unlike the policy pursued by the less powerful but still influential states of Asia vis-à-vis China. The United States worked to advance its own position while counseling—and, to the extent it could, intervening—to sustain stable relations among the powers.

The interwar years thus saw a diplomacy more active than had been seen hitherto and aimed primarily at trade agreements, development of an international financial and economic system (particularly around the reparations schedules imposed on Germany by Britain and France after World War I), and disarmament. The country stayed out of the League of Nations—which was seen as entanglement in affairs it could not shape—but expressed willingness to be a member of the World Court, a forum in which normative power was thought to be predominant. Vigorous efforts were made, with mixed results, to consolidate U.S. trade hegemony in South America. The dollar diplomacy of the pre–World War I era was recast in the context of managing the contradictory trends of high(er) tariffs, war-debt-repayment schedules, and reparations payments in the face of a worldwide depression. Disarmament policies were motivated in large measure by concerns over rising Japanese power, dwindling British power, and the collapse of Russia under the Bolsheviks.

The success of these policies is debatable. The point to be taken is that U.S. security policy in the era leading up to World War II was an active one, reflecting an appreciation for (if not always a good use of) the basic elements of its power—economic power conferred by its status as the world's lender, trading power, and a claim to moral rectitude appealing at home and acceptable abroad—and carefully avoiding policies that depended on military strength.

During the 76 years between the end of the Civil War and Pearl Harbor, this "official" approach to security policy was mirrored in the activities of private citizens. Particularly after the turn of the century, the United States was a source of considerable international NGO activity that built on the activities of missionaries in the Sandwich Islands and the Far East. These NGOs did bring on revolution in Hawaii and, for alleged subversive activity, were targeted for discrimination and persecution by the last of China's dynasties. During this same era the Red Cross was given life and the Hague conventions gained status. Increased government, or government-sponsored, activity abroad was mirrored during this time by an increasingly Progressive attitude toward the role of the federal government in the administration and regulation of everyday domestic life; thus Departments of Commerce and Labor were established to give force to the new way of life in America. During the depression of the 1930s the federal government assumed additional responsibility for social security.

By the outbreak of World War II, the United States was a leading power based on its financial and economic interests and its normative leadership. Its diplomatic power and commercial power were acknowledged. Its military power (recently displayed in World War I) was appreciated for its potential more than for its actual strength. It had a fleet in being—one that other powers had to take into consideration but that by itself could not decisively alter the conduct of affairs in a region of interest to the United States, as the Japanese decisions to make war against China and then the United States amply demonstrated. It had no army to speak of and only nascent air forces.

As noted, the conduct and outcome of World War II ushered in an era unique in U.S. history and, with it, dramatic changes in the apparatus used by the United States to pursue its security policies. American military power, made strong by its industrial and economic base and legitimate by the political morality of the nation, dominated the formation of U.S. security policy. This was less a matter of choice than of necessity. The preferred U.S. choice was represented in the plans for demobilization and downsizing of the military establishment during the post–World War II years. From a peak of some 12–15 million men and women under arms in 1945, the Truman administration proposed the creation of a unified national military of 1.5 million men and women (with the percentage of gross domestic product spent on defense falling from 41.9 in 1944 to 4.9 in 1947). In the immediate aftermath of the war, economic power and normative power were championed first, with military power confined to the background. Between 1946 and 1954, U.S. foreign aid for nonmilitary purposes ($30 billion) far outstripped military aid ($12.2 billion).[3] But the role of military power in security policy grew substantially as the ideological differences with the USSR led first to suspicion of and then to opposition to its expansionist policies, Chiang's forces collapsed in the face of Mao's Communist forces in China, civil war commenced between Communists and nationalists in Greece, the government in Czechoslovakia was subverted, similar subversive attempts were made in France, the Korean War broke out, and the Soviet Union acquired atomic weapons.

Even as the military component of security policy loomed larger and was reflected in the growth of the armed forces and the Pentagon work force and, in particular, in the size of the Office of the Secretary of Defense (OSD), so too did the Department of State grow in size and in the range of issues it addressed. But much of this growth at State was directly related to the administration of new programs spawned by World War II, the post–World War II effort to contain the USSR with aid programs, and the management of new alliances created for the same purpose.

As we leave the Cold War era behind and consider whether the focus of security policy, and with it the policy machinery left over from the Cold War, is in need of overhauling, it is worth considering whether that effort might profitably draw its orientation from the security policy experience of the past. It is clear that the Cold War militarization of U.S. security policy has been reversed as the immediacy of the threat has receded. At the same time, there is an increased, and increasing, emphasis on the more traditional bases of U.S. security policy, namely financial, economic, and normative power. As in the past, military power has come to be complemented by other forms of power as the United States seeks to secure itself so that it may act in the world in a manner appropriate to its principles and supported by its citizens.

Notes

1. The interpretation of history provided in the following paragraphs is the responsibility of the author. Among the sources consulted were Thomas A. Bailey, *A Diplomatic History of the American People,* 8th ed. (New York: Appleton-Century-Crofts, 1969); Sean Dennis Cashman, *America in the Gilded Age: From the Death of Lincoln to the Rise of Theodore Roosevelt,* 3rd ed. (New York: New York University Press, 1993); John S. D. Eisenhower, *Intervention! The United States and the Mexican Revolution, 1913–1917* (New York: Norton, 1993); John S. D. Eisenhower, *So Far From God: The United States War With Mexico* (New York: Anchor Books, 1989); John Lewis Gaddis, *We Now Know: Rethinking Cold War History* (New York: Oxford University Press, 1997); John D. Hicks, *Republican Ascendancy, 1921–33* (New York: Harper & Row, 1960); Akira Iriye, *The Globalizing of America, 1913–1945,* Vol. 3 of *Cambridge History of American Foreign Relations* (Cambridge: Cambridge University Press, 1993); Walter LaFeber, *The American Search for Opportunity, 1865–1913,* Vol. 2 of *Cambridge History of American Foreign Relations* (Cambridge: Cambridge University Press, 1993); Arthur S. Link, *Woodrow Wilson and the Progressive Era, 1910–1917* (New York: Harper & Row, 1954); Walter A. McDougall, *Promised Land, Crusader State: The American Encounter with the World Since 1776* (Boston: Houghton Mifflin, 1997); Walter A. McDougall, *Let the Sea Make A Noise…A History of the North Pacific from Magellan to MacArthur* (New York: Basic Books, 1993); John C. Miller, *The Federalist Era, 1789–1801* (New York: Harper & Row, 1960); Bradford Perkins, *The Creation of a Republican Empire, 1776–1865,* Vol. 1 of *Cambridge History of American Foreign Relations* (Cambridge: Cambridge University Press, 1993); Matthew Spalding and Patrick J. Garrity, *A Sacred Union of Citizens: George Washington's Farewell Address and the American Character* (New York: Rowman & Littlefield, 1996).

2. This was not a small difference. Theodore Roosevelt's nationalism led him to mediate the Russo-Japanese War without attacking the moral foundations of the international system. Indeed, he exploited that system to broker the peace and advance the U.S. interest in Asia. Roosevelt was far less impressed with the shortcomings of the international system or its members than was Wilson. Both were impressed with America's unique form of power. But Roosevelt wanted to use power for U.S. interest. Wilson believed the country had an interest in using it to reform the international system within which it operated.

3. Thomas A. Bailey, *A Diplomatic History of the American People,* 8th ed. (New York: Appleton-Century-Crofts, 1969).

4

Organizing for Security

THE PRECEDING REVIEW of past security approaches, brief as it was, was meant to underscore the unique character of the Cold War era in U.S. security policy. The Cold War gave rise to an enormous increase in the size of the government agencies committed to conducting it. But of interest here is not the size to which the government grew but the tendency of government organization to emphasize the steady and economical application of U.S. capabilities in pursuit of Cold War objectives. This tendency is clear in the original organization of the security establishment under the National Security Act of 1947.[1]

Under the act, a national military establishment was created. Within it were grouped the Joint Chiefs of Staff (JCS), the War Council, the Munitions Board, and the Research and Development Board. These were in addition to the Departments of the Army, the Navy, and the newly created Air Force. The JCS was to be supported by a staff of some 100 officers. The secretary of defense was to have a smaller staff (one aide and four special assistants) that reflected the secretary's role as assistant to the president for national security matters. The act also created the National Security Council (NSC), which was to consist of the president; the secretaries of state, defense, army, navy, and the air force; and the chairman of the newly created National Security Resources Board. The newly established Central Intelligence Agency (CIA) was subordinate to the NSC.

This structure was altered considerably with subsequent amendments to NSA '47. Likewise, changes in the organization of the Department of Defense (DOD), the State Department, and the CIA have substantially changed the shape of the wiring diagrams used to represent the national security apparatus. Those changes have also affected the locus of the center of gravity within the apparatus and within agencies. For example, the role of the secretary of defense has evolved from that of an adviser to the president and coordinator of essentially independent service departments to that of an executive authority subordinate to only the president in the military chain of command. The responsibilities of the JCS and the CJCS have been increased, less to enhance their roles in the chain of command than to provide them with the authority to plan and provide for the requisite military capabilities. The role of the DCI in the intelligence community grew substantially in the 1960s, only to begin to wane in recent years. The role of the national security adviser has fluctuated, depending on the wishes of the president and the character of the individual in the post.

Through this evolution, one predominating characteristic has been apparent: The comprehensive nature of the Cold War required a comprehensive establishment to fight it. Steadiness of purpose and direction, not agility, were the hallmarks of the approach to the war. At the same time, through one administration after another, presidents sought means and methods by which they could be more flexible and agile in dealing with the issues before them, bring more imagination to the planning for national security, and inspire a faster response from agencies during periods of quiet as well as crisis. The result is that the history of the security apparatus is studded with examples of ad hoc arrangements created by presidents to get around the very organization created to provide them with the assets to fight the Cold War.

Like the Cold War itself, the apparatus created to fight it is unique in U.S. history. Again, this judgment is rendered less with respect to its size than to its complexity. Until NSA '47, including the periods of World Wars I and II, no apparatus approaching that which evolved during the Cold War existed. From the founding of the Republic until 1947 the conduct of national security affairs by the executive branch was directed by the president and the president alone, who did so by operating directly through (mostly around) the War Department and Navy Department secretaries and sometimes with the secretary of state. One need only recall the conduct of George Washington in the 1790s, Jefferson's purchase of Louisiana, Madison's nearly direct conduct of the War of 1812, Polk's domination of the planning and conduct of the Mexican War, and

Lincoln's exasperated (and no doubt exasperating to some) direction of the Civil War.

It might be expected that this would have changed with World War I, but that was not the case. Woodrow Wilson served as his own secretary of state and, when war finally came, he did not dramatically alter the command organization of the War and Navy Departments. More surprising to a contemporary audience is that Franklin D. Roosevelt (FDR), perhaps having learned his lessons as a Navy Department assistant secretary under Wilson, followed the approach of his World War I predecessor. In World War II the State Department played virtually no role in the conduct of the war. The War and Navy Departments were likewise ignored. FDR worked through the Executive Office of the President and, within it, the Office of Emergency Planning. Under this arrangement he organized his advisers under Admiral William D. Leahy, with Admiral Ernest J. King overseeing naval affairs, General George C. Marshall army affairs, and Harry Hopkins acting as his personal emissary to foreign governments. Intelligence was centralized in the Office of the Coordinator of Intelligence, which was upgraded to the Office of Strategic Services; both reported to the president through the JCS.

The drive for steadiness and economy in the post–World War II period led to an explosion in the extent of the government's operations: the Marshall Plan, the outbreak of the Korean War, and the growth in the scope and intensity of the Cold War. This explosion in the extent of operations was paralleled by a growth in the size and number of the agencies managing those operations. The watchwords of steadiness and economy continued to prevail—despite appearances to the contrary. Policymakers were reluctant to increase the size of the armed forces. The commitment of forces to NATO, the Southeast Asia Treaty Organization (SEATO), and other military alliances was tentative and until the mid-1960s relatively small. No expense was spared on the strategic forces—both the offensive retaliatory capability and the intelligence assets for surveillance—but even so they represented a small fraction of the defense budget and, as domestic spending began increasing in the 1960s, of the national budget overall. Except for the special spending for the Korean War and Southeast Asia, it was not until the 1980s that the United

States experienced a substantial year-on-year increase in defense spending.

But the desire for steadiness (if not economy) allowed for stodginess within the bureaucracy. Every president since Eisenhower has complained of his inability to move the bureaucracy in the directions he wished to go. To overcome impediments they have used the NSC and its adviser to create committees, boards, senior and other interagency groups, and working groups. They have created crisis management cells and advisory boards. Yet no satisfactory method for restoring the kind of authority, flexibility, and agility enjoyed by pre-1947 presidents has been found.

Under the post-1947 system, responsibility is assigned to a lead agency; other agencies are required to support development of policy but they are not subject to lead-agency authority with respect to the execution of policy or the conduct of operations. The result is most frequently a set of parallel efforts that are more or less coordinated but never controlled by a single authority. All too often, however, the coordination process is stymied by lower-level failures of coordination or attempts by agency heads to sabotage efforts.

The result is that, in the end, major initiatives that require a mix of department and agency skills end up being coordinated by the White House; that is, the national security adviser, who has no constitutional authority, becomes the de facto leader of critical policy development and operational efforts. Although such an approach might have been adequate when the critical issues (arms control, space policy, and crisis management, to mention but three prominent examples) that fell outside of or could not be managed by a single department were few, in an era when the range of issues is much broader, with few issues of an absolutely critical nature but all of substantial interest, such an approach is a recipe for gridlock or disaster. Gridlock occurs because the White House does not have the personnel to apply to the full range of issues; disaster occurs because the complexity of issues requires more talent and information than can be contained within a White House structure, the current law and practices are ignored, or the execution of an operation is complicated and requires more professional direction.

Note

1. See Appendix B for a brief history of the act and the departments and agencies it created. Appendix D provides the text of the act.

5

A New Model

T HE IMPLICATIONS OF THE DISCUSSION thus far might be summarized as follows:

- Factions within the national security policy community are
  the result of differences not about what the nation should
  do in a particular instance but about the very purpose and
  object of policy and, therefore, of the character of the regime and, for that reason, are nearly irreconcilable.

- The Cold War was a unique experience in U.S. history, and
  in the foreseeable future the United States is unlikely to
  confront an adversary both able to do the United States (or
  its allies) grievous harm and determined to confront the
  United States as an ideological enemy.

- Although the focus of U.S. national security policy has var-
  ied in the past, enduring hallmarks have been assertions of
  moral authority and economic power and the prudential
  use of military power.

- The future security environment, measured in terms of im-
  minent threats and ideological adversaries, is more likely to
  represent the pre–World War II past than the unique Cold
  War experience.

- Throughout U.S. history, irrespective of the international
  situation, U.S. presidents have been the principal, and in
  many cases the sole, authorities on the direction and execution of security policy.

- The organization of the Cold War security apparatus might
  have suited the unique situation of the Cold War, but its

virtues then might now be impediments to the president's flexibility in developing security policy.

These implications do not by themselves demand a change in the security apparatus although they are sufficient to warrant such consideration. To them might be added the following five changes in the security environment that policy experts, irrespective of their factional affiliation, would agree have occurred:

- Although military operations are expected to be smaller in scale than were anticipated during the Cold War, they require standing military forces far in excess of those fielded before World War II. Today the range of military missions is greater than in the past, with forward presence and power projection for combat added to the classic operations other than war (OOTW) of the pre–World War II era, e.g., pacifying the frontier, chasing bandits, defending embassies, extracting personnel and citizens, and stabilizing neighboring governments. Today's OOTW do not include frontier pacification although military patrols of the air approaches and borders of the United States for the interception of drug traffickers and illegal immigrants would not be unknown to the men of General Pershing's command.

- Security relations with states can no longer be based exclusively on bilateral ties or occasional alliances of convenience. The combination of finance, trade, security, environment, culture, and political developments has made regional approaches to affairs far more common than in the past as states organize themselves into regional associations, alliances, and unions. This is not saying that bilateral relations do not matter but that they need to be developed in light of larger U.S. goals toward regions of interest.

- A set of threats has emerged that is not of the traditional variety and whose origin may be abroad but whose impact can be felt in the United States by U.S. citizens. These threats include terrorism, the use of WMD, organized crime (including drugs), and illegal immigration. Measures for addressing them may require actions at home and abroad. What distinguishes them from traditional security concerns is that in the United States they would be considered crimes, not acts of war. Therefore they need to be addressed as such while they are integrated into a broader security policy.

- The evolution of the international finance, trade, and monetary systems—driven primarily by the information revolution (a combination of hardware and software)—has created both new opportunities and new vulnerabilities for the United States. Protecting the livelihoods of U.S. citizens while maintaining a stable and secure international economic environment requires a careful blending of both domestic and international policy. Although this has been true in the past, what is different now is the volume and pace of international economic activity and the need to defend it against disruption or abuse.

- The importance of maintaining a base of scientific and technological capability has increased. In the pre–World War II era, this base was nearly the exclusive domain of the private sector although investments made by the government in roads and harbors, government's liberal (sometimes too liberal) encouragement of railroad and telegraph development, the country's industrial growth and consolidation, and federal tariff policies cannot be discounted. In the Cold War era, direct investment in science and technology related to the means of waging the war found their indirect outlets in the civil and commercial sectors. In the post–Cold War era, government investment is relatively lower and the range of potentially important sectors for development is very broad indeed. Thus, relative to the past, neither a laissez-faire approach nor a targeted one is likely to be appropriate.

These changes in the environment suggest that, although the steadiness and economy of the Cold War era are much to be admired, flexibility, foresight, and agility in a fiscally constrained environment are more to be desired. The convenient (though never truly appropriate) segmenting of domestic and security policy and (within the latter) of foreign and defense policy, common to the Cold War era, hardly seems appropriate. In each of the five areas of change noted, it is apparent that domestic and political policies, economic policies, and military and public safety policies are confluent. Moreover, experience during the past decade has demonstrated that the relative balance among them may shift quickly and radically.

Given the experience of the nation in its foreign affairs—a reliance on its moral force and its economic strength protected by appropriate military force—and its experience with an executive authority able to shape and guide the nation's security policy directly, the suggestion to be offered here for a new organization for national security focuses on restoring flexibility and agility to the president. The reason for this preference was put forward in the earlier reflection on the genius of the U.S. constitutional system, which makes it possible to bring together "a man and his place"; that is, it provides offices from which individuals are able to govern in ways necessary to provide for the nation's good. In the field of security affairs that responsibility rests with the Office of the President. This office can be organized and its affairs conducted in ways that are infinitely variable to meet the changing circumstances. This privilege of office, in turn, fairly demands that its occupant organize it to permit the fulfillment of the presidential responsibilities to the nation.

In light of the current lack of consensus on security policy, that leadership extends beyond mere administration of the nation's security affairs to taking steps to meet the exigencies of the era while building support for the current president's view of policy direction. Those measures, however, must meet the accountability standards of the political system, which means that in times of dispute those charged by the president with conducting policy must be accountable not only to the president but to the Congress as well. That accountability, in the first instance, is with respect to the law. But where lawful conduct is not itself enough to be persuasive to the public, that accountability must extend to accommodating—to the limit of presidential prerogative—the political concerns and interests of different factions within the polity.

The conceptual point of departure, therefore, is less concerned with a sweeping departmental reorganization à la NSA '47 than with a new approach to the development of policy and the execution of critical operations by the president. The reasons are twofold: first, the lack of consensus on security policy makes a broad reorganization highly unlikely to succeed. More important, it would divert attention from the purpose of the effort—reestablishing a base in public opinion for the conduct of security affairs—to the politics of the effort itself. We need only recall the fate of the numerous "roles and missions" efforts of the past decade to take the point.

Second, a vigorous effort by a president to reorder the Office of the President and strike a different course in the development and execution of security policy focuses attention on the objectives of the president, the purposes of the office, and how the president intends to use the latter to discharge constitutional responsibilities in the field of security policy. In such a discussion it is difficult to stray from the fundamental questions. Although such discussions can sometimes be difficult, once begun they are even more difficult to conclude without a resolution. Building a consensus on security policy given the divergent views of the protagonists will require such a discussion. The president's choices can prompt and guide the discussion with respect to the organization and operation of the office.

The approach for organizing and operating the president's office in the field of security affairs borrows liberally from the approach taken by the armed services in the development of their concepts of the services, which are designed to provide manpower, as well as the training and equipment for that manpower, to the combatant commanders. These combatant commanders or commanders in chief (CINCs) in turn direct the operations of forces supplied to them by the services. Those forces are used in a joint fashion to achieve the missions assigned the CINCs. It is possible for a CINC to serve in any operation as either the "supported" or the "supporting" CINC. In the former position, the supported CINC leads an operation, and the forces of the supporting CINC are "chopped" and placed under the direct authority of the supported CINC. The chopped forces are returned to the supporting CINC at the conclusion of the mission. There are two kinds of CINCs—unified, who control all forces within their areas of responsibility; and specified, who have forces assigned to them by direction for performance of a specific mission.

Under this arrangement the services provide administrative, training, and equipping functions in response to CINC requirements. A service may organize itself under various commands. For example, the air force has established the Air Combat Command, under which it organizes its forces for the purposes of training and doctrine development. Under the current U.S. approach, the requirements of the CINCs are harmonized among the services under the direction of the Joint Requirements Oversight Council (JROC) made up of the vice chairmen of the services and led by the vice chairman of the JCS. Requirements are addressed by the JROC in light of the statutory roles and missions of the services. The apportioning of responsibility among CINCs is accomplished via the command plan issued by the CJCS, by direction of the secretary of defense, under the authority of the president as commander in chief.

Congress authorizes and appropriates funds for the DOD and for each of the services and conducts oversight of the department, its officers, and their actions.

The system is sufficiently flexible that a single CINC can wear multiple hats. Thus, under the current arrangements, the commander in chief, Europe (CINCEUR) is also the supreme allied commander, Europe (SACEUR) for NATO. The commander in chief, U.S. Atlantic Command (CINCACOM) is also the supreme allied commander, Atlantic (SACLANT) for NATO. This arrangement permits the development of headquarters staffs devoted to specific policy and planning activities with forces that can be combined and joined as needed. Force levels are maintained on the basis of the aforementioned apportioning of forces by the CJCS, and force capabilities are adjudicated by the JROC and the services in consultation with the CINCs. So-called end-strengths are decided by the Congress through the annual appropriations and authorization bills.

Figure 1
The National Security Directorate

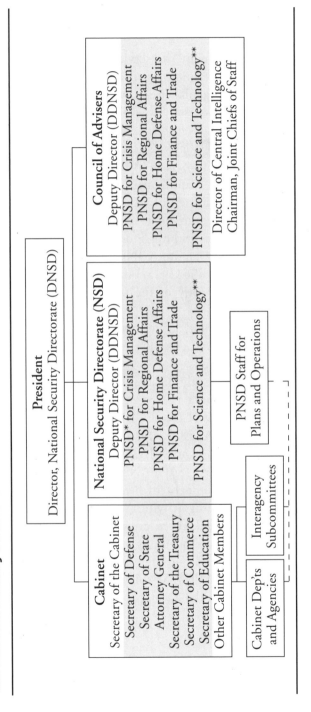

Note: Shaded area indicates members of the Cabinet who would also serve on the NSD and the Council of Advisers.

* PNSD stands for principal member of the NSD.

** The PNSD for science and technology could be either the secretary of commerce or the secretary of education.

6

Applying the Model

A SIMILAR CONCEPT applied to the security policy apparatus of the United States, more broadly defined, that takes into account the newer features of security policy outlined above is developed below as Option 1, the National Security Directorate (NSD).[1] The NSD (see figure 1 on preceding page) is charged with developing, planning, and executing policies and operations as assigned and directed by the president. But, because the NSD is meant to provide the president with the flexibility to manage those affairs of greatest relevance to the nation's security in a rapidly evolving environment, the NSD is not intended to be responsible for the day-to-day affairs of national security. That task would fall to a newly tasked cabinet organization.

The National Security Directorate (Option 1)

In addition to the roles of head of government and commander in chief, the president would be the director, National Security Directorate (DNSD).

As DNSD the president is supported by five directorates, each led by a cabinet secretary:

- Directorate for Crisis Management (D/CM); secretary of defense

- Directorate for Regional Affairs (D/RA); secretary of state

- Directorate for Home Defense Affairs (D/HDA); attorney general

- Directorate for Finance and Trade (D/F&T); secretary of the treasury

- Directorate for Science and Technology (D/S&T); secretary of commerce or secretary of education

This NSD is directed by the president (as DNSD) and on a day-to-day basis is overseen by a deputy director (DDNSD) of cabinet rank. The choice of DDNSD is the president's. It could be the vice president. If not, the DDNSD would require confirmation by the Senate. The deputy director is tasked to serve as a coordinator of the principal members of the NSD (PNSDs). The staff of the DDNSD would be limited by statute to a small number needed to serve as a secretariat to prepare papers for the president's signature, to assure that directives are legal and do not contain overlapping responsibilities, and so forth. The DDNSD has no directive authority over the principals nor operational authority over any component of the national security apparatus. But, given the cabinet rank, the DDNSD possesses a voice equal to that of the other principals in giving advice to the president. In this the deputy director serves in a capacity not unlike that of the CJCS relative to the secretary of defense.

In addition, the president has available the advice of the DCI. The DCI is not, however, a principal of the NSD and, like any other "service" chief, is obliged to provide support to a PNSD as directed by the president through the DDNSD.

Each PNSD is dual-hatted: each also serves as a cabinet secretary. In this capacity every PNSD is responsible for the conduct of a specific department. The roles and missions that are the exclusive purview of that department are established by statute and would be revised only through a process of review in the NSD and new legislation.

The president would assign roles and missions to every PNSD, who would be directed to execute the instructions by means of a joint organization. That is, each cabinet secretary would chop to the PNSD the personnel and resources needed to perform the assigned role and execute the mission. The specific objectives of a PNSD and the limits of a PNSD's requirements would be set by the DDNSD through the equivalent of a command plan negotiated among the PNSDs. These personnel and resources would be drawn from those components within the current department structure that are evidently engaged in interdepartment activities or whose activity is obviously related to the role and mission assigned the PNSD. This directorate staff would perform the equivalent of a headquarters function, designing policy for approval by the NSD and directing operations in the assigned mission areas.

The PNSD would have the option of assigning the execution of the mission to a single department or retaining it within the directorate. In either case, the PNSD retains controlling authority over the operational director (OPDIR) assigned to execute the mission.

The PNSD–OPDIR arrangement initially would be implemented on an ad hoc basis for crisis management and on a permanent basis for a select number of issues or problems as designated by the president. That is, although statutes establishing the NSD and PNSDs would be broadly written, the operational control of a PNSD would be by direction of the president. Over time, the structure could evolve into a transitional one, allowing for a more complete reorganization of the government.

The Cabinet

The day-to-day tasks of national security affairs, as well as the other affairs of government, would fall to a revamped cabinet. The cabinet would continue as a vehicle for coordinating the affairs of government. It might take on the character of the JCS; that is, serving under the direction of the president's chief of staff acting as secretary of the cabinet (in lieu of the CJCS), cabinet members would sit as the policy coordination body for the government. To meetings each cabinet department would bring the issues and decisions related to the administration of the department that needed the attention of the president. The president, in turn, would charge the cabinet with preparing the executive to conduct the day-to-day administration of the law and the ordinary affairs of government. The work of the cabinet—to include that brought forward by the departments and charged by the president—would be conducted within subcommittees made up of cabinet representatives working under the direction of the secretary of the cabinet; the subcommittees would reflect the current practice of creating interagency working groups. These subcommittees would be led by a member of the cabinet secretariat and meet as needed to prepare the issue and decision papers. In addition, the secretariat would staff the president on the matters assigned to the cabinet and the ordinary affairs of government.

Within this construct the existing departments of government would not be abolished. They provide the expertise and manpower needed to manage the nation's national security assets—its armed forces, embassies, trade delegations, and so forth—as well as, through the cabinet, its day-to-day affairs and major initiatives that cannot be as well conducted by the NSD.

The organization of the cabinet secretariat is not fully developed here. There are two broad choices. The first would be to organize around specific policy initiatives the president might wish to undertake, creating subcommittees to oversee each one. Although this suits the president's needs, it may not serve the needs of the departments, which have far fewer grand issues and decisions to be addressed by the president—budgets, personnel, diplomatic postings, negotiating positions, preparations for foreign travel, and the like.

An alternative would make use of the model of the Joint Staff, where labor is divided on functional instead of topical grounds. The functional divisions of the Joint Staff address a fairly narrow field of regard, however; they are not obliged to include within their deliberations many of the traditionally domestic concerns of a president.

A combination might be considered. A number of offices that currently operate for the president but independently of the cabinet departments might be brought under the control of the secretary of the cabinet. For example, the Office of Management and Budget (OMB)—which effectively operates as comptroller of the government —could perform its function within this structure. So too might the science adviser, the Office of Personnel Management, the Council of Economic Advisers, the President's Foreign Intelligence Advisory Board, and so forth. An office would need to be created to address the peculiar concerns of the Defense and State Departments that are beyond those that could be addressed by the units listed above. This might be a political-military policy office or a smaller version of the Arms Control and Disarmament Agency charged with coordinating foreign negotiations, not only arms control.

The point here is that the cabinet secretariat would take on the ordinary administrative and day-to-day functions of the government, including those related to security affairs. The secretary of the cabinet would become, by virtue of the position, a chief of staff to the president for the operation of the government. In security affairs, however, the secretary of the cabinet could become the rival of either the cabinet secretaries or the DDNSD. However, the work related to security affairs overseen by the secretary of the cabinet would in all cases arrive through the subcommittees on which the appropriate departments are represented and would be on subjects that have been left in the departments for work because they are not central to the policies of the president.

Two Objectives Accomplished

The approach outlined above aims to accomplish two objectives. First, it seeks to assure that future presidents possess the kind of hands-on control exercised by U.S. presidents in the century and a half before 1947. It does so, however, without diminishing executive accountability to the rest of the government or to the American people. In this regard, the role of the department secretaries as PNSDs is critical. As confirmed constitutional officers, they would be examined by a Congress mindful of their dual hatting. And, with respect to their own cabinet departments, they are not able to ignore the bureaucratic imperatives of modern government.

Second, the approach seeks to free the NSD from the day-to-day management of affairs. Members are charged with planning and executing policy and operations that are essential to the national security of the nation in the modern era. Day-to-day tasks of government are assigned to the cabinet and the secretary of the cabinet. The secretary of the cabinet becomes a true chief of staff in this arrangement, running not the president's office but the president's government. There may still be a need for chief doorkeeper; but the task of running the government is taken out of the politics of the office and put into the politics of the government. Moreover, the increased importance of the cabinet provides a check on the power of the NSD. Dual-hatted department heads must sit in both forums. In the cabinet they must be accountable to their opposite numbers to sustain the budgetary, programmatic, personnel, and administrative clout essential to the health of their own agencies.

A New Possibility Created

In this proposed reorganization, two new positions are created—the secretary of the cabinet and the DDNSD. Each has a perspective across the government. The former is focused primarily on domestic affairs but cannot ignore the impact on the government of security affairs. The latter is focused on security affairs but is required to coordinate the work of traditional domestic agencies with traditional defense and foreign affairs agencies. Together, the DCI, the CJCS, the five PNSDs, and the DDNSD would constitute a council of advisers that could be called on to provide counsel on a schedule congenial to the president. These advisers could be constituted either as a formal or informal committee in the Office of the President or as a subcommittee of the cabinet. In either case their role would be advisory, not executive, in function.

In this sense, the advisory committee might replace the current NSC (constituted as its principals, without any staff analogous to that of the NSC). But the council of advisers would not take on any of the functions of the current NSC, which would have been dispersed to the NSD and the cabinet.

Note

1. In an effort to determine whether organizational theories and methods might suggest alternative structures, a number of sources were consulted, including Selwyn W. Becker and Duncan Neuhauser, *The Efficient Organization* (New York: Elsevier, 1975); Raymond Cohen, *Theater of Power: The Art of Diplomatic Signaling* (London: Longman, 1987); Stanley Deetz, *Transforming Communication, Transforming Business: Building Responsive and Responsible Workplaces* (New York: Hampton Press, 1995); Roy L. Harmon, *Reinventing the Business: Preparing Today's Enterprise for Tomorrow's Technology* (New York: Free Press, 1996); Stephen Kern, *The Culture of Time and Space* (Cambridge: Harvard University Press, 1983); Thomas Lewis, *Empire of the Air* (New York: Edward Burlingame Books, 1991); Al Gore, *Common Sense Government: Works Better and Costs Less* (New York: Random House, 1995).

7

Roles and Missions of the NSD

IN THEIR DUAL-HAT CAPACITY, the members of the NSD would convene for two purposes, broadly defined:

- As cabinet secretaries, to negotiate the command plan. Here they would present the president and the DDNSD with their judgments on how they would fulfill the responsibilities assigned to their directorates and what resources they would require from the cabinet departments.

- As PNSDs, to coordinate their areas of responsibility on a day-to-day basis and their operations in time of crisis or conflict.

The DDNSD is the coordinator of the NSD, the functional equivalent of the CJCS. As such, in addition to the duties outlined above, the deputy director might be tasked to draft the annual national security strategy document. But the DDNSD is not to perform staff work for the DNSD beyond the preparation of papers forwarded by the PNSDs; otherwise, a new organization will be created not unlike the current NSC staff. This is to be prevented through a statutory limit on the number of staff.

The DCI continues as the head of the intelligence community and director of the CIA and retains the responsibility of advising the president on intelligence matters. The DCI is not, however, a member of the NSD and the DCI's status as cabinet member is at the president's discretion.

The Five Directorates

Directorate of Crisis Management

Headed by the secretary of defense, the Directorate of Crisis Management (D/CM) would be charged with the planning and execution of all missions abroad when the preponderance of assets to be used belong to the DOD and there is a high probability of organized, armed resistance to U.S. personnel by state or nonstate actors. Once the area or theater of operations is declared stable or upon direction of the president, responsibility and authority for the operation within the NSD would shift to another PNSD or be terminated.

Directorate of Regional Affairs

Headed by the secretary of state, the D/RA would be charged with planning for U.S. policy on a regional basis. Staff of the D/RA would assure that policy and operations in such fields as political-military affairs, economic affairs, and environmental and population affairs are coordinated on bilateral and multilateral bases. The D/RA likely would have more of a coordination function among the directorates with less direct operational responsibility; however, major initiatives such as General Agreement on Tariffs and Trade, North American Free Trade Agreement, NATO enlargement, and European Union–U.S. political and diplomatic agreements could be directed by the D/RA as the president would choose.

Directorate of Home Defense Affairs

The formation of the D/HDA would be premised on the belief that new threats to the people and territory of the United States have emerged ; the directorate would be headed by the attorney general. Threats include WMD attacks by nonmilitary means, acts of terrorism, activity of international organized crime, undermining of infrastructure security, and illegal immigration. What distinguishes these threats is their status as crimes when committed on U.S. soil by nonstate actors or foreign nationals acting in the absence of a state of war. Because they are seen as crimes, the criminal justice system's procedures must be followed in protection of U.S. citizens' constitutional rights. The D/HDA would be assigned the missions of reducing U.S. vulnerability, protecting assets and populations, and apprehending and prosecuting perpetrators.

Directorate of Finance and Trade

Headed by the secretary of the treasury, the D/F&T would be charged with identifying and countering threats to the stability of the international financial and trade system and reducing U.S. vulnerability to threatening actions by foreign governments, NGOs, or hostile nonstate actors. In addition, the D/F&T would coordinate and, as necessary, direct policies designed to promote U.S. interests within the world of finance and trade. It would not have directive authority over the Federal Reserve Board.

Directorate of Science and Technology

Headed by either the secretary of commerce or the secretary of education, the D/S&T would be shaped by the choice of its PNSD. If it was directed by the commerce secretary, the directorate would be geared to tasks such as identifying methods of keeping the United States competitive and increasing the emphasis on one sector or another. If the education secretary was the director, the emphasis would be on building a longer-term base along the lines of the National Defense Education Act of the late 1950s. The D/S&T would be charged with long-range planning in the science and technology sector with respect to government investment in civilian and commercial sectors, military dual use, government industrial support, and government spending in the public- and private-education sectors.

Tasking to the Directorates

The president, as the DNSD, would reserve the right to direct the activity and operations of the directorates within the NSD. Unless directed otherwise by the president through the DDNSD, the directorates might undertake the following activities and operations:

Deputy Director of the NSD. The DDNSD would coordinate the activities of the directorates, assure that requests from one to another are promptly acted on, and provide advice to the president.

Directorate of Crisis Management. The D/CM would be the focal point in the U.S. government (USG) for planning and managing foreign contingencies and crises in which the preponderance of assets deployed belong to the DOD or U.S. assets and personnel are likely to be resisted by force of arms by state or nonstate actors.

The D/CM would form a joint planning agency. The joint staff would comprise a number of experts to provide military, diplomatic, political, social-cultural, intelligence, financial, and industrial advice to planning efforts. The size and composition of the staff would be determined by consensus among the PNSDs. The contingency planning staff would perform two functions: prepare plans for activating an operations staff to manage crises, and develop a methodology for forecasting the emergence of crises affecting the interests of the United States and courses of action by which the United States and its allies might forestall or prevent the emergence of the crises.

The DNSD, through the DDNSD and D/CM, would retain control of all crisis management operations. The D/CM would exercise operational control through an OPDIR, who would exercise command of all joint assets made available by the D/CM acting on authority granted by the DNSD. The D/CM would take care to treat the OPDIR as a joint billet, to be occupied by a professional with skills appropriate to the nature of the crisis. Therefore it would be possible for a civilian to be placed in this billet even when U.S. armed forces provide the preponderance of assets to the operation. In such a case, the D/CM would take all measures necessary to assure that the U.S. armed force remain under the tactical command of military personnel and that the force commanders have access to the D/CM through the OPDIR.

The crises to be managed by the D/CM would be limited to those in which the War Powers Act has not been, or is unlikely to be, invoked.

The methodologies and courses of action developed by the D/CM would be reviewed by the NSD and, when approved, would serve as the bases for crisis-management planning as well as for planning by other directorates as ordered by the DDNSD.

Directorate of Regional Affairs. The D/RA would be the focal point for planning U.S. security policy goals by region and for assuring their integration on a global scale; for overseeing the implementation of those goals by the departments and agencies of the USG, particularly the embassies and consulates of the State Department; and for managing regional security policy initiatives as directed by the DNSD.

The D/RA would form a joint planning staff drawn from the Departments of Defense, State, Commerce, Justice, Treasury, and others, with the size and composition of the staff to be determined by consensus among the PNSDs. The staff would focus on the following regions of interest: Europe, to include European Russia and the Middle East and the Mediterranean littoral of Africa; Southwest, Central, and South Asia, to include Russian interests in this region; the Pacific Rim, to include the islands of the Pacific Ocean; the Americas, to include the Caribbean area; and sub-Saharan Africa.

Policy planning would focus on integrating the tools of U.S. diplomacy—military, political, economic, cultural—to address issues affecting the interests of the United States in regions that are

- themselves subject to challenges that can be resolved only through multidisciplinary operations;

- of concern to the United States and one state or a small set of states in the region but with issues not subject to solution through bilateral operations;

- affected by problems that are pan-regional in their sources or solutions: sources might include environmental or health-related issues, immigration, and the like; solutions might include coordinated changes to national laws and regulations, funding, or resources.

The D/RA would appoint an OPDIR to oversee the implementation of policy initiatives in each region. The OPDIRs would lead the planning staff for each region and would themselves form the D/RA's planning staff for integrating regional policy on a global scale. The OPDIR would have directive authority over all USG components in a specified region on matters placed under the purview of the D/RA by the NSD. The OPDIR also would be charged with the oversight of U.S. public diplomacy in the region, to include USG public affairs programs and the relationship between USG components and NGOs.

For regional security initiatives specifically assigned to the D/RA by the DNSD, the PNSD would appoint an OPDIR with the authority to implement the initiative, including the authority to draw on personnel of USG components within the region. For such initiatives, the specified OPDIR would serve only until the initiative is completed or is sufficiently advanced to permit its oversight by normal staff arrangements; this determination will be made on the basis of consensus by the NSD. Any PNSD would be able to place the status of a specified initiative on the agenda of the NSD.

Directorate of Home Defense Affairs. The D/HDA would be the focal point for all USG efforts to reduce the vulnerability of the territory, people, public and private property, and facilities of the United States to threats posed within the boundaries of the United States by foreign sources.

The D/HDA would be responsible for identifying the vulnerabilities of the United States to threats posed by

- terrorism directed at the infrastructure—physical and virtual —of the United States, U.S. public and private institutions and industries, or U.S. citizens;

- organized crime dedicated to the importation of drugs and other contraband, to include illegal immigrants;

- acts of state-sponsored aggression against the infrastructure —physical and virtual—of the United States, U.S. public and private institutions and industries, or U.S. citizens; and

- other sources identified by the DNSD.

The D/HDA also would develop policies and plans to reduce these identified vulnerabilities. Policies would include government–private-sector partnerships for reducing vulnerabilities and the establishment of procedures for responding to the effects of crimes perpetrated on U.S. soil.

Plans would include the formation of investigative and reaction teams intended to warn of threats; to prevent and, if necessary, respond to an attack; and to assess crimes, arrest perpetrators, and prosecute them to the full extent of the law. The investigative teams would be permitted to extend their investigations to foreign locales; D/HDA reaction teams would confine their preventive and response work to the territory of the United States. The D/HDA would appoint an OPDIR to lead the investigative and reaction teams. The OPDIR would have directive authority over the assets assigned by the departments and agencies of the USG for the purpose of the investigation or operation.

The D/HDA could request that the D/CM or the D/RA undertake foreign operations—overt or covert—when its preventive and response activities need to be extended beyond U.S. borders.

Plans for reducing vulnerabilities would include proposals for government efforts and funding and for programs to complement private-sector initiatives, as well as for action by the USG to reduce or eliminate the sources of the threats.

The D/HDA would create a staff to carry out these policy and planning functions. The staff, like other such staffs, would be drawn from the appropriate departments and agencies of the USG, with size and composition settled by consensus in the NSD.

Directorate of Finance and Trade. The D/F&T would be the focal point for all policies and plans related to protecting the security and stability of the international finance and trade system and, in particular, the points at which U.S. public and private institutions, U.S. business and industry, and U.S. citizens interface with the international system. The D/F&T would not engage in efforts to manage the international finance and trade system or the activities of U.S. institutions, business community, industry, or citizens. It would review international agreements (to which the United States is and is not a party) to assure that the system is constructed and operates fairly and to reduce the vulnerability of the United States to organized efforts to corrupt the system or to target U.S. institutions, firms, or individuals for criminal action.

The D/F&T would create a staff to carry out these policy and planning functions. The staff, like other such staffs, would be drawn from the appropriate departments and agencies of the USG, with size and composition to be determined by consensus in the NSD.

Directorate of Science and Technology. The D/S&T would be the focal point for policies and plans for sustaining the leadership of the United States in important areas of science and technology. It would identify the key areas in the fields of scientific research and technology and develop, in conjunction with U.S. academic and industry leaders in those fields, plans and programs to assure that federal funding is available to support those areas when necessary. Emphasis will not be confined to traditional areas of defense research. Science and technology related to information-system hardware and software, environmental status and evolution, biomedical research, and materials and structures, among others, are all candidate areas of activity.

The D/S&T would not confine its effort to advanced research only. It would include in its plans and programs attention to education from the primary through the secondary levels as well as applied and engineering sciences. The objective of the directorate would be to keep the United States at the leading edge of science and technology. It would push U.S. research and help support a defense and nondefense base from which to respond to a pull from either the private or the public sector.

The D/S&T would present a national plan for S&T development. It would have oversight authority for the implementation of the plan by the laboratories of the USG and in USG-contracted research.

As directed by the DNSD, the D/S&T would direct research in specified areas through an OPDIR. As in the case of other specified OPDIR activity, the OPDIR ceases to function once the mission has been certified as accomplished by a consensus decision of the NSD.

Cabinet

The cabinet would serve as the focal point within the government for discussions and decisions related to the ordinary operations of the government. Cabinet tasks in the area of security affairs would include all matters not assigned by the president to the NSD. Resolution of turf conflicts would be the responsibility of the DDNSD and the secretary of the cabinet.

The secretary of the cabinet would establish, as appropriate, subcommittees of the cabinet to prepare decision papers and oversee the execution of policy. These can be standing subcommittees or ad hoc subcommittees. In the field of security affairs, a subcommittee might include representation from State, Defense, the Joint Staff, and CIA. Depending on the issue, it might be augmented with representatives from other departments or other agencies within the Office of the President, for example, OMB. The subcommittees would be chaired by the secretary of the cabinet or the deputies of the secretary. The secretary of the cabinet would have directive authority over the subcommittees with respect to the process of preparing decision papers and oversight of policy execution. The range of activity that might be assigned the cabinet and its subcommittees includes the implementation, monitoring, and verification of treaties and agreements; the conduct of bilateral affairs; and departmental organization.

Council of Advisers

The council would provide advice to the president. Its core members—the secretaries of state, defense, treasury, commerce, education and the attorney general—would be able to take a national perspective because of their dual roles as members of the cabinet and heads of their respective directorates. The CJCS holds an advisory position independent of both the cabinet and NSD, and the DCI might have a cabinet position but is the president's intelligence adviser.

The agenda for the council's meetings would be prepared by the secretary of the cabinet or the DDNSD, depending on the reason for the meeting. On most issues, it is likely that the NSD would lead because it was formed to tackle the preeminent issues facing the nation.

Roles and Missions for the Existing Departments

Except as noted, the departments and agencies of the USG would continue to operate under existing legislation, presidential guidance, and department and agency directives.

Departments and agencies would provide personnel and resources as requested by PNSDs, including housing personnel and providing overhead support. The NSD would make maximum use of information technologies to allow a minimum disruption of personnel.

Department secretaries would be directed to institute personnel and management changes within their departments to reflect the responsibility and authority granted the directorates of the NSD as well as the need of those directorates for trained personnel and resources.

Many of the details of restructuring of departments would be left to the secretaries but would require approval from the NSD before legislation would be sought to restructure the department. The following changes, however, would be instituted:

- Assignment of personnel to the directorates of the NSD would be for a fixed period, not to exceed three years.

- Personnel could be reassigned to an NSD after a three-year hiatus but could serve no more than three tours.

- Each department would create a "joint career" class of professionals to assure that the highest quality personnel are assigned to the directorates and to provide a professional career path for such personnel. These individuals would be selected from among participants in at least one joint task force under an OPDIR. Selection would make use of standard career civil service practices for personnel at the GS-13 level.

- Personnel thus selected would be eligible for assignment to any directorate. The DNSD would provide the personnel evaluations for the staff of the directorate.

- Only personnel who have served in a joint career assignment will be eligible within their departments for assignment to positions equivalent in rank to deputy assistant secretary and assistant secretary.

- This preferred status would apply only to billets designated by the department as operational; administrative or technical billets—finance, legal, intelligence, personnel, acquisition, or procurement—would not qualify.

8

Evaluation of the Proposed Organization

Advantages

- The proposed organization provides the president with a line-management capacity with respect to issues assigned to the directorates. This capacity should put an end to the lament that presidents "command nothing but the Marine Band."

- The structure operates only by direction of the president; that is, it has no bureaucratic life of its own other than the specific charges the president gives to the PNSDs. If the president has no security policy agenda, the staff work in the directorates is academic at best, and the OPDIRs will have no standing.

- Day-to-day responsibility for oversight of the NSD is given over to the DDNSD. The choice of DDNSD belongs to the president, who could choose the vice president. If the president chooses someone else, that candidate must undergo the Senate's advise-and-consent process. PNSDs do not require a second confirmation; their confirmations as a department secretaries would suffice. As a result, the security policy of the nation is entrusted through constitutional processes to a chain of command fully accountable to the American people, which might make a presidential candidate's security policy a matter of greater interest to the electorate, particularly if the candidate intends to give the post of DDNSD to the vice president.

- Dual-hatting the cabinet secretaries reinforces the chain of command; requires that each secretary separate department missions and functions from assigned directorate missions and functions; and gives the secretary, as a PNSD, control over the key security issues within a specific area.

- The establishment of a joint career path creates a cadre of senior civil servants that can operate across department lines even when acting in a department, instead of a directorate, capacity.

- Assigning responsibility to the DNSD for senior staff evaluation reports (ERs) assures responsiveness while staff are in the directorate; and, because the ER is a part of the selection process for promotion within the parent department, good performance in a joint position will not penalize a staff member on return to the department.

- The requirement of prior service on a task force under an OPDIR as a prerequisite for selection to a directorate staff is meant to provide department secretaries with an incentive, from the beginning, to provide quality people to the task forces. If only second-rate personnel are assigned, the secretaries will have only second-rate people from which to draw for the staffing of both their departments and directorates.

- The focused responsibility of the directorates permits their use for tackling issues not amenable to a standard, intergovernmental solution. It is not a structure meant to change the current departmental organization or to replace existing departments. Nor does it attempt to resolve the contentious matters associated with the role of the DCI—other than to prohibit the director from acquiring the status of a PNSD. Although it would be good if the directorates provided incentives for transferring components from one department to another, that is not the principal intent of the structure. Its intent is to make a meaningful and manageable change to the process of government that, in turn, would stimulate extant organizations to respond so that they too might accommodate to the new process. At the same time, the change needs to be sufficiently large and insulated so that it is not subject to piecemeal absorption by the extant organizations and processes.

- The Council of Advisers assumes the advisory role that the NSC plays today. Because the PNSDs are also cabinet secretaries, their bureaucratic loyalties will be diversified. They cannot simply promote their directorate interests at the expense of their department interests, and vice versa. Directorates are composed of representatives from various departments and the cabinet is composed of subcommittees on which the PNSDs will need the support of other cabinet members. The presence on the council of the DCI and CJCS adds two actors with wholly different bureaucratic interests who have in their hands the means for the PNSDs and secretaries to accomplish their tasks. Tension within the council, between the secretary of the cabinet and the DDNSD, is possible; but that tension ought to be useful to the president who is attempting to maximize control over the government as a whole while concentrating on the matters of critical and urgent importance to national security.

- The role of the cabinet is substantially increased in this organization plan because of the underlying premise of the NSD—that it is to concentrate on the critical and urgent affairs of security. Within this organization the ordinary business of government, particularly in the security realm, is transferred from the old NSC to subcommittees of the cabinet. As noted earlier, this might include much of the work currently done within the traditional Interdepartmental Group and Senior Interdepartmental Group structures of the NSC and the National Economic Council. This makes the selection of department secretaries who will sit as cabinet members more important than it has been to date. It also invests a good deal of importance in the position of the secretary of the cabinet.

The increased responsibility of the cabinet and the creation of the Council of Advisers are meant to create centers within which dual-hatting concerns can be addressed. The enhanced role of the cabinet provides those secretaries who are not in the NSD with increased weight in the government and requires the NSD members to take steps to win their support on matters of administration—budgets, personnel assignments, policy—as well as in areas where subcommittee assignments affect mutual interests. For example, it is not difficult to imagine that the Departments of Agriculture and Interior might have substantial influence on trade matters relating to farm products or natural resources in a subcommittee that includes Treasury and/or Commerce. In short, the PNSDs cannot be cavalier toward those not on the NSD. Likewise the Council of Advisers establishes a venue in which the PNSDs will need to demonstrate appreciation for their colleagues if they expect to receive support in staffing their respective directorates and arriving at a satisfactory command plan, that is, the assignment of roles and missions to the directorates, overseen by the DDNSD.

Critique

- Should the vice president be made DDNSD it could become very difficult for the president to control the vice president because of both the political embarrassment associated with firing the nation's only other nationally elected constitutional officer and the very likely possibility that the vice president would establish an independent network of support within the Congress and in the departments and agencies in support of the vice president's, as opposed to the president's, national security strategy and policies.

- A DDNSD raised to cabinet rank and confirmed by the Senate would undoubtedly seek to establish a personal constituency, independent of the president, on Capitol Hill. Such a DDNSD would be less likely than a vice president to be able to pretend to a national mandate in the conduct of policy but, like any cabinet officer, the standing of this type of DDNSD would not be dependent solely on the pleasure of the president.

- Perhaps more troubling in the case of a cabinet-level DDNSD is the reverse side of the confirmation coin: such a DDNSD would be accountable to the Congress and not to the president for the conduct of security affairs. Under the current arrangements, the NSC is bound by the nation's laws but is a creature of the president, who is accountable to the Congress. Devolving accountability is contrary to the purpose of the proposed reform and could create crippling constitutional battles over which branch of government controls the nation's foreign and defense policy.

- The dual hatting of the selected cabinet secretaries as PNSDs increases accountability—they are directly charged by the president with policy development and implementation, with all the necessary assets placed at their disposal—and has the potential of reducing interdepartment and interagency friction. At the same time, it could create significant problems:

  Who is in charge? Ambitious PNSDs could seek to enlarge their influence in the government by seeking to assume authority over an issue on their own initiative; this would impose on the president the need to adjudicate among the PNSDs in assigning tasking. Although this might raise the level of the president's involvement, it also could result in a substantial waste of time as the traditional interagency battles, once conducted below the presidential threshold of regard, now take place within the president's areas of immediate concern. Because these areas are of highest priority, their treatment becomes a matter of the political prestige of the president, at home and abroad.

  Separating the secretary from the PNSD. The model for the proposed reform was that of the CINC; but CINCs are military officers who serve in capacities subordinate to civilian control in a system that separates the formulation of policy from its execution. CINCs can be viewed as supreme only within a (relatively) narrowly defined sphere of action. It could be argued that a secretary is more like a CINC than a PNSD and that a PNSD is actually entrusted with far more authority than a secretary over a wider range of activity. Such a structure could possibly create confusion in the chain of command—a PNSD's orders could be self-originating. A dual-hatted CINC could never be in this situation. Of equal concern is that a secretary, despite having an obligation to perform in a joint role when operating as a PNSD, could impose the department on the directorate —or vice versa. In either case, one of the organizations is likely to suffer, as would the other directorates and/or departments by comparison.

Of these criticisms, the most troubling is related to the role of the vice president and the confirmability of the DDNSD. As a matter of principle, no structure that invites a struggle over constitutional responsibilities should be put in place. Any structure must provide the president with the clear capacity to direct the nation's foreign policy and preserve presidential prerogatives with respect to the role of commander in chief of the nation's armed forces.

The complications arising from dual hatting the secretaries are not constitutional but political and procedural. They are no less important for that reason. But in a well-legislated structure they should not pose insuperable impediments to the conduct of security affairs within the areas identified.

These criticisms can be addressed by altering some of the features of the reforms that were described in Chapter 6 as Option 1. One description of these alterations is provided in Option 2, below, along with a discussion of their implications for the approach that guided the development of Option 1.

Alternatives

Option 2

Although Option 2 would seek to preserve the functional areas identified in Option 1, several adjustments might be made:

- Instead of designating the vice president as DDNSD or requiring that the post of DDNSD be confirmable by the Senate, the DDNSD would serve at the pleasure of the president. This would preserve the DDNSD's independence from the Congress, on the one hand, and guarantee a role distinct from that of the PNSDs.

- The PNSDs would not be dual-hatted but would be appointed by and accountable to the president although they would still take their direction from the DDNSD.

- Tasking for the directorates would come from the secretaries meeting as the NSD and chaired by the DDNSD. Only in cases where agreement could not be reached would tasking be done by the president; however, the president as DNSD would still be responsible for setting the charter of each of the directorates. In practice, the DDNSD would be responsible for developing those charters.

- Staffing for the directorates would still be provided by the departments and agencies.

- The single most substantial change would be to forgo the cabinet arrangements. Instead of having the ordinary business of security conducted in the cabinet, that activity could take place through a secretariat in the Council of Advisers. In effect, then, the Council of Advisers would take on the functions of the present NSC, with the directorates serving as specified commands (to use DOD language) within the council. The DDNSD would lead both the council and the NSD.

Implications of Option 2. These features of Option 2 would have a profound effect on the capacity of the NSD to formulate and execute policy.

In policy formulation the key difference is the altered interplay between the DDNSD and the PNSDs. The PNSDs, relative to the department and agency heads, would have little more real authority in the formulation of policy than current NSC staff members. Their authority would be directly dependent on the relationship of the president and DDNSD with the cabinet secretaries. (In a strong presidency, NSC staff authority can be enormous; in a weak one the tendencies of the departments and agencies to chart their own courses will continue to dominate policymaking.)

But it is not in the formulation of policy but instead in its execution that Option 2 suffers most by comparison with Option 1. The dual hatting of the PNSDs and the accountability of the DDNSD made it possible to consider giving the PNSDs executive responsibility—direction—of the highest-priority operations. In Option 2 that is not possible—no chain of command or accountability exists for either the DDNSD or the PNSDs.

Under such conditions it is less likely that a secretary will want to assign the best personnel to the directorates; secretaries will need them in their own departments to execute policy.

Nonetheless, the functional grouping of the NSD tends to preserve the focus on the highest priorities of the administration. Interagency task forces and backstopping groups can be fashioned around the functional groups. The DDNSD would have considerable latitude in deciding how far to separate the ordinary from the extraordinary business of national security that is suggested by the creation of these functional directorates. That is, instead of maintaining a second organization for the conduct of ordinary business, the president could direct the DDNSD to organize security affairs in a manner that forces all department and agency heads to cast the issues requiring presidential attention so they fit within the functional framework.

Should a president adopt such a course, it would be an attempt, in effect, to create the consensus on security affairs that is lacking. Because the president would be insisting that the departments and agencies adjust their several approaches to accommodate presidential priorities, the presidential will would be imposed in the conduct of business within areas of department and agency responsibility. This in turn would result, inevitably, in hearings before the Congress with respect to the president's intentions as they are represented in budget, personnel, and policy directives and actions. But the difficulty that can be encountered in such an attempt might be discerned from the reactions to Secretary of Defense Les Aspin's plans to restructure the DOD in the early days of the Clinton administration. Absent a consensus on the implied policy objectives the proposed reorganization was to serve, the reorganization plan had virtually no chance of being accepted by what was then a Democratic-controlled Congress.

It might be argued, nevertheless, that the DOD has undergone some reorganization along the lines laid down by Aspin. But even the most conspicuous success—the rechartering of OSD/International Security Policy (ISP) to concentrate on the issue of "loose nukes" instead of the larger portfolio of NATO, multilateral arms control, strategic arms control, and so forth, of former years—has been modest at best.

Assessment of Option 2. The adjustments to Option 1 reflected in Option 2 might address the most troubling objections raised by Option 1, but they do not serve to address the underlying problem Option 1 was designed to manage—the lack of a consensus with respect to foreign and defense policy.

Hence, if the objections to Option 1 cannot be reconciled but the underlying problem is accepted as persistent, an entirely different approach may be required.

Option 3

An alternative that might satisfy the twin objectives of building a consensus about security policy while better marshaling the assets of the government is the creation of ministers to oversee the critical planning and operations related to national security.

That is, rather than dual hatting the current secretaries and placing them on an NSD, it might be better to amalgamate relevant functions under officials known as ministers, who receive their commissions from the president and are confirmed by the Senate. These ministers would assume a role more analogous to that of the CINCs; that is, within their specific areas of responsibility they would be responsible for the planning and execution of national policy.

Direction for the activities of these ministers would come from the president (with the advice of the department secretaries and the

DCI); the ministers would now be sitting in the position equivalent to the service chiefs of staff when they are convened as the JCS. The role of the DDNSD would be analogous to the CJCS—first among equals and an independent adviser to the president—but the DDNSD would hold a warrant from the president.

Under this arrangement the secretaries would serve as the supporting component to the ministers within the ministers' areas of responsibility. Staffing for the ministers would be the same as in Option 1. Staff for the DDNSD would be seconded from both the Office of the President and the departments.

In contrast with Option 1, the DDNSD would be the only dual-hatted official in the system and would oversee both the specified activities of the ministers as well as the more general and extensive activities of the department secretaries in the performance of their responsibilities.

As in Option 1, the area of responsibility and the extent of executive authority to be granted the ministers would be subject to legislation and congressional oversight.

Implications of Option 3. This option has the virtues of preserving the independence of the DDNSD and avoiding the complications—political and constitutional—associated with Option 1 with respect to the dual hatting of the department secretaries.

This option has the added advantage of setting in legislation the areas of responsibility to be treated by the ministers and, by extension, the support to be provided by the departments to the ministers. Hence, Option 3 could make internecine warfare among the dual-hatted secretaries less likely than in Option 1—or at least confined within accepted bureaucratic boundaries. In so doing it goes a long way toward minimizing the overlap of jurisdiction between department and directorate; for example, between the DOD and D/CM over control of a peace-enforcement operation.

At the same time Option 3 creates competing centers for authority and resources within the security apparatus. Option 1 created the risk that a secretary might favor directorate over department, or vice versa; but in the end the secretary would be accountable for both, and success as either a secretary or a PNSD would depend on sustaining a proper balance between the two.

There would be an obligation, as both secretary and PNSD, to maintain correct (if not cordial) relations with security colleagues when no special advantages could be asserted.

Option 3, however, separates the ministers from their bases of support. This could favor either the minister or the secretaries obliged to support the minister. Which would hold the advantage might depend on such factors as the areas of responsibility assigned the minister or denied the secretary; the salience of the responsibility assigned the minister; the extent to which a minister might be able to act independently of the secretaries owing to a minimum requirement for support; and the determination of a secretary to assert prerogatives or refuse to man, train, and equip the supporting assets required by a minister.

The requirements of the ministers would need to be adjudicated by the DDNSD. For example, the DDNSD might form the policy equivalent of the JROC used by the Office of the Joint Chiefs of Staff to integrate the technical requirements of the CINCs. That is, the objectives, policies, programs, and operations to be undertaken by the ministers and their requirements for assets—manpower, legislation, and so forth—could be reviewed and integrated across the ministries. The product of this staff exercise would be approved by the president in consultation with the department secretaries.

From a congressional point of view, it is altogether likely that the more explicit the responsibility granted a minister, the better it is for the purposes of oversight. From a presidential point of view, this ought not impose any particular burden or undue constraint. In fact, it ought to create an opportunity for consultation with the Congress on the particular responsibilities the president has assigned to the ministers. By carefully choosing the issues or interests assigned to ministers, the president can create a process to establish a consensus with respect to security affairs.

As was the case in Option 1, an important question regarding legislation is whether it is permissive or restrictive. Although in Option 1 the preference would be for a permissive approach, in Option 3 the preference might be for a restrictive approach. That is, only that activity specifically authorized can be undertaken by the ministers; but within the specific area of responsibility the minister is supreme, subject of course to the president's direction.

Assessment of Option 3. Option 3 provides a less complicated set of relations among the DDNSD, the PNSDs, and the secretaries. By creating ministers for specific purposes, the president reaches a level of flexibility in the pursuit of security policy that is not currently attainable.

At the same time, the lack of complication comes with a narrowing of the scope of activity for a minister. It is easy to imagine a minister being reduced to the status of a czar, which in the past has meant a presidential emissary lacking bureaucratic clout. To avoid such an outcome, a minister would need to be both confirmed and supplied with a regular, competent, and appropriately sized staff.

Option 3 does not fully resolve the problem associated with the president's role in the adjudication of disputes. Whereas in Option 1 the chief executive would have been compelled to adjudicate among the secretaries in their roles as PNSDs, in Option 3 the president would need to protect the ministers against the encroachments, or outright hostility, of the secretaries. The tension need not be intolerable or even counterproductive; but if it is to be put to good use it must be managed by the president. The DDNSD will not have the authority to fill this role.

Congressional oversight in Option 3 is less complicated and more likely to be focused on specific issues and interests than in Option 1. This is a decided advantage.

9

The Long View

THIS ESSAY BEGAN WITH A REFLECTION on the factionalized state of thinking about U.S. national security policy. This reflection was prompted by research to support the assumption that prompted this study: with the distance of some six or seven years from the end of the Cold War and the reelection of the first post–Cold War president, a consensus—perhaps nascent, but a consensus nonetheless— would have emerged on the purpose, object, and conduct of U.S. national security policy.

Close inspection has suggested that the assumption was unwarranted. In the debate on national security policy, the issues faction and the interests faction appear to be firmly entrenched and unwilling or unable to seek reconciliation. The reasons are both conceptual and practical, which can mean political. The conceptual differences are stark. The issues faction continues to pursue concepts and policies that would raise international standards and norms to such a height that the sovereign authority of the government and people of the United States would be subordinated to it. Members of this faction argue that this subordination would be for particular purposes or activities only; they do not suggest the creation of and obedience to "world government." But it is a small step, in the view of members of the interests faction, from propositions put forward by prominent members and supporters of the Clinton administration (in publications like *A New Concept of Cooperative Security* and *Self-Determination in the New World Order*) to a loss of sovereign control over issues of war and peace, intervention and neutrality.

For its part, the interests faction persists in seeing the "new world order" as an unfortunate "vision thing" of the last Cold War president. Henry Kissinger remarked in the early 1990s that the problems of immigration, environment, humanitarian concerns, and international organized crime do constitute new security concerns. But adherents of the interests faction are at a loss about how to address the new concerns in any context other than what critics from the issues faction would call the Westphalian state system. Moreover, they have yet to reconcile their insistence on maintaining a large and (mostly) conventionally oriented military force in the absence of an adversary that warrants such preparation. But these particular differences mark the interests faction less than does its continued insistence, in opposition to the views of the issues faction, that there is a peculiarly American way of life that need not be and should not be modified to meet the demands of the post–Cold War era—whatever these demands might be and whether they are generated by domestic requirements or foreign preferences.

The policies and rhetoric of President Clinton can be seen as the best evidence of the fact of this factional split and of the irreconcilable nature of it. From the time of his inaugural address to his most recent speech to the UN General Assembly, the president has consistently put forward the issues-based concept and agenda. During the same period he has repeatedly tacked across the issues in the need to accommodate the interests faction. This raises the practical and political concerns that militate against reconciliation of the factions. The president's tacking, hardly objectionable or unusual in its own right, has given rise to mistrust and charges of duplicity by the interests faction; and proponents of the interests point of view, who are currently centered in the Congress, have produced legislation aimed at trimming the president's sails.

Thus has a dispute about the purposes of U.S. national security policy been transformed. It has evolved from a heated debate among elites, going back at least as far as Woodrow Wilson's time, into a contemporary struggle between the nation's two political parties, themselves animated by differing views of what America is, what it should become, and how it ought to be governed. That party struggle, owing to the fact that each party controls a separate branch of government, in turn has metamorphosed into a classic struggle between the executive and legislative branches for control of not only security policy but of domestic policy as well.

This last point is of some significance for appreciating the depth of the split between the factions. Proponents of the interests faction are associated, in the main, with the view that government should be smaller and less intrusive and that its main task abroad is to protect what Americans have at home. How others govern themselves is a matter of little concern to them except when the domestic affairs of other states affect their security policies and make them a threat to America's security. If there is no threat, the interests faction sees little requirement for the United States to do any more than demand civility and reciprocity among nations.

The issues faction has a different view of government. Associated primarily with those who believe the U.S. government has a positive role to play in the improvement of the daily lives of its citizens and taken with the notion that democracy has emerged triumphant as the conceptual basis of modern politics everywhere, the issues faction is prepared not only to espouse new norms of international democracy but, where necessary, to intervene in the affairs of other states to assure that the new norms are adopted and followed. This intervention can take the form of humanitarian assistance, peace making, and nation building or multilateral–multinational agreements.

As is often the case with a dispute on national security policy, the lack of a consensus can be traced to a difference on domestic affairs. From George Washington's day through Madison's difficulties with the New England states, the opposition to Polk's war, the resistance to Wilson's progressivism, and the left–right split in the decade after World War II, the state of the nation's domestic affairs and politics has played an important role in the struggle over the formulation and execution of security policy.

That so much should be at stake—control over both the domestic and foreign agenda—is not unusual. Nor is the fact that two factions, well-matched, should contend for that control. But it means that, barring catastrophe, the likelihood for consensus being reached in the near term is not very high.

This analysis left the object of this study—an inquiry into the need to alter the apparatus of the government to better address the national security affairs in the post–Cold War era—without a solid foundation in public (i.e., political) opinion. The National Security Act of 1947, although it established the apparatus with which the United States fought and won the Cold War, was not itself a creature of the Cold War. Its origins lay in the lessons learned from fighting an industrial-age global war; an unshakable consensus that U.S. power would be needed to organize the state-based, post–World War II international system; and the belief that discharging this responsibility with minimum domestic disruption called for a combination of military downsizing, efficient organization, and a process for rapid mobilization of industrial resources. NSA '47, with subsequent revisions, met the requirement.

The radical character of NSA '47 is easily overlooked. Its three key provisions—the creation of the NSC, the formation of the DOD, and the establishment of the DCI—eliminated 150 years of practice with respect to the War and Navy Departments and ended forever the conceit that "gentlemen do not read each other's mail." NSA '47 created a structure within which formal consultation and coordination were to take place. Moreover, the reorganization was intended to provide the president—in the future—with the power to plan for the use of and effectively control the nation's resources in wartime and to direct the collection and assessment of intelligence to assure that those resources could be mobilized in time and be applied in ways that would bring victory. In doing so, NSA '47 created new centers of opinion and authority with which the president was then required to consult and coordinate; this was intended to reduce the kind of independence exercised by FDR during World War II. The time when that planning would be tested, when resources were mobilized, and intelligence needed came sooner than many in 1947 expected. But the system put in place proved effective in fighting the Cold War although the United States had only mixed success in conducting the numerous armed conflicts waged during it.

The fundamental changes of NSA '47 depended on the established consensus. Because such a consensus is lacking today, this study would make little contribution to the public policy debate if it recommended a substantial and extensive change to the national security apparatus. The current bureaucracy being cumbersome and often unable to respond in a timely manner, changes have been thought needed to increase the flexibility of the president in response to what are undoubtedly new security challenges. Moreover, changes have been thought needed to adapt the security apparatus so its organization more nearly approximates what both the issues faction and the interests faction agree are the more immediate areas of security concern: crisis management, regional security, home defense, finance and trade, and science and technology.

The suggestion that the two factions agree on these areas of concern does not imply that agreement exists on how to meet them. Therefore, now is not the time to recommend the elimination or merger of whole departments or the reassignment of responsibilities among departments. Instead, a more modest proposal has been made.

The proposal draws from the notion, raised at the outset and validated by NSA '47, that the genius of the U.S. system of government is that it provides a place for people of ambition. This is particularly so in the executive branch and most especially in the field of security policy, where the Constitution and historic practice endow the president with the authority to set and execute the policy of the government. This immense power can attract ambitious leaders, as it has in the past. But it is a power that is also subject to accountability to the Congress in the name of the citizenry.

Constitutional checks and balances, however, do not change one immutable fact of U.S. politics: only the president can lead on security policy. A Senate full of prime ministers and a House of Representatives full of chancellors of the exchequer, if you will, have never been, and show no prospect of ever being, able to conduct security policy. Therefore the United States must find a way to provide the president with an apparatus that brings under presidential control the requisite government resources for developing and executing policy on security concerns believed to be of a defining character. If the position of president today both explicitly held the direct authority that it previously had enjoyed in forming and executing policy and could exercise increased flexibility to shape and respond to events, ambitious presidents would attempt to assert that authority and use that flexibility. But precisely because ambition is balanced by congressional oversight, the president's success would depend on the ability to persuade the public of the correct direction to take. Put another way, under the proposal put forward here, any ambition felt by the president either to transcend faction or to reach accommodation with factional rivals would not be restricted by the question of who controls the bureaucracy, by congressional intent, or by restrictive legislation. It would rest on the power of the president and the presidential advisers to persuade the public that the use to which the new apparatus is put is in their interest. In short, it would depend on the president's ability to lead.

The proposed NSD is an organization within the Office of the President that an ambitious chief executive might use to shape the nation's security policy for the coming decades and that itself requires attention to the limits of policy imposed by domestic requirements and foreign circumstances. The appeal to ambition is manifested in a structure that places at the president's disposal the staff and resources to plan and also carry out a small number of initiatives key to the success of executive policies. Under the proposed arrangements, a president is not bound to navigate the impossible corridors of the Pentagon and the State, Treasury, and Justice Departments, the details of the War Powers Act, and so forth. Instead, within the NSD reside the means for accomplishing presidential tasks with dispatch.

The chief executive's ambition is modified by two factors, however. The first is the process of appointment of the principal members of the NSD. Their status as confirmed officers of the government, preferably also as department secretaries, is born of the country's need to have the power of the executive branch overseen and checked when necessary by the Congress. The confirmation process is meant to impose on the president, through the choice of nominees and the points of view they agree to present to the Congress, the obligation to be clear about the nature and object of the presidential security policy. Because the executive is being granted authority to pursue cherished policy ambitions through the directorates, the president and the nominees must be able to persuade the Congress that those ambitions are not detrimental to Congress's own or to the ambitions of the constituents it represents.

The choice of cabinet officers therefore becomes a matter of political moment for a president, and perhaps even for the candidates for president. That is, a public knowing that the president and the highest-level officers will be invested with considerable power in the directorates might find a greater interest in the political characters of both the candidate they would choose for office and the cabinet officers to be selected. If so, the public accountability of the politicians and the professional security policy experts is much increased.

And that accountability must be presented on two grounds: first, the public must find the policy direction and prescription acceptable in terms of the policy's effect on their domestic circumstances, and, second, the public must not be embarrassed by the consequences abroad of U.S. policy. These are, after all, the criteria upon which the credibility of the president in security affairs is based.

The proposal is not without its problems, and alterations of the basic proposal are presented. But it must be admitted that each alteration reduces the integrity of the concept. For example, altering the confirmable status of either the DDNSD or the PNSDs reduces the accountability of those actors and the president, preventing them from taking full advantage of the authority and flexibility conferred by the proposal.

But this study is not about the one correct choice for reorganizing or adapting the nation's security apparatus. Instead, it aims to raise a number of critical questions about the base on which security policy in fact rests and to argue that any effort to revise the NSA '47 must be, at its heart, a political undertaking. Security policy today and in the past has been an essential component of the nation's understanding of itself. What is done abroad is a reflection of what the American people think about themselves and the role of their government at home. Hence, in restructuring the security apparatus, an effort must be made not so much to assure the correct outcome as to assure that the American people can recognize it as an effective apparatus that is ultimately, and directly, accountable to them. The foregoing has been offered in that spirit.

Appendix A

Interests and Issues: Perspectives on Future Challenges to U.S. Security

Patrick J. Garrity

THIS PAPER REVIEWS BRIEFLY the major analytic perspectives concerning the changing character of the international environment. It is obviously impractical to consider every viewpoint, but for the purposes of thinking through the future requirements of the U.S. national security apparatus, two broad ways of understanding the post–Cold War world can be identified.

The first perspective on the future international environment might be characterized as interests-based. This approach assumes that the nation-state essentially remains the central unit of account in world affairs, that nations pursue their national interests first and foremost through the accumulation of power, that nations are sensitive to their relative positions in the structure of international relations, and that nations will react in more or less traditional fashion to perceived threats to their national security and position in the international system (e.g., through attracting support or balancing, seeking to deter or reassure). From this perspective, the most critical trends in international politics involve the manner in which various nation-states are adjusting to the change in power relationships caused by the collapse of the Soviet Union, by the prospective rise of new major centers of power (e.g., China, Japan, Germany–Europe, India), and by the alignment of important regional actors (e.g., Iran, Ukraine, a united Korea).

The other broad perspective focuses on issues as opposed to interests. From the issues perspective, the traditional, Westphalian structure of international politics—dominated by the relationships among nation-states and by the balance of military power—is relatively less important. Peoples (however defined) and individuals are struggling to find their places in a world that has become much smaller, much more interdependent, and much less amenable to control by sovereign states and traditional political structures. Instead of the familiar *threats* to the sovereignty and independence of states, peoples and individuals now face functional *dangers* to their collective and singular well-being. Such dangers include the proliferation of weapons of mass destruction (WMD), terrorism, ethnic and tribal conflicts, global climate change, the asymmetrical effects of a globalized economy, and the like.

The different ways of assessing critical trends in world affairs can be illustrated by two recent books by the historian Paul Kennedy. The first book, *The Rise and Fall of the Great Powers* (1987), was written during the latter stages of the Cold War. As the title indicates, Kennedy sought to understand international politics in terms major states or empires; he was particularly interested in understanding the tendency of great powers to decline because of "imperial overstretch" (i.e., the loss of political and economic vitality at home due in part to excessive commitments abroad). By contrast, Kennedy's second book, *Preparing for the Twenty-First Century* (1993), was concerned with transnational developments— demographic, social, technological—that traditional political mechanisms will struggle to accommodate.[1]

To be sure, these two basic orientations are not mutually exclusive. The interests-based perspective generally acknowledges the importance of the changing character of power and the impact of transnational (and subnational) forces on international affairs. And for most of those who see the world in issues, the nation-state, or power politics, is not going to disappear. The analytic focus on interests over issues (or vice versa) tends to be a matter of relative emphasis. The two are often given equal weight. For example, in a recent major report on U.S. foreign policy, the Center for Strategic and International Studies (CSIS) listed two international problems (one stated as an issue, the other an interest) to which the United States should give its highest immediate priority: first, preventing the spread of WMD and the missile technology required to deliver them; and, second, maintaining peace among the major powers.[2]

It is also important to note that there is no necessary ideological (i.e., left–right, isolationist–internationalist) division between the two approaches. This is especially true of the interests category. Also, the issues–interests controversy is by no means a new one. For many decades—at least as far back as Woodrow Wilson (issues) and Theodore Roosevelt (interests), if not to Thomas Jefferson and Alexander Hamilton—Americans have debated how best to understand the world.

A New Structure for National Security Policy Planning is designed to explore the adequacy of a security structure that was designed essentially to fight the Cold War. The U.S. Cold War strategy of containment and deterrence was by no means devoid of concern with issues, but its core elements—and structure—involved managing alliances and conducting large-scale military operations in the defense of traditional national interests. If one believes that the emerging international environment will still be dominated by interests and threats, the current national security structure is probably adequate as a point of departure, with appropriate modifications at the margin. But if one decides that the new global issues and dangers take precedence, this implies that a major restructuring of the U.S. government might be in order.

Interests

In general terms, those who focus on interests assume that the post–Cold War environment will continue to be defined essentially by the relationships among the major powers and between greater and lesser states, although many other factors obviously enter into the equation. The central question from this perspective is whether the structure of international politics—relations among nations—will be peaceful or competitive or conflictual. Peace now prevails among the great powers, and none are actively preparing for war with others; but this situation could change, and international relations will be affected decisively by efforts to avoid such competition (or to maximize one's position in a prospective competition). An alternate interests-based perspective, considered below, argues that the dominant dimension of great-power relations and conflict will be economic rather than military.

Henry Kissinger, for instance, argues:

victory in the Cold War propelled America into a world which bears many similarities to the European state system of the eighteenth and nineteenth centuries.... In an international system characterized by perhaps five or six major powers and a multiplicity of smaller states, order will have to emerge much as it did in past centuries from a reconciliation and balancing of competing national interests.[3]

Former senator Sam Nunn asserts:

Great power politics did not end with the Cold War. In fact, the international relations of tomorrow may in some ways be more like the 19th century balance of power system...war and interstate conflict are not obsolete. The means of conflict may have changed, but the sources of human conflict and cruelty remain.[4]

Peter Rodman acknowledges that there are many centrifugal forces, some old (like nationalism and religious fundamentalism) and some new (like economic and technological trends), that further weaken the traditional sovereign actors on the world scene. But it is too early to write the obituary of traditional actors; the international system is still in a state of flux, and it is on this structural problem that U.S. global strategy should focus.

The "New Age" agenda of environmental, humanitarian, and other non-traditional issues is important. But if relations among the great powers go sour, we invite a recurrence of big-league international conflict.... If we take for granted the present moment's relatively benign balance among the major powers, in other words, we will lose it. Similarly, if trade disputes among the industrial democracies are not contained or resolved in accordance with an overriding sense of common strategic interest, they will unravel the international order.[5]

Owen Harries concludes that global politics will still be characterized by the relationship among states that has existed since the time of Thucydides:

Interdependence, transnational institutions, the spread of democracy, the obsolescence of war, the new primacy of economics, the dilution of sovereignty—take your pick, all have been nominated as revolutionizing international politics and falsifying classic realist premises.... Similar or identical claims have been advanced in earlier periods and proved spectacularly and dangerously wrong. They invariably underestimate the durability and tenacity of the past.[6]

Those who see the world in a geopolitical context tend to view the emerging international system in structural terms, as either unipolar or multipolar. There is also the special case of those who follow the logic of interests but who assign growing importance to cultures instead of nation-states.

The Geopolitical Structure

The collapse of the Soviet Union and the political-military performance of the United States during the Gulf War led some analysts to describe the emerging strategic environment as unipolar. Charles Krauthammer, for example, has written that at the center of world power is the unchallenged superpower, the United States, attended by its Western allies. The notion that economic power inevitably translates into geopolitical influence has proved to be a materialist illusion—a fact fully illustrated during the Gulf War. U.S. preeminence is based on the fact that it is the only country with the military, diplomatic, political, and economic assets to be a decisive player in any conflict in whatever part of the world it chooses to involve itself.

For Krauthammer, the fact that the collapse of the Soviet Union created a unipolar moment does not mean that the United States will dominate a new world order, however. He anticipated two threats to U.S. hegemony: first, the resurgence of isolationism on both the right and the left of U.S. politics, and, second, the rise of small aggressive states armed with WMD that they are able to deliver. In a shrunken world, the divide between regional superpowers and great powers is radically narrowed. Missiles shrink distance; WMD devices multiply power. Relatively small, peripheral, and backward states will be able to emerge rapidly as threats to not only regional security but also world security. It is the United States that must address this threat because, for Krauthammer, the alternative to American unipolarity is not stable multipolarity but chaos.[7]

Most interests-based analysis suggests that, instead of the world being unipolar, it consists of asymmetric poles; one pole (the United States) is much the strongest but the other poles are nonetheless important independent actors. The important powers are Western Europe, Russia, China, and Japan, although India may join the group within a decade or so. There are strong geopolitical incentives for the lesser poles to seek equality with the United States. The dominant trend, as seen from the late 1980s and early 1990s, was the rise of Germany–Europe and Japan. The possible reemergence of a nationalist Russia and a newly powerful China have been of more recent concern.

Kenneth Waltz, the dean of academic neorealists, notes that with the waning of Soviet power the United States is no longer held in check by any country or combination of countries. Balance-of-power theory leads to the prediction that other countries, alone or in concert, will try to bring U.S. power into balance. The way in which nations can try to do so, however, has changed because of nuclear weapons: even economically inferior powers can compete militarily if they adopt a status quo policy and a deterrent strategy. At the same time, "economic competition is often as keen as military competition, and since nuclear weapons limit the use of force among the great powers at the strategic level, we may expect economic and technological competition among them to become more intense." And, in the end, "with the use of military force negated at least among the nuclear powers, the more productive and technologically advanced countries have more ways of influencing international outcomes than do the laggards."[8]

Thus, at both the military and the economic levels, the great-power club is open if the European Union (EU), Germany, China, or Japan seeks entrance; and there is little reason to think that some or all will choose not to join. Waltz does not accept the argument that globalization has meant that states have lost the ability to manage stable economies within their frontiers. "To manage 'globalization,' leading states are likely to strengthen their economic influence over states on which they depend or to which they are closely connected. Because incentives to compete are strong, the likely outcome is a set of great powers forming their own regional bases in Asia, Europe, and America, with Russia as a military power on the economic fringe." In a multipolar world, the strongest power (the United States) will find other states edging away from it: Germany moving toward Eastern Europe and Russia, and Russia moving toward Germany and Japan.

Waltz focuses on Germany and Japan as the most important, and assertive, new poles, but there are other possibilities. In the past, the greatest danger within the international system has been created by a revisionist great power—either a nation that has sustained defeat in war but seeks to reestablish itself (e.g., Germany after World War I) or that is growing economically and militarily and seeks its place in the sun (e.g., Germany before 1914). Today two candidates seem obvious: Russia in the first category and China in the second.

Many experts assert that Russia is suffering from something similar to the Versailles syndrome that afflicted Germany after World War I. It feels isolated and is bitter about the contrast between its post–Cold War situation and its past superpower status. Moscow thinks it is the victim and others are taking advantage of its temporary difficulties. It resents being treated as a loser in the Cold War when it feels that, instead of losing, it evolved in a way advantageous to all. Its military is in decline if not disarray. And, as important as any other factor, its economy has shrunk by half over the last decade while the rest of the world has grown stronger. Yet Russia remains a nuclear power that can threaten the survival of the United States as a nation. Russia is recovering geopolitically before it recovers economically; it has begun to throw its weight around, asserting a "special responsibility" to keep order in the turbulent sphere of the former Union of Soviet Socialist Republics (USSR).[9]

China, by contrast, is often said to fill the role of Wilhelmine Germany. David Shambaugh, for example, writes:

> China today is a dissatisfied and non–status quo power which seeks to change the existing international order and norms of inter-state relations. Beijing is not satisfied with the status quo, sees that the international system and its "rules" were created by Western countries when China was weak, and believes that the existing distribution of power and resources is structurally biased in favor of the West and against China. It does not just seek a place

at the rule-making table of international organizations and power brokers; it seeks to alter the rules and existing system.[10]

China's strength is being manifested most notably in terms of the rapid economic growth of the People's Republic, and also in terms of the selective modernization of China's conventional and nuclear capabilities. Unlike the Japanese or the German, the current Chinese leadership apparently is not attracted by the image of becoming a civilian power or a trading state. The world is viewed, in the main, as a conflictual place where security and material interests are best served through self-help. In this regard, the Chinese hold to the traditional formula of rich nation, strong army: the wealthier and, relatively speaking, militarily stronger the state, the more secure it is.

This realist view of international relations is coupled with an extreme sensitivity over perceived threats to Chinese sovereignty and over the fragility of China's domestic "fourth revolution."[11] Chinese assertiveness masks a fundamental domestic vulnerability. The Chinese are especially concerned with the prospect that the United States has embarked on a policy of containing China while pursuing a rhetorical policy of engagement designed to undermine socialism and the political integrity of China. Chinese officials and scholars publicly characterize U.S. diplomacy as power politics and hegemonism that imperialistically bullies the weak and fears the strong. The People's Republic thus has an interest in weakening the preponderant power of the United States in international relations.

Many Chinese concurrently believe that U.S. staying power in the Asia-Pacific region will be limited over the long term and that the inevitable U.S. withdrawal will correspondingly lead to the militarization (and nuclearization) of Japan, a process that many believe is already well under way. In either case, whether the threat comes from Washington or Tokyo, the Chinese are determined not to be bullied.

But not everyone believes that the emerging multipolar system will be, or need be, conflictual. There is a school of optimists that focuses on the possibility of an emerging concert of powers, particularly in Europe, that is "primed for peace." The European wars of the twentieth century resulted mainly from military factors and domestic conditions that are largely gone and will not return in force. The nuclear revolution has dampened security motives for expansion, and the domestic orders of most European states have changed in ways that make renewed aggression unlikely. The most significant domestic changes include the waning of militarism and hypernationalism; other important changes include the spread of democracy, the leveling of highly stratified European societies, and the disappearance of states governed by revolutionary elites. In particular, Germany has undergone a social transformation that removed the roots of its past aggressiveness. To be sure, there are risks of renewed ethnic conflict in Eastern Europe, but these are manageable with prudent political strategies.[12] Europe has become, or is capable of becoming, a security community.

To support this case, some Russia experts challenge the view that Russia is a Weimar in the making, with economic collapse and political reaction on the horizon. Democracy is slowly but surely taking hold. From this perspective, Russia's foreign policy line is a simple one: it needs to be able to direct its resources to the successful completion of massive internal tasks and not to a quixotic effort to reestablish the old empire, much less reconstitute the old Soviet military threat to the West. There is neither a groundswell of public opinion for a revival of the old Soviet Union nor a more assertive or aggressive foreign policy. Nor are the Russian elites excessively nationalistic.[13]

Former U.S. ambassador to Russia Thomas Pickering argues that Americans have a tendency "to underestimate this great peoples' quick adaptability, in the same way that they underestimated Japan in the 1950s." Pickering argues that Russia will achieve its transition to democracy and to a free market and take its place as a leading partner in world trade and world affairs. He predicts, for example, that within three years the Russian Far East will become an economically vibrant area; indeed, perhaps as vibrant as other parts of the Pacific Rim, including Singapore, Japan, Taiwan, Korea, and California's Silicon Valley. Russia will become one of America's top trading partners, and the United States will consider its trade relationship with Russia to be as important as its relationships with Europe and Japan and other huge and significant markets.[14]

Is great-power peace and cooperation possible in other regions? The Asia-Pacific region lacks the intrusive and formal cooperative security mechanisms that exist in Europe. Nevertheless, it is argued, modest building blocks are beginning to take hold: the Association of Southeast Asian Nations (ASEAN) and the ASEAN Regional Forum (ARF), the Asia-Pacific Economic Cooperation (APEC) process, and the Council for Security and Cooperation in Asia-Pacific. China will clearly be the key to the success of cooperative security, and not all analysts are pessimistic about its future. Henry Rowan, for instance, argues that China's economic success will lead it to become a democracy within the next several decades (following the path of Taiwan and South Korea). The process may not be smooth or easy, but democracies are less dangerous interlocutors for other democracies than are dictatorships.[15]

Civilizational Politics

Samuel P. Huntington has advanced the controversial thesis that the fundamental sources of conflict in the future will not be primarily ideological or economic but, instead, cultural. Nation-states will remain the most powerful actors, but the great sources of division among humankind will be civilizational. Huntington argues that cultures in some ways are replacing states: peoples and countries with similar cultures are coming together, whereas peoples and countries of dissimilar cultures are coming apart. As a result, "culture and cultural identities…are shaping the patterns of cohesion, disintegration and conflict in the post–Cold War world…. Global politics is being reconfigured along cultural lines." For Huntington, "the principal conflicts of global politics will occur between nations and groups of different civilizations. The clash of civilizations will dominate global politics. The fault lines of civilizations will be the battle lines of the future."[16]

A civilization by this account is the highest cultural grouping of people and the broadest level of cultural identity people have short of that which distinguishes humans from other species. The heart of a culture, in turn, involves language, religion, values, traditions, and customs. Huntington identifies seven or eight major civilizations: Western, Slavic-Orthodox, Confucian, Hindu, Japanese, Islamic,

Latin American, and possibly African. (Western civilization includes the United States, Britain, Western Europe, Australia, and
New Zealand.)

It is argued that the emergence and division of distinct civilizations creates interests, and threats, not dissimilar to those faced by
nation-states. Or, put differently, particular nation-states will come
to see their interests (and perceive threats) in the context of where
they fit into the larger patterns of civilization. This is analogous, at
least in part, to the manner in which the United States, the Soviet
Union, and their allies identified interests and threats according to
the larger patterns of ideology (democracy versus communism).
And for a majority of civilizations, there is a single dominant
nation-state: the United States, Russia, China, India, and Japan.[17]

For Huntington, the dominant civilizational division will be
"the West and the Rest." This is caused by a number of factors, the
most important of which is "the efforts of the West to promote its
values of democracy and liberalism as universal values, to maintain
its military predominance and to advance economic interests,"
which will "engender countering responses from other civilizations." Other conflicts will develop as nations (e.g., the former Yugoslavia) come apart because the fault lines between civilizations
run through their territory. Others, like Turkey, are "torn countries,"
that have a fair degree of cultural homogeneity but are divided over
whether their society belongs to one civilization or another. And
there might be direct conflicts between particular civilizations or
coalitions of civilization; for instance, Huntington argues that a
Confucian–Islamic connection has emerged to challenge Western
interests, values, and power.[18]

Economic Nationalism

The growing importance of economic power relative to traditional
indexes of military capability is often cited as a trend or issue that
will transform the competitive, geopolitical structure of international relations. Some scholars contend that the devaluation of military power does not mean the end of competition among nation-
states, however. Edward Luttwak, for instance, argues that we are
witnessing an era in which geopolitics is being replaced by

"geoeconomics." According to Luttwak, "the methods of commerce are displacing military methods—with disposable capital in lieu of firepower, civilian innovation in lieu of military–technical advancement, and market penetration in lieu of garrisons and bases." Geoeconomics is competitive and dominated by logic of conflict (zero sum). In this world, states and blocs of states extract revenues, regulate economic as well as other activities, and finance or otherwise sponsor the development of new technologies and new products for their national advantage. Contrary to the common wisdom, this pursuit of economic advantage will not be undertaken by entrepreneurs or corporations. Economic regulation is as much a tool of statecraft as military defenses ever were.[19]

States are inherently inclined to strive for relative advantage against like entities on the international scene, Luttwak argues. As bureaucracies writ large, states are themselves impelled by the bureaucratic urges of role preservation and role enhancement to acquire geoeconomic substitutes for their decaying geopolitical role. Economic interest groups, in turn, seek to manipulate the state for their own purposes.

The pursuit of geoeconomics is for Luttwak not quite the same as mercantilism. Whereas the goal of mercantilism was to maximize gold stocks, the goal of geoeconomics is to provide the best possible employment for the largest possible segment of the population. Mercantilism was limited and governed by the ever-present possibility that the loser in the commercial competition would shift to war. The resort to force is no longer conceivable for advanced states, however. For some decades now the dominant elites of the greatest powers have ceased to consider war a practical solution for military confrontation between them: conventional war is highly likely to escalate into nuclear war and nuclear war is self-inhibiting.

In the new paradigm, the instruments as well as the causes of conflict must be economic. The weapons of geoeconomic warfare include the more or less disguised restriction of imports, subsidization of exports, funding of competitive technology projects, the support of selected forms of education, and the provision of competitive infrastructures. Some of the tools are distinctly offensive in nature: for example, the predatory financing and sale of new technologies during their embryonic stage and the manipulation of the standards that condition their use.

John B. Judis and Michael Lind characterize the result:

> Now that the contest between capitalism and socialism has been settled, a new ideological contest is emerging between national variants of capitalism—American free-market radicalism, Japanese economic nationalism and German social-market capitalism.[20]

The notion that we are entering an age of geoeconomic competition is supported by the so-called revisionist school of scholarship about Japan. These scholars and journalists, including Chalmers Johnson, Karel van Wolferen, and James Fallows, argue that Japan is not a "normal" democratic country by U.S. standards (i.e., one in which the polity is designed to guarantee the political and civil rights, and maximize the economic well-being, of individual citizens). Instead, the Japanese government—controlled by a bureaucracy with a xenophobic outlook that goes far back in Japanese history—seeks to create national self-sufficiency and independence at the cost of the good of the Japanese consumer as well as of Japan's trading partners. Essentially, Tokyo is trying to realize its vision of a Greater East Asian Co-Prosperity Sphere and dominate the global economy through predatory economic practices, the subsidizing of key industries and technologies, and the like. Japan would prefer to be relatively better off than other nations in economic terms, even if its citizens are absolutely worse off than they would be if Tokyo participated in a regime of international free trade. By the same token, Japan actively seeks to weaken the economies (or the strategic industries) of other nations as a means of strengthening its own position.[21] In the words of one revisionist, the Japanese economic bureaucracy manages and wages "a deliberate, humorless, and relentless economic war" against the United States.[22]

Issues

The second perspective on the international security environment focuses on what this paper calls issues—trends in global affairs that profoundly affect the ability of nation-states to retain their traditional sovereign status and to meet the needs of their peoples. The threats created by such issues—the diffusion of technology, weapons proliferation, and interdependence—"are a greater source of danger than any immediate threat of deliberately calculated aggression."[23]

Joseph Nye contends that "the realist view of world order, resting on a balance of military power, is necessary but not sufficient, because it does not take into account the long-term societal changes that have been slowly moving the world away from the Westphalian system." In that system, "order was based on the sovereignty of states, not the sovereignty of peoples." But the growth of nationalism, democracy, transnational communications, migration, and economic interdependence makes more relevant the liberal conception "of a world society of peoples as well as states, and of order resting on values and institutions as well as military power."[24]

In this vein, John Lewis Gaddis views the dominant trends, or issues, as involving contradictory developments above and below the level of the nation-state. He believes that "another form of competition has been emerging that could be just as stark and just as pervasive as was the rivalry between democracy and totalitarianism at the height of the Cold War: it is the contest between forces of integration and fragmentation." For Gaddis, integration "involves breaking down barriers that have historically separated nations and peoples in such diverse areas as politics, economics, religion, technology, and culture." Integration is occurring in a variety of ways: the communications revolution, economic globalization, collective security actions, and the growing acceptance of liberal democratic and free market ideas. All this points toward the possibility of peace, at least among the great powers.[25]

But the forces of integration are being challenged by forces of fragmentation: these forces "are resurrecting old barriers between nations and peoples—and creating new ones—even as others are tumbling." The most important fragmenting force is nationalism, whose pressure is felt by the West as well as the non-West: witness the breakup of the Soviet Union and Yugoslavia and the continuing separatist pressures in Ireland, Spain, Belgium, and Canada. The forces of fragmentation also show up in the economic field, in the form of protectionism: the effort, by various means, to insulate individual economies from the workings of world market forces. Racial and religious differences also manifest the resistance to integration.[26]

For Gaddis, the relationship between integration and fragmentation is complex. For example, in the case of the Soviet Union, one of the great integrative ideas—liberalism—had profoundly disintegrative consequences. Saddam Hussein used Iraq's integration into the international market—and the inability, or unwillingness, of highly industrialized states to control their own entrepreneurs—to obtain sophisticated technology that nearly permitted him to acquire a nuclear weapons capability. Thus it is not clear which tendency the United States should want to prevail: for Gaddis, the best course may be one of balancing integration and fragmentation.

Stanley Hoffmann writes similarly that

> [T]oday's world is post-Westphalian: myriad normative restraints and a huge loss of autonomy resulting from transnational forces are eroding state sovereignty generally, and the sovereign state itself, the very floor of the Westphalian construction, is collapsing in many parts of the world.[27]

Pierre Hassner argues:

> [T]he great achievement of the modern state—the establishment of a neutral authority that ensures the primacy of common citizenship over privileges based on blood-lines and over religious divisions—is being jeopardized both by the trends towards transnational de-territorialization and by the trend towards national, subnational and ethnic re-territorialization. The multiplication of different types of actors, loyalties, and conflicts leads to a return in some respects to the sixteenth century, to the power of merchant towns and religious wars. In other respects, it is a return to the Middle Ages when, in contrast to the modern nation-state and its monopoly of violence, order was based on a variety of actors, of authorities, territorial and not territorial.[28]

Jessica T. Mathews contends that the end of the Cold War resulted not merely in an adjustment among states, but "a novel redistribution of power among states, markets, and civil society.... The steady concentration of power in the hands of states that began in 1648 with the Peace of Westphalia is over, at least for a while." For good or ill, those things that matter—money, information, pollution, popular culture—circulate and shape lives and economies with little regard for political boundaries. "International standards of conduct are gradually beginning to override claims of national or regional singularity. Even the most powerful states find the marketplace and international public opinion compelling them more often to follow a particular course."[29]

In this sense, President Clinton has spoken of the twenty-first century as one in which "the blocks and barriers that defined the world for previous generations will continue to give way to greater freedom, faster change, greater communications and commerce across national borders, and more profound innovation than ever before; a century in which more people than ever will have the chance to share in humanity's genius of progress."[30]

In a 1996 speech, presidential science advisor John Gibbons argued that the end of the Cold War meant that the "battle for peace" had shifted from "the security front" to the "economic and social front." This second front has grown continually "in both size and complexity, shaped by the forces of globalization, technological advance, population growth, environmental degradation, and social change." According to Gibbons, it is "human wants—for jobs, education, health, a sound environment—and threats—infectious disease, illiteracy, mass migration, terrorism, and global change—which now define the second front of security policy." As a consequence, the United States "faces a set of regional and global challenges which transcend agency missions, disciplinary divides, and political boundaries.... Our work increasingly involves building new linkages; sorting out the appropriate division of labor between the public and private sector; beginning new partnerships between old adversaries and forming new combinations of people, places, and ideas."[31]

Paul Kennedy has also described the situation: "Today's global society...confronts the task of reconciling technological change and economic integration with traditional political structures, national consciousness, social needs, institutional arrangements, and habitual ways of doing things." For Kennedy, all this will be complicated by trends that "now threaten to exacerbate social relations in all manner of ways, and may even threaten the long-term existence of humankind itself."[32] These trends include the proliferation of

WMD and advanced military technologies, ethnic and tribal warfare, international crime, global terrorism, overpopulation and migrations, and global climate change.

This requires a change in the definition of security, which has been "closely tied to a state's defense of sovereign interests by military means. At its most fundamental level, the term security has meant the effort to protect a population and territory against organized force while advancing state interests through competitive behavior."[33] By contrast, global security—defined as "the absence or avoidance of threats to the vital interests of the planet"[34]—means that security must be treated from a global rather than from a national or even an international perspective.

> In essence...security applies most at the level of the citizen. It amounts to human well-being; not only protection from harm and injury but from access to water, food, shelter, health, employment, and other basic requisites that are the due of every person on Earth. It is the collectivity of these citizen needs— overall safety and quality of life—that should figure prominently in the nation's view of security.[35]

Vertical Issues

For most issues-based analysts, the notion of polarity does not adequately capture the dynamics of the emerging international system(s). Instead, the strategic environment is characterized more by a division, and potential conflict, between the center and the periphery. The economically and politically dominant great powers— including the United States, the European Union, Japan, China, and (now at the margin) Russia—form the "center" of the international system. The center's monopoly on power allows it to determine the system's rules; the weak, underdeveloped states of the "periphery" have no choice but to operate within those rules. Within the center, superpower bipolarity has been replaced by a complex, multipolar distribution of power where power resides not only with several actors but takes multiple forms—military, economic, cultural, and the like. With the collapse of the Soviet Union and Marxism-Leninism, the peripheral states are struggling to find ways to gain the attention of the center and keep from becoming even further marginalized or coerced by the center.[36]

A 1996 study by the Institute for National Strategic Studies (INSS) of the National Defense University (NDU) concluded that states fall into three categories according to how successful they are at achieving the almost universally proclaimed goals of democracy and market-based prosperity.[37]

First are the market democracies of free and prosperous—or at least rapidly developing—nations. These were once found only in North America, Japan, and much of Europe; but large parts of Latin America, the newly industrialized nations of East Asia, and Central Europe are now joining this group. Second are the transitional states of ex-Communist lands as well as countries such as India and South Africa. These states are progressing from a low economic baseline, and they run the risk of becoming frozen short of freedom and prosperity with authoritarian politics, heavily politicized economies, and relatively low levels of economic development.

Finally come the troubled states, primarily in Africa, the Middle East, and parts of Asia. These states are falling behind the rest of the globe economically, politically, and ecologically, and they are often plagued with rampant ethnic and religious extremism. Some of the troubled or transitional states may be tempted to divert attention from domestic problems by means of external aggression aimed at the establishment of regional hegemony. In the case of a nation such as Iraq or North Korea, this could lead to a major regional conflict. The proliferation of WMD, particularly nuclear weapons, could increase the propensity of aggressive states to threaten their neighbors and increase the risks for the United States. Also, conflict within troubled states is likely to be a common occurrence and, in some cases, the state will fail—the government will cease to function effectively and civil society will degenerate into near chaos.

Anthony Lake, President Clinton's first national security adviser, considers some in this latter category as "backlash states." The end of the Cold War and the emergence of newly independent states in Eastern Europe have created the potential for a dramatic enlargement of the family of nations now committed to the pursuit of democratic institutions, the expansion of free markets, the peaceful settlement of conflict, and the promotion of collective security.[38]

But recalcitrant and outlaw states—Cuba, North Korea, Iran, Iraq, and Libya come to mind—not only choose to remain outside the family but also assault its basic values. These states lack the superpower's resources that would enable them to seriously threaten the democratic order being created around them. Nevertheless, their behavior is often aggressive and defiant. The ties among them are growing as they seek to thwart or quarantine themselves from a global trend to which they seem incapable of adapting.

According to Lake, these backlash states have some common characteristics. Ruled by cliques that control power through coercion, they suppress basic human rights and promote radical ideologies. Although their political systems vary, their leaders share a common antipathy toward popular participation that might undermine the existing international regimes. These nations exhibit a chronic inability to engage constructively with the outside world, and they do not function effectively in alliances—even with those that are like-minded. They are often on the defensive, increasingly criticized and targeted with sanctions in international forums. Finally, they share a siege mentality. They are accordingly embarked on ambitious and costly military programs—especially in WMD and missile-delivery systems—in a misguided quest for a great equalizer to protect their regimes or advance their purposes abroad.

Transnational Dangers

A second dimension of issues consists of a variety of dangers created by adverse global trends and developments characteristic of the post-Westphalian world.

Proliferation. The relative discipline and general predictability of the bipolar Cold War relationships have been replaced in several key regions of the world by the expansion of regional arms races, including the aggressive pursuit of WMD and missile-delivery capabilities. In several regions, the Persian Gulf and Northeast Asia, for example, there appear to be no limits on the ambitions of unstable actors to acquire the most advanced and deadly weapons available, either through internal or external sources. Possession of WMD is perceived as both a status symbol and an instrument of political and military power for the pursuit of hegemonistic objectives.[39]

In some regions, to be sure, the trend is positive. Argentina and Brazil have apparently resolved their security concerns and abandoned their nuclear programs. South Africa has agreed to dismantle its nuclear weapons program and the six nuclear weapons it already possesses and to join the Nuclear Non-Proliferation Treaty as a non-nuclear weapons state. But despite these successes, at least 20 countries have or are seeking the capability to produce and deliver nuclear weapons. Some potential proliferators are pursuing chemical weapons (CW) and biological weapons (BW) programs, often at the same time they are pursuing nuclear weapons. CW and BW offer a number of advantages over nuclear weapons for such states. First, although nuclear weapons are very expensive, CW and BW provide a much cheaper route to WMD capability. Second, almost all the technologies and materials required to produce CW and BW are dual-use in nature and are widely available for commercial purposes. Third, CW and BW programs are much easier to conceal from international inspectors and are much more secure from air strikes.

Finally, the majority of potential WMD proliferators see missiles, and especially ballistic missiles, as the delivery system of choice. More than a dozen of these countries have operational ballistic-missile programs. Although the missiles possessed by today's proliferators are generally limited in range to approximately 600 km, much longer range missiles are being pursued. And as cruise-missile technology becomes available with growing access to navigational aids such as the global positioning system, cruise missiles will become more attractive as a low-cost but highly effective WMD delivery system.

On the supply side, the diffusion of advanced technologies has become exceptionally difficult to control despite the strengthening of export-control regimes directed at preventing WMD and missile proliferation. The emergence of alternate suppliers, the development of greater indigenous capabilities, and the consequences of the collapse of the Soviet Union make it unlikely that those countries determined to acquire such weapons can be stopped. Many of the technologies and materials used for WMD production are also used for legitimate nonweapons purposes. Such dual-use technologies are increasingly available on the open market and, where they cannot be openly bought or bartered, appear also to be increasingly available through illicit channels. In this context, the exponential growth of organized crime in Russia and the possible leakage of formerly tightly controlled nuclear weapons materials indicate a larger problem.[40] Although a decade or more might be needed to acquire nuclear weapons, a determined leadership with sufficient resources is likely to succeed. For chemical and biological weapons, the time and costs are significantly less.

Concerns about terrorist groups and organized crime coming to possess WMD have intensified in recent years. The end of the Cold War has heightened fears that terrorists could acquire such weapons, threaten their use, and perhaps even be prepared to use them under certain circumstances. Moreover, concerns about a loss of control over the former Soviet Union's stocks of weapons-grade nuclear material have led to fears that organized crime elements could begin to traffic in nuclear materials as they have already done in other arms. Senators Nunn, Lugar, and Domenici have argued that the proliferation threat is changing: the cast of proliferation characters has gradually expanded beyond the declared and undeclared nuclear states and the outlaw states such as Iraq and North Korea and now includes religious, ethnic, and nationalist groups; other politically disaffected groups and nonstate actors; terrorists; and, possibly, criminal organizations. Further, previously distinct issues or trends—proliferation, terrorism, and organized crime—are now merging.[41]

Ethnic, Tribal, or Religious Warfare. Some commentators believe that the dominant forms of conflict in the future will not be those between nation-states but will reflect a "new world disorder," resulting from the loss of discipline that had been imposed by Cold War bipolarity.

For instance, ethnic hatreds can erupt into genocide and ethnic cleansing, as in Rwanda and the former Yugoslavia. A related phenomenon has been the collapse of organized government under the pressure of warlords and clan rivalries. Robert Kaplan notes:

Central Asia looks more like a medieval map, in which geography and ethnicity—defined by highly ambiguous and ever-shifting centers of power—will matter increasingly more and fixed borders will matter less. Pakistan's relations with the Taliban [in Afghanistan] is an illustration: Pakistan's security services, cooperating with the Islamic movement, have re-opened a traditional caravan route through southern Afghanistan to Iran. Thus although Pakistan is unraveling as a state, it is increasingly able to exert its influence on the region. In the new Central Asia, power will not be defined by a country's borders. Influence will not be exerted as much within states as within ethnicities and clans, and no ethnic group may be strong enough to dominate.[42]

Tribalism is on the rise worldwide, from Bosnia to India, from the former USSR to Rwanda. Americans themselves had a short lesson in its ugly course during the 1992 Los Angeles riots, when inter-group violence spread from a confrontation between African-Americans and whites into a wave of violence that also engulfed Korean-American and Hispanic communities.[43]

Traditional states and societies in the Middle East and Asia are especially threatened by radical, or political, Islam. According to Peter Rodman, the fertile soil for its growth may be the deep-seated social and economic frustrations of Arab societies struggling with the dislocations of modernization. But its upsurge in the Sunni world has been in part a function of the seeming erosion of legitimacy of Arab governments whose performance has been weak and whose moral and political authority had rested on the secular ideology of the now discredited Arab socialism. Islamic radicalism filled the vacuum. Although this is not some centrally directed radicalism, its contagion is not a mirage. An Islamist takeover in Algeria could destabilize Tunisia and Morocco; send reverberations through France, Italy, and Spain; and, most important, have a shock effect in Egypt.[44]

International Crime. International criminal organizations and conspiracies—especially drug cartels that operate on a scale large enough to threaten governments—are emerging or are being strengthened. Walls that came down with the defeat of communism have also, in many instances, removed barriers to the spread of syndicated and freelance crime in the forms of gangsterism, drug trafficking, money laundering, narcoterrorism, smuggling of aliens, large-scale black marketeering and counterfeiting, and the proliferation of armed bands. These are symptoms of a general breakdown of law and order within societies, which threatens to extend its reach even to places where the infrastructure of law enforcement is still intact. Indeed, the seemingly impenetrable cycle of drugs and violence in the United States cannot be divorced from the global criminal networks, which are well organized, flexible, and highly efficient.[45]

Terrorism. Terrorists take advantage of more open societies to mount increasingly brazen attacks, such as the 1993 bombing of New York's World Trade Center. Senator Sam Nunn argued that the March 1995 Tokyo subway attack by the Aum Shinrikyo cult "demonstrates the threat a well financed, sophisticated and international terrorist group poses [and is the] greatest national security concern in the years ahead."[46]

In a recent article, Walter Laqueur discussed the outlines of what he calls a "new terrorism."[47] Today's society faces not one terrorism but many terrorisms. The past few decades have seen the birth of dozens of aggressive movements espousing varieties of nationalism, religious fundamentalism, fascism, and apocalyptic millenarianism. Most international and domestic terrorism today is not ideological (in the sense of extremists of the left or the right) but is ethnic–separatist in inspiration. Apocalyptic movements are also on the rise: sects and movements that preach the end of the world gain influence toward the end of a century, and all the more at the close of a millennium. In the past, terrorism was almost always the province of groups of militants that had the backing of political forces; in the future, terrorists might be individuals on the pattern of the Unabomber or like-minded people working in very small groups.

The targets of terrorism might differ. Society has become vulnerable to attacks on the advanced networks of electronic storage, data retrieval, analysis, and transmission of information. In addition, the line between politically motivated terrorism and the operation of national and international crime syndicates is often impossible for outsiders to discern in the former Soviet Union, Latin America, and other parts of the world.

If terrorists have used chemical weapons only once and nuclear material never, to some extent the reasons are technical—the problems inherent in the production, manufacture, storage, and delivery of WMD. Given these difficulties, terrorists are less likely to use nuclear devices than chemical weapons, and they are least likely to attempt to use biological weapons. But difficulties could be overcome, and the choice of unconventional weapons will in the end come down to the specialties of the terrorists and their access to deadly substances. To be sure, terrorists may draw the line at WMD. But a single successful act could claim many more victims, do more material damage, and unleash far greater panic than anything the world has yet experienced.

Some analysts contend that the motivation for using WMD has changed. New proliferators, especially terrorist groups, do not necessarily acquire such weapons to deter aggressors; they are more likely to acquire them for actual use. Religious, ethnic, nationalist, criminal, or simply disaffected groups have become more aggressive in seeking to further their aims by using weapons that cause large-scale casualties. There is little care for garnering public sympathy or support. Punishment, not discrete objectives, becomes the object of the new terrorism.[48]

Overpopulation and Migrations. The surge in global population and the rising demographic imbalances between rich and poor countries are creating a new set of international problems. World population may be heading toward 10 billion or more by the middle of the next century, with most of the growth occurring in the poorest regions of the world. "The result is a growing mismatch between where the world's riches, technology, good health, and other benefits are to be found and where the world's fast-growing new generations, possessing few if any of these benefits, live. A population explosion on one part of the globe and a technology explosion on the other is not a good recipe for a stable international order."[49]

Sudden mass migrations are becoming more common, partly in response to state failure and ethnic violence. These waves of people, who might or might not fit the traditional definition of refugees, can overwhelm poor neighbors. As illustrated by the experience with Haitians and Cubans, migrants can pose an unacceptable burden on industrial nations like the United States that are concerned that the refugees may become permanent residents. The result in advanced countries may be strained cohesion, turning immigration into a controversial issue in both foreign and domestic policy and influencing the foreign policies of the host nations toward the regions from which the migrants flow.[50]

At the opposite end of the spectrum are the so-called failed states like Somalia. A downward spiral of development is taking place in parts of the Third World (sub-Saharan Africa, South Asia, and the Caribbean) where gross domestic product has slipped steadily behind population growth. The downward spiral includes increased poverty, population growth, and environmental degradation, all interacting negatively to compound one another. Then there are diseases—HIV/AIDS is but one of the many widespread diseases capable of societal disruption.[51] Robert Kaplan views this as the "coming anarchy"—a spreading global impoverishment in which the entire world's future will come to resemble the disease, poverty, tribalism, crime, overpopulation, and general social breakdown now afflicting West Africa.[52]

Environmental Problems. The population explosion also produces environmental challenges qualitatively different from those of 60 years ago. There has been an exponential growth in industrial emissions, the draining of wetlands and aquifers, the onslaught on tropical forests, and the overgrazing of plains and savannas. Evidence is at hand of a greenhouse effect that could affect ecologies in all sorts of ways—as the climate changes and sea levels rise, even the most environmentally responsible societies will be affected. For scholars like Paul Kennedy it is inconceivable that the Earth can sustain a population of 10 billion people devouring resources at the rate enjoyed by rich societies today—or at even half that rate.[53]

In some cases, shortages of vital resources such as water may lead directly to interstate conflict. The Middle East, for example, is facing a serious water shortage due to population growth that averages 3 percent annually, recent drought, and groundwater resource depletion.[54] The Jordan, the Ganges, the Nile, and the Rio Grande have been at the center of dozens of international disputes. In 1990, Turkey threatened to restrict water flow to Syria to force it to withdraw support for Kurdish rebels operating in southern Turkey. But most scholars conclude that the connection between resource scarcity, environmental degradation, and conflict is not direct. "Resource scarcities do not, by themselves, send angry mobs into the streets. Rather, such scarcities help to generate secondary effects such as poverty, ethnic tension, migration, and weak social and governmental institutions that help make conflict more likely."[55] Environmental change produces social change, leading to the fragmentation of states or, conversely, to a more authoritarian "hardening" of the state.[56]

One of the most politically visible aspects of environmental security involves concerns about global climate change. The Intergovernmental Panel on Climate Change (IPCC), in its Second Assessment Report, articulated what its supporters claim to be a scientific consensus of the impact of humankind on the global environment.[57] The Earth's climate has changed in the past owing to a variety of natural phenomena, but now human activities have caused new and comparatively sudden changes. The IPCC report asserts: "the balance of evidence suggests that there is a discernible human influence on global climate." That is, the "signal" of global warming is beginning to emerge from the "noise" of normal variability. The long atmospheric lifetime—on the order of decades to many centuries—of many greenhouse gases coupled with the centuries-long lag time for the oceans to equilibrate mean that the warming effect of anthropogenic emissions will be long lived. Even after a hypothetical stabilization of the atmospheric concentrations of greenhouse gases, temperatures would continue to increase for several decades, and the sea level would continue to rise for centuries. Reversing the effects therefore would also take centuries, and some impacts, such as species loss, are irreversible.

Changed patterns in precipitation will lead to more floods and droughts. According to a U.S. insurance industry estimate, even modest levels of global warming could result in increased storm damage to the United States to a level where "no foreign army has done that much damage to our territory since the War of 1812."[58]

In the view of Gibbons, "climate change will be a significant new stress on ecological and social systems that are already affected by pollution, increasing resource extraction, massive population growth, and non-sustainable management practices." The effects will vary by region, and they may even be beneficial in some areas. The mostly negative consequences of climate change unfortunately are likely to affect the economy and the quality of life for this and future generations. Gibbons argues:

- Human health will be adversely affected. There will be increases in the incidence of heat waves with high humidity like the episode in Chicago in 1996 that resulted in several hundred deaths. Vector-borne diseases such as malaria, and non-vector-borne diseases such as cholera, are likely to spread as conditions for their survival change. To give just one example, the world could face an additional 50 million cases per year of malaria near the end of the next century.

- Food security will be threatened by changes in weather in some regions of the world, especially in the tropics and subtropics where many of the world's poorest people live.

- Human habitat loss will occur in regions where small islands and coastal plain and river areas are particularly vulnerable to sea level rise. For example, Bangladesh is in danger of losing 17 percent of its land, while the combination of sea-level rise and storm surges could create 50 million environmental refugees in China.

- The composition, geographic distribution, and productivity of many ecosystems will shift as individual species respond to changes in climate. This may lead to loss of biological diversity and threaten the ability of ecosystems to provide the purification of air and water upon which we depend.[59]

In 1996, Secretary of State Warren Christopher argued that environmental concerns ought to be an integral part of U.S. diplomacy. The U.S. ability to advance its global interests is inextricably linked to how the Earth's natural resources are managed. According to Christopher, the environment has a profound impact on U.S. national interests in two ways. First, environmental forces transcend borders and oceans to threaten directly the health, prosperity, and jobs of U.S. citizens. Second, U.S. efforts to address natural-resource issues are frequently critical to achieving political and economic stability and to pursuing U.S. strategic goals around the world.

> Across the United States, Americans suffer the consequences of damage to the environment far beyond our borders. Greenhouse gases released around the globe by power plants, automobiles, and burning forests affect our health and our climate, potentially causing many billions of dollars in damage from rising sea levels and changing storm patterns. Dangerous chemicals such as PCBs and DDT that are banned here but still used elsewhere travel long distances through the air and water. Overfishing of the world's oceans has put thousands of Americans out of work.[60]

According to Christopher, for the nations of the former Soviet Union and Central Europe to build stable market democracies, they must overcome "the poisonous factories, soot-filled skies, and ruined rivers that are one of the bitter legacies of communism. The experience of this region demonstrates that governments that abuse their citizens too often have a similar contempt for the environment." Equally important are the environmental challenges faced by China. "With 22 percent of the world's population, China has only seven percent of its fresh water and cropland, three percent of its forests, and two percent of its oil. The combination of China's rapid economic growth and surging population is compounding the enormous environmental pressures it already faces."

The Information and Economic Revolutions

At the same time that transnational dangers have emerged or have become more prominent, computers, faxes, fiber-optic cables, and satellites speed the flow of information across frontiers. Ideas, people, and goods are moving across borders at an unprecedented rate. A 1996 report by the INSS at NDU reports:

> What makes the information explosion so revolutionary is not that technology is advancing but the pace at which it improves. Although societies have often been confronted with profound social changes owing to advancing technologies, never before have societies been forced to adapt to a technology which for decades has been improving by an order of magnitude every three or four years. The speed at which computers function—the rate at which information can be transmitted over long distances—looks set to continue increasing at the rate of tenfold every three to four years, which translates into up to 1,000-fold per decade.

According to the NDU report, it is impossible to foretell all the ways in which information technologies will enhance (or mitigate) traditional venues of national power, but some themes are beginning to emerge.[61]

First, access to information is being recognized as a sine qua non of economic growth. Mastery of information technology—whether exercised through commercial or military channels—is surpassing mastery of heavy industry as the primary source of national power. The new wave of computers and communications will be the key to future economic growth, but the older waves of agriculture and industry will remain indispensable elements of national economic life. Because the United States possesses the richest information flux, other countries have become increasingly interested in tapping into these flows. Linkages to sources of expertise (Silicon Valley), sources of finance (Wall Street), or sources of knowledge (universities, think tanks, and selected government agencies) are considered desirable and one more reason for nations to cultivate good relations with the United States.

Second, the information revolution will affect decisively the way in which the United States and other nations attempt to use military power. Defense requirements will demand more investment in information systems and less in industrial-era configurations of tanks, planes, and ships. Information may come to rival explosive force as a factor in warfare. The development of an integrated approach—a system of systems—that combines sensors, communications, and processors with weapons delivery will allow further advances in the precision with which U.S. forces can strike. With more precise information about where to strike, weapons delivery systems can shrink in size, facilitating the trend toward striking from a long distance, possibly directly from the continental United States to the battlefield. The ability of the Defense Department to generate and distribute vast quantities of intelligence permits the United States to influence even the outcomes of conflicts in which it chooses not to intervene directly. At little direct risk, the United States can provide an "information umbrella" to its friends by providing imagery and weather data, software and other systems integration services, and, within the next few years, simulation and other training tools.

How the information revolution will affect the military forces of other nations or groups is less clear. The United States holds such a commanding edge in many of these technologies that other parties may well seek to develop offsets to U.S. information dominance by, for example, seeking cheap and effective means to bring down the complex and interdependent U.S. information network.

Third, technology is making traditional jobs redundant, replacing them with entirely new systems of production, all in the face of the demographic explosion. This will occur while multinational corporations, freeing themselves from their local roots, increasingly compete for global market shares and make use of every device—for example, relocating production—to achieve that aim. Local communities in the developed world, and entire societies in the developing world, will have difficulty in accepting the logic of the global marketplace if it works to their disadvantage. Instead of economic and technological trends leading to that all-embracing unity of activity—the borderless world—they could provoke commercial clashes and social instability.

Finally, the global communications revolution is affecting people across the globe. Where it once appeared that the new media would enhance the power of the government, their effect has been the opposite recently: breaking state monopolies of information, permeating national boundaries, allowing peoples to hear and see how others do things differently. More than was possible a half century ago, the new media have also made richer and poorer countries more aware of the gap between them and have stimulated legal and illegal immigration. As a result, communities and even entire countries appear to have less and less control of their own destinies. Traditional power structures have unsatisfactory answers—or no answers at all—to job losses caused by the technology revolution. They find it hard to prevent companies from relocating to other regions, much less muffle information from transnational television and radio.

Because the established structures are fumbling with these challenges, peoples around the globe are responding with resignation (the decreased percentages of voters), searching for new structures (from the EU experiment to the dismantling of the USSR and Yugoslavia), demanding protection from global forces for change (pressures from French farmers and U.S. textile workers), and turning angrily against recent immigrants.

The global information revolution, especially in its economic dimension, has winners and losers.[62] The winners are those who focus on companies and individuals (chiefly professionals providing high-value services), who benefit from current socioeconomic developments, and who are keenly positioning themselves to gain further advantages. The losers are the billions of impoverished, uneducated individuals in the developing world and the tens of millions of unskilled nonprofessional workers in the developed world. As a result, the gap between the rich and the poor will steadily widen as we enter the twenty-first century, leading to not only social unrest within developed countries but also growing North–South tensions, mass migration, and environmental damage from which even the winners might not emerge unscathed.

The information revolution also tends to accelerate the weakening of the nation-state. Information technologies disrupt hierarchies, spreading power among more peoples and groups. This favors decentralized networks over other types of organization. Jessica Mathews argues that "in a network, individuals or groups link for joint action without building a physical or formal institutional presence."

> Networks have no person at the top and no center. Instead, they have multiple nodes where collections of individuals or groups interact for different purposes. Businesses, citizens organizations, ethnic groups, and crime cartels have all readily adopted the network model. Governments, on the other hand, are quintessential hierarchies, wedded to an organizational form incompatible with all that the new technologies make possible.[63]

The growing gap between rich and poor, even within developed societies, also reflects the fact that recent economic growth in the developed world has been unusually slow compared with growth during the previous decades of the industrial age.[64] In the United States, the economy during the century after the Civil War grew at an annual average of a little more than 3 percent, and from 1945 to 1973 the figure was more than 4 percent. Since the early 1970s, though, average annual growth has been just over 2 percent. Productivity in the United States from the Civil War to the Vietnam era grew similarly at approximately 2 percent per year; since 1973 it has been an anemic 0.9 percent per year, on average. There is little agreement on what might be causing this slowdown, but some observers have hinted recently that technological change and the information revolution might itself be a prime culprit.

In any case, many economists and policy analysts have noted an increasing imbalance of wealth in U.S. society, dating from around the early 1970s. A series of studies has shown rising poverty rates, a widening gap between the richest and the poorest Americans, and stagnating or even declining incomes and wages for U.S. workers in approximately the bottom third of the income distribution ladder. Most economists, in other words, find empirical support for the conventional wisdom of political discourse that the rich have gotten richer and the poor have gotten poorer during the past three decades. What studies of this phenomenon find alarming is that there may not be enough high-skill, high-earning positions to go around, thus increasingly helping to split U.S. society between a privileged, prosperous minority and an anxiety-ridden, low-paid majority.[65]

Democratization

It can be argued that one of the singular trends of the past several decades has been the expansion of democratic forms of government. In 1974, less than 30 percent of the world's countries were democratic; today the figure is more than 61 percent. A slim but clear majority of the world's population (54 percent) lives under democracy.[66] This third wave of democratization began in the mid-1970s with the demise of right-wing dictatorships in Europe, and in the 1980s it gathered and spread, notably to Latin America.[67] Democracy has also spread because it can help countries modernize their economies, ameliorate social conditions, and integrate with the outside world. Democratic authorities, unlike authoritarian regimes, have an important source of legitimacy that can reinforce their ability to make painful but necessary economic choices, including the allocation of scarce national resources.[68]

Promoting economic growth while monopolizing political power is an almost impossible balancing act over the long term, especially in a world increasingly linked by communications and trade. As people's incomes rise and their horizons broaden, they are more likely to demand the right to participate in government and enjoy full protection under the rule of law.[69] This seems to be an iron law of politics, refuting the argument that democracy is exclusively a Western phenomenon.

To be sure, there are obstacles to further democratization. Specifically, political progress is a hostage to economic disadvantage. In many countries, the gap between poverty and wealth is widening as the states undergo a double transition from authoritarian to democratic politics and from centralized to market economies. This has created an undertow, especially in the post-Communist world where there is widespread resentment at what often seems to be the capriciousness and inequity of the market and insecurity about the absence of a safety net.[70]

Some observers contend that today's global economy, with its transnational corporations, interest groups, and other supranational trends, works against democracy, at least on a national basis. The rise of representative democracy was deeply intertwined with the development of the nation-state; but as nation and state weaken, liberal democracy ceases to be a viable political system. Decisions made by other political communities and actors interfere with representative forms of government, which have no obvious recourse when the individual rights and interests of their citizens are not respected by others. One author advocates the establishment of "cosmopolitan democracies" that can democratically control these forces, just as welfare states were developed earlier this century to control capitalism at the national level.[71]

The Effects of Interdependence

As noted above, much issue-based analysis assumes that the growing interdependence of the global economy and politics has made the nation-state (or the central government) a much less important instrument for achieving personal or group security. In this respect, G. John Ikenberry argues the "second American agenda" of the Cold War succeeded and remains the dominant fact of international life. (The first agenda involved the containment of the Soviet Union.) America's international objectives involved the commitment to an open world economy and its multilateral management and to the stabilization of socioeconomic welfare, so as to "domesticate" the dealings of the industrial democracies through a dense web of multilateral institutions, intergovernmental relations, and joint management of the Western and world political economies. The success of the second agenda explains why realist assessments of international politics—which predict the breakdown of relations among the Western powers—have proved false. Instead of the autarkic regional blocs of the 1930s, we are witnessing "the forces of business and financial integration...moving the globe inexorably toward a more tightly interconnected system that ignores regional as well as national borders."[72]

Richard Rosecrance argues[73] that "international civilization worthy of the name is the governing economic culture of the world market.... Yet the world's attention continues to be mistakenly focused on military and political struggles for territory," that is, the traditional agenda of the nation-state. In fact, according to Rosecrance, nation-states are functionally downsizing as they struggle not for cultural dominance but for a greater share of world output. The state no longer commands resources as it did during the mercantilist period; "it negotiates with foreign and domestic capital and labor to lure them into its own economic sphere and stimulate its growth." The virtual state "specializes in modern technical and research services and derives its income not just from high-value manufacturing, but from product design, marketing, and finance." Virtual nations "will likely supersede the continent-sized and self-sufficient units that prevailed in the past." The world is embarked on a progressive emancipation from land as a determinant of production and power.

In time, this shift in the basis of production will have an impact on the frequency of war. "Land, which is fixed, can be physically captured, but labor, capital, and information are mobile and cannot be definitively seized." When land is the major factor in production, the temptation to strike another nation is great. When the key elements of production are less tangible, the situation changes. The taking of real estate does not result in the acquisition of knowledge, and aggressors cannot seize intellectual capital.

After decades of increasing state involvement in area after area of society, central governments have been on the retreat, according to a 1996 study by NDU.[74] Publics in many countries seem to have changed their views about national priorities and the role of the government in achieving those national goals. The most obvious characteristic of the retreat of the state has been the end of the totalitarian systems in the Warsaw Pact, in which the state dominated all aspects of life, stifling the institutions of civil society. But in many other countries as well, a dramatic change has taken place in what citizens expect from their governments. After decades in which the power of central governments grew steadily, those central governments are now reinventing themselves, and power is diffusing from the center. Two changes stand out in particular.

First, central governments are ceding more power to regional and local governments. For instance, not only did the Soviet Union break up into its constituent republics, but Moscow has had to permit regions freer reign. In post-Mao China, the provinces acquired a large measure of economic independence that they used to deny resources to the central government, which finds that its budget is growing only modestly while the national economy races ahead. In the EU, after years of defining detailed Unionwide directives, the new principle is "subsidiarity," under which responsibility for each problem is to be assigned to as local a level of government as possible—preferably local instead of national, and then national instead of Unionwide. In the United States, the 1994 House of Representatives Republican Party members' Contract with America exemplified the strong interest in devolving to the states responsibility for programs that the federal government previously controlled.

Second, central governments are shedding functions, partly to reduce expenditures and thereby contain budget deficits. The most important reduction in the role of the state has been a wave of privatization that has swept Western Europe, the former Soviet bloc, and Latin America and has created ripples elsewhere. In 1994, governments privatized approximately $80 billion in assets. The general mood is that states are poor managers of factories and selling off such enterprises is a way to raise growth rates. The change in attitude in Latin America has been particularly sharp, from a general assumption that the state must organize economic development to enthusiasm for the rule of the markets.

Fareed Zakaria has commented on the rise and fall of what he calls the command state. For most of history, he observes, the state was only one of the many entities within a society that claimed legitimacy and power. (The church and feudal lords and princes also competed for the control of territory.) During the past few centuries, the state slowly crowded out its competitors by taking greater control of the core functions of society—especially preparing for and waging war. But the era of war—in the sense of intense and sustained ideological, political, and military conflict among great powers—is now in the past, at least for the next several decades. Without the tensions and emergency needs of great war and struggle, it will be difficult for the state to maintain its dominance in society. The decline of the command state has already begun: across the Western world, people are choosing to enter private contractual arrangement for those things that the state has provided: police, financial security, education, and especially communications.[75]

No single entity is likely to replace central government, but organizations are stepping into the vacuum. Mathews notes that the dramatic increase in the number and influence of NGOs, which "breed new ideas; advocate, protest, and mobilize public support; do legal, scientific, technical, and policy analysis; provide services; shape, implement, monitor, and enforce national and international commitments; and change institutions and norms. Increasingly, NGOs are able to push around even the largest governments." International organizations are building constituencies of their own and, through NGOs, are establishing direct connections with the peoples of the world. There is a growing class of international civil servants—lawyers, scientists, diplomats, NGO representatives—responsible for implementing, monitoring, and enforcing international agreements. The EU is neither a union of states nor an international organization; yet its councils, committees, and working groups penetrate and weaken the internal bonds of member states. And units below the national level are taking on formal international roles—for example, nearly all 50 states of the United States have trade offices abroad, and all have official standing in the World Trade Organization.[76]

Will the effects of interdependence—and the weakening of the nation-state—have a positive or a negative effect on international security? Mathews argues that in a time of enormous change, NGOs may be "quicker than governments to respond to new demands and new opportunities. Internationally...NGOs, when adequately funded, can outperform government in the delivery of many public services.... And they are better than governments at dealing with problems that grow slowly and affect society through their cumulative effect on individuals—the 'soft' threats of environmental degradation, denial of human rights, population growth, and lack of development." On the economic front, expanding private markets can avoid economically destructive but politically seductive policies like excessive borrowing. International organizations, with adequate funding, could take on larger roles in global housekeeping, security, human rights, and emergency relief.

In Mathews's opinion, however, the continuing diffusion of power away from nation-states could mean more conflict and less problem solving both within states and among them. NGOs suffer often from tunnel vision, judging every act by how it reflects their particular interest. Global civil society might become "fragmented, producing a weakened sense of common identity and purpose and

less willingness to invest in public goods, whether health and education or roads and ports." Excessive pluralism could become unman-
ageable. And more international decisionmaking will also exacerbate the so-called democratic deficit, as decisions that elected
representatives once made shift to unelected international bodies.

> With citizens already feeling that their national governments do
> not hear individual voices, the trend could well provoke deeper
> and more dangerous alienation, which in turn could trigger new
> ethnic and even religious separatism. The end result could be a
> proliferation of states too weak for either individual economic
> success or effective international cooperation.... The shift from
> national to some other political allegiance, if it comes, will be
> an emotional, cultural, and political earthquake.[77]

Policy Prescriptions

Interests

Those who advocate looking at the world in more traditional, geopolitical (or geoeconomic) fashion tend to focus on the tried-and-
true methods—hegemony, equilibrium, or concert—by which
competition among states can be prevented, managed, or success-
fully conducted.

Hegemony. Benevolent global hegemony should be the U.S.
objective, advises the unipolar school. The first objective of U.S.
foreign policy should be to preserve and enhance U.S. strategic and
ideological predominance "by strengthening America's security, supporting its friends, advancing its interests, and standing up for its
principles around the world."[78] Potential challengers are deterred by
overwhelming U.S. power and influence even before they contem-
plate confrontation. "The ubiquitous post–Cold War question—
where is the threat—is thus misconceived. In a world in which
peace and American security depend upon American power and the
will to use it, the main threat the United States faces now and in the
future is its own weakness." For William Kristol and Robert Kagan,

this requires a "remoralization of American foreign policy," following from the American belief that the principles of the Declaration of Independence are not merely the choice of a particular culture but are universal, enduring, self-evident truths. In response to those who recall John Quincy Adams's warning that America should not go abroad in search of monsters to destroy, they answer:

> But why not? The alternative is to leave monsters on the loose, ravaging and pillaging to their hearts' content, as Americans stand by and watch.... Because America has the capacity to contain or destroy many of the world's monsters, most of which can be found without much searching, and because the responsibility for the peace and security of the international order rests so heavily on America's shoulders, a policy of sitting atop a hill and leading by example becomes in practice a policy of cowardice and dishonor.

Equilibrium. Those who view the world more in multipolar terms look toward a strategy designed to maintain an equilibrium among the great powers. Samuel Huntington, before publishing his argument about the clash of civilizations, wrote that "in this new environment, the overall strategic interest of the US does not lie in deterring an existing threat, but rather in preserving an equilibrium and in preventing the emergence of new threats. Pursuing equilibrium rather than containment requires less emphasis on military force and more and diplomatic, economic, and institutional means."[79]

The conservative Heritage Foundation advocates a doctrine of selective engagement. With this strategy, the United States "would engage its military power primarily to maintain a balance of power in regions that are most vital to U.S. interests." Although no single power can challenge the United States globally, "smaller powers in Europe, Asia, and the Persian Gulf can threaten U.S. security interests in these vitally important regions." Selective engagement provides that "the U.S. would bear principal responsibility for the collective defense of these regions, while U.S. allies in the regions, with U.S. support, would become responsible primarily for collective security, peacekeeping, and settling lesser conflicts that are essentially regional or limited in nature."[80]

A more liberal analyst, Charles William Maynes, writes:

> The United States [should] center its foreign policy on the countries that determine the overall character of the international system—China, Japan, Russia, members of the European Union, and some of the emerging powers, such as India and Indonesia. Only states of this size and power can mount or prevent the kind of regional or global struggle that could jeopardize world peace. So long as such states are at peace, surface turmoil in the international system can continue without shaking its foundations. It is only when such states engage in the type of "great game" that was played before World War I or when some great power seeks a hegemonic role that regional or global peace is endangered.[81]

Many who favor the geoeconomic approach agree on the need for political as well as economic equilibrium, which requires first-order attention to America's domestic economic strength. Beyond this, as Chalmers Johnson argues, the United States must understand that "global commerce will acquire the logic of war. This has always been true for the developmental states; it will now become true for all states. The most logical way to promote peace, stability, and continued prosperity under these conditions will be through some form of the balance of power." For Johnson, in the case of Asia and the Pacific, this means seeking "a balance among China, Japan, and ASEAN, with the United States shifting its strength in order to achieve and maintain it, while supporting Korea and Vietnam as the two most important buffer states in East Asia."[82]

Concert. An alternative geopolitical approach would involve the concerting of power, at least in key regions such as Europe. A concert-based collective security system would rely on a small group of regional powers that would guide the operation of a regionwide security structure. Members of the concert would meet on a regular basis to monitor events and, if necessary, orchestrate collective initiatives. Decisions would be taken through informal negotiations, through the emergence of a consensus.

This flexibility and informality would allow the structure to retain an ongoing current of balancing behavior among the major powers. A great-power concert requires a broadly compatible view of a stable international order, but it allows for subtle jockeying for position to take place. This has the advantage of enhancing stability by institutionalizing, and thereby promoting, cooperative behavior and ameliorating the security dilemma. In Europe, such a concert might involve the United States, Russia, Britain, France, and Germany under the rubric of the Organization for Security and Cooperation in Europe. The concert would take on tasks such as prevention of both nuclear proliferation and regional-conflict escalation.[83]

Many interests-based analysts favor national means to assure national ends. Former senator Robert Dole argued in 1995 that "international organizations—whether the United Nations, the World Trade Organization, or any others—will not protect American interests. Only America can do that. International organizations will, at best, practice policymaking at the lowest common denominator—finding a course that is the least objectionable to the most members. Too often, they reflect a consensus that opposes American interests or does not reflect American principles and ideals." For Dole, this did not mean going it alone; "the real choice is whether to allow international organizations to call the shots—as in Somalia or Bosnia—or to make multilateral groupings work for American interests—as in Operation Desert Storm. Subcontracting American foreign policy and subordinating American sovereignty encourage and strengthen isolationist forces at home—and embolden our adversaries abroad."[84]

Many, but not all, of those with the interests-based perspective would concur with Colin S. Gray's view that "it is more likely than not that the United States will find that there is a superpower of quantity and quality of menace in its future." As a result, the United States needs to maintain its high value to others as a prospective ally in the case of potential balance-of-power troubles in Eurasia. Second, the United States needs to preserve the ability to effect timely and decisive intervention in some regional or local quarrels. Third, for a wide range of reasons in support of its foreign policy, the United States needs the ability to use force deftly in very precise and limited ways that are short of any common-sense definition of war.

This requires the United States to maintain a strategic force posture second to none, a navy able to enforce the right of maritime passage virtually everywhere, the ability to project power from the air on a massive scale and globally, and the ability to project land power on a modest scale but with great ability and precision."[85]

At bottom, the central point of policy departure for the interests perspective is the view held toward the two powers—China and Russia—that are believed capable (in one form or another) of challenging the strategic position of the United States. Some analysts remain concerned with the possibility of a Japanese or a European–German threat, but it is generally presumed that any future hostility on the part of Tokyo or Berlin would result from a failure of the United States to deal with challenges by China or Russia or both. The task for the United States is to sustain the alliance among the Western democracies and other friendly nations, to deter any challenges from one or both of these revisionist powers, and to provide the basis on which one or both can be integrated into the international community if the strategic posture proves to be moderate. The interests proponents are by no means united on which—China or Russia—represents the greater short- and long-term challenge.

Some from the traditionalist geopolitical or realist perspective argue for a much more modest U.S. approach to the world. They are particularly critical of the U.S. penchant for crusades ("Wilsonianism")—a tendency to strive for overambitious ends with only modest means. The danger they see is a political coalition between the conservative nationalists, who argue that the United States should exercise a benevolent hegemony over the world, and the liberal issues school, who believe it is now safe to resume the moralistic activism that was held in check by the Cold War. The lack of U.S. restraint would not only squander the nation's prestige and credibility, but it would also backfire because "hegemons are always regarded with great suspicion and resentment by other states. Unless they make a special effort to abstain from throwing their weight around, they are likely to bring into being hostile coalitions formed to balance and contain them."[86] Robert Tucker argues that "if the ends of policy are to be scaled down significantly, we will have to entertain a more modest vision of international order and of our role in that order than we have entertained in the past and continue to entertain today.... [A]n adjustment to a more modest concept of order, and of America's role in that order, [seems] appropriate." This requires a recognition that U.S. power is in relative decline and the United States must focus on how that decline may best be arrested. Washington will require the greater cooperation of others, chiefly its principal allies of the past half century in Europe and Asia, which will in turn require a greater willingness to compromise.[87]

Those of the interests perspective caution in particular against ready U.S. intervention in regional conflicts or for controlling the effects of anarchy. "What happens in Liberia or even Bosnia cannot affect the underlying stability of the international system so long as the great powers refuse, as they have to date, to intervene in these crises for diplomatic advantage, which would renew the kind of struggle for supremacy that unsettled Europe prior to 1914."[88] Absent such an obvious connection, equilibrium and stable great-power relations in the face of regional disputes can be maintained by mutual forbearance.

Issues

Those who focus on global security rather than national security tend to be much more activist, but they argue that such a course actually will require fewer resources than one aimed at U.S.-led geopolitical hegemony or equilibrium.

> As the leading power in the international system, the U.S. has the opportunity, especially in the wake of the end of the Cold War, to help shape elements of the system in directions that favor the achievement of greater political and economic development and stability. It has long been clear that the emergence of a highly interdependent international system mandates the creation of institutions to facilitate myriad interactions and tradeoffs that must be made every day in the normal course of international relations. This strategy seeks to accelerate these developments in the expectation that they can, over time, help the U.S. to secure its national objectives at less cost and with a more equitable sharing of costs than is the case today.[89]

Joseph Nye observes that "the ability of great powers with impressive traditional power resources to control their environment is...diminished by the changing nature of issues in world politics. Increasingly, the issues today do not pit one state against another; instead, they are issues in which all states try to control non-state actors." The solutions to these issues "will require collective action and international cooperation." Creating and resisting linkages between issues when a state is either less or more vulnerable than another becomes the art of the power game:

> Political leaders use international institutions to discourage or promote such linkages; they shop for the forum that defines the scope of an issue in the manner best suiting their interests....
>
> Although force may sometimes play a role, traditional instruments of power are rarely sufficient to deal with the new dilemmas of world politics. New power resources, such as the capacity for effective communications and for developing and using multilateral institutions, may prove more relevant....
>
> ...A state may achieve the outcomes it prefers in world politics because other states want to follow it or have agreed to a situation that produces such effects. In this sense, it is just as important to set the agenda and structure the situations in world politics as to get others to change in particular cases. This second aspect of power...might be called co-optive or soft power in contrast with the hard or command power of *ordering* others to do what it wants.[90]

Cooperation, not competition, between states represents the best strategy for effectively and actively addressing global challenges. From this perspective, nongovernmental and intergovernmental organizations have emerged as critical actors that enable cooperation in addressing transnational and subnational issues.

Transnational trends feed a growing sense that individuals' security may not in fact reliably derive from national security, traditionally defined. Jessica Mathews suggests:

> A competing notion of "human security" is creeping around the edges of official thinking, suggesting that security be viewed as emerging from the conditions of daily life—food, shelter, em-

ployment, health, public safety—rather than flowing downward from a country's foreign relations and military strength.[91]

President Clinton told an audience in Detroit:

As walls come down around the world, so must the walls in our minds between our domestic policy and our foreign policy. Think about it. Our prosperity as individuals, communities, and a nation depends upon our economic policies at home and abroad—on Detroit's empowerment zone and your commitment to an airport facility that will connect you better to the rest of the world. Our well-being as individuals, communities, and a nation depends upon our policies to fight terrorism, crime, and drugs at home and abroad. We reduce the threats to people here in America by reducing the threats beyond our borders. We advance our interests at home by advancing the common good around the world.[92]

This is consistent with President Clinton's argument that U.S. foreign policy should be based on the enlargement of democracy.[93] From the perspective of multilateralism: "The history of the world, after all, chronicles smaller social subgroups successively relinquishing their autarky and sovereignty to larger institutions that then assume governing functions, including security, at the expense of individual or local power, even when the larger institutions are not omnicapable." The key is that such institutions be democratic, or governed by democratic values. In that case, international organizations "should be the primary vehicle for gradual extension of democratic governance and expansion of the democratically oriented international community."[94]

Stanley Hoffmann disagrees with those who would take a narrow interests-based approach because, for example, "the campaign against nuclear proliferation is at least as much about a world order as about protecting American lives." Certain levels and kinds of distress in other countries are morally unacceptable and certain political, economic, and social breakdowns too dangerous to world order to be ignored. This requires certain carefully selected interventions in foreign domestic crises.

For we live in a world in which apathy about what happens in "far away countries of which we know nothing" can all too easily lead—through contagion, through the message such moral passivity sends to troublemakers, would-be tyrants, and ethnic cleansers everywhere—not to the kind of Armageddon we feared during the Cold War but to a creeping escalation of disorder and beastliness that will, sooner or later, reach the shores of the complacent, the rich, and the indifferent.[95]

Zbigniew Brzezinski also makes the case for broad activism:

Threats to international security have traditionally been defined in terms of state-to-state relations. That was especially the case in an age in which the nation-state was the principal vessel of decisive political action. But in the emerging age of organic global politics, it is just as likely that major threats could originate from within states, either through civil conflicts or because of the increased technological sophistication of terrorist acts.... Accordingly, in determining when and how to address such problems the international community may have to be guided less by traditional notions of sovereignty (i.e., is one state violating the sovereignty of another?) and more by the scope of the threat itself. In other words, there may develop situations in which external intervention in the seemingly internal affairs of states—as in Yugoslavia yesterday and perhaps elsewhere tomorrow—may be necessary and justified by the potential consequences of activities that are otherwise of internal character and do not, of themselves, involve interstate collision.[96]

In a national security policy concerned with issues and dangers, the ends and means of national defense would be significantly different. Forces and activities will be directed more

to support the preventive management of security conditions, a task significantly different from responding to a specific attack....

If the cold war could be summarized as an era of competition in military development and the quest for military advantage, the emerging era can credibly be projected as a search for reliable control over the results of that competition. The primary security objectives that have guided the major military establishments for decades—the deterrence of nuclear aggression and territorial defense against organized aggression—are no longer the overriding concerns. What has been left for resolution is the question of how to manage the secondary consequences of existing deployments, advanced technical developments, excess military production capacity, and the residual effects of large-power decisions on the character and direction of regional security agendas.[97]

To be sure, military conflicts will occur, but the focus should still be on cooperation rather than competitive advantage. According to a 1994 Brookings Institution study, cooperative engagement is "a strategic principle that seeks to accomplish its purposes through institutionalized consent rather than through threats of material or physical coercion. It presupposes fundamentally compatible security objectives and seeks to establish collaborative rather than confrontational relationships among national military establishments." The basis for such collaboration is

> mutual acceptance of and support for the defense of home territory as the exclusive national military objective and the subordination of power projection to the constraints of international consensus.... To be useable and effective against new security contingencies, even military force will require internationally agreed-upon norms to guide the composition and objectives of force postures.[98]

In a cooperative security regime,

> the use of military force would be a last resort, to be invoked only after the full range of other instruments of influence or coercion had been exhausted. The threat of force would be maximally effective in discouraging aggression if military forces were configured in a broadly based coalition equipped with modern weapons born of political consensus. This broad international support would make the threat of military action politically credible.[99]

An example of this cooperative approach is what former secretary of defense William Perry calls preventive defense. Just as preventive medicine creates the conditions for individual health and makes disease less likely, "so preventive defense creates the conditions that support peace, making war less likely, and deterrence unnecessary." Preventive defense includes efforts to discourage the proliferation of WMD but, perhaps more important, it also engages the U.S. defense establishment in "building democracy, trust, and understanding in and among nations." In almost every new democracy, Perry explains, the military is a major force in domestic politics, and "if a crisis occurs, the United States wants that nation's military to come down on the side of democracy and economic reform and play a positive role in resolving the crisis...." Regular contacts between the U.S. military and those of other nations demonstrate how armed forces function in a democracy and serve to build openness and trust between nations:

> [C]onfidence-building measures build trust between countries. Among the most important of such measures are the ones promoting openness about military budgets, plans, and policies.... Openness, after all, is an unusual concept in defense, for the art of war involves secrecy and surprise. The art of peace, however, involves exactly the opposite—openness and trust. Through openness about security matters, nations gain insights into each other's strategic intentions, reducing pressure to engage in arms competition and chances for miscalculation.

Perry uses the North Atlantic Treaty Organization's Partnership for Peace and military-to-military dialogue with the Chinese People's Liberation Army as examples of this sort of use of the U.S. defense establishment for the purposes of positive engagement.[100]

Notes

1. Paul Kennedy, *The Rise and Fall of the Great Powers: Economic Change and Military Conflict from 1500 to 2000* (New York: Random House, 1987); and *Preparing for the Twenty-First Century* (New York: Random House, 1993).

2. Douglas Johnston, ed., *Foreign Policy into the 21st Century: The U.S. Leadership Challenge* (Washington, D.C.: CSIS, 1996), 35–36. For a similar

report, see *America's National Interests* (Washington, D.C.: The Commission on America's National Interests, July 1996).

3. Henry Kissinger, *Diplomacy* (New York: Simon and Schuster, 1994), 805.

4. Sam Nunn, "Surveying the Strategic Landscape," *Aviation Week and Space Technology* (November 25, 1996): 66.

5. Peter Rodman, *America Adrift: A Strategic Assessment* (Washington, D.C.: Nixon Center, 1996), 10–11.

6. Owen Harries, "Fourteen Points for Realists," *The National Interest* (Winter 1992/93): 109.

7. Charles Krauthammer, "The Unipolar Moment," *Foreign Affairs* 70 (America and the World 1990/91): 23–33. In his more recent writings, Krauthammer has become increasingly pessimistic about the willingness of the United States to maintain a unipolar status.

8. Kenneth Waltz, "The Emerging Structure of International Politics," *International Security* 18 (Fall 1993): 44–79. See also Christopher Layne, "The Unipolar Illusion: Why New Great Powers Will Arise," *International Security* 17 (Spring 1993): 5–51.

9. Institute for National Strategic Studies (INSS), *Strategic Assessment 1996: Elements of U.S. Power* (Washington, D.C.: National Defense University, 1996); Rodman, *America Adrift*, 14–15.

10. David Shambaugh, "Containment or Engagement of China? Calculating Beijing's Responses," *International Security* 21 (Fall 1996): 186–187.

11. Gerrit W. Gong, "China's Fourth Revolution," *The Washington Quarterly* 17 (Winter 1994): 29–43.

12. For an early articulation of this point of view, see Stephen Van Evera, "Primed for Peace," *International Security* (Winter 1990/91): 7–57. Those making this argument may fit into the issues camp, in that they believe that it is transnational trends that make peace possible. For their model, however, such analysts often point to the Congress of Vienna system, which is one of great-power cooperation.

13. Stephen Sestanovich, "Geotherapy: Russia's Neuroses, and Ours," *The National Interest*, no. 45 (Fall 1996): 3–13.

14. Thomas Pickering, "Farewell Speech at American Chamber of Commerce (Moscow) Luncheon" (Federal News Service transcript, October 21, 1996).

15. Henry S. Rowen, "The Short March: China's Road to Democracy," *The National Interest* (Fall 1996): 61–70.

16. Samuel P. Huntington, "The Clash of Civilizations," *Foreign Affairs* 72 (Summer 1993): 22–49. See also Huntington, *The Clash of Civilizations and the Remaking of World Order* (New York: Simon and Schuster, 1996).

17. This is my interpretation, not necessarily that of Huntington, which is why I put his assessment of culture into the category of "interests" instead of

"issues" although it could be argued that it could fit into the latter as well or better.

18. Huntington, *The Clash of Civilizations and the Remaking of World Order,* 183–206, 308–321. See also Kishore Mahbubani, "The West and the Rest," *The National Interest* (Summer 1992): 3–13.

19. Edward Luttwak, "From Geopolitics to Geo-Economics: Logic of Convex, Grammar of Commerce," *The National Interest* (Summer 1990): 17–23.

20. John B. Judis and Michael Lind, "For a New Nationalism," *New Republic* (March 27, 1995): 26. See also Lind, *The New American Nation* (New York: Free Press, 1995).

21. For a recent review of the revisionist position, see R. Taggart Murphy, "Making Sense of Japan," *The National Interest* (Spring 1996): 50–63.

22. Ivan Hall, "Samurai Legacies, American Illusions," *The National Interest* (Summer 1992): 22.

23. Janne Nolan, ed., *Global Engagement: Cooperation and Security in the 21st Century* (Washington, D.C.: The Brookings Institution, 1994), 3.

24. Joseph Nye, "What New World Order?" *Foreign Affairs* 72 (Spring 1992): 89.

25. John Lewis Gaddis, "Toward the Post–Cold War World," *Foreign Affairs* 70 (Spring 1991): 102–122.

26. Benjamin Barber characterizes this as a case of "jihad versus McWorld"—the main conflicts now and in the future will be between the values of tribe and locality on the one hand, and the global values of technology and democracy on the other. Barber, *Jihad versus McWorld* (New York: Random House, 1995).

27. Stanley Hoffmann, "In Defense of Mother Teresa: Morality in the National Interest," *Foreign Affairs* 75 (March/April 1996): 174.

28. Pierre Hassner, "Beyond Nationalism and Internationalism: Ethnicity and World Order," *Survival* 35 (Summer 1993): 53.

29. Jessica T. Mathews, "Power Shift," *Foreign Affairs* 76 (January/February 1997): 50–51. For an earlier version of this argument, see Mathews, "Redefining Security," *Foreign Affairs* 68 (Spring 1989): 162–177.

30. Bill Clinton, "Remarks by the President to the People of Detroit" (White House transcript, October 22, 1996).

31. John Gibbons, "Climate Change, U.S. Business, and the World Environment," speech at the Department of State (White House transcript, June 8, 1996).

32. Kennedy, *Preparing for the Twenty-First Century,* 329–349.

33. Geoffrey D. Dabelko and David D. Dabelko, "Environmental Security: Issues of Conflict and Redefinition," in *Environmental Security and Secu-*

rity Debates: An Introduction, Environmental Change and Security Project, report no. 1 (Washington, D.C.: Woodrow Wilson Center, 1995), 3.

34. Michael Intrilligator, "Defining 'Global Security'" (Los Angeles: University of California, 1991, unpublished).

35. Norman Myers, *The Ultimate Security: The Environmental Basis of Political Stability* (New York: W. W. Norton & Co., 1993), 31.

36. Barry Buzan, "New Patterns of Global Security in the Twenty-First Century," *International Affairs* 67, no. 3 (1991): 431–451.

37. INSS, *Strategic Assessment 1996.* These categories are not firm; some important countries, like China, combine characteristics of two or even three groups.

38. Anthony Lake, "Confronting Backlash States," *Foreign Affairs* 73 (March/April 1994): 45.

39. The following analysis is drawn principally from INSS, *Strategic Assessment 1995: U.S. Security Challenges in Transition* (Washington, D.C.: National Defense University, 1995).

40. The situation in the former Soviet Union is considered by Graham T. Allison et al., *Avoiding Nuclear Anarchy: Containing the Threat of Loose Russian Nuclear Weapons and Fissile Material,* CISA Studies in International Security, no. 12 (Cambridge, Mass.: MIT Press, 1996).

41. For a discussion of this viewpoint, see John Sopko, "The Changing Proliferation Threat," *Foreign Policy,* no. 105 (Winter 1996–97): 3–21.

42. Robert D. Kaplan, "Countries Without Borders," *New York Times,* October 22, 1996.

43. Amitai Etzioni, "The Community of Communities," *The Washington Quarterly* 19 (Summer 1996): 127–128.

44. Rodman, *America Adrift,* 39.

45. Johnston, *Foreign Policy,* 146.

46. Quoted in INSS, *Strategic Assessment 1996.*

47. Walter Laqueur, "The New Terrorism," *Foreign Affairs* 75 (September/October 1996): 24–36. Laqueur pointed out that fears about the disruptive effects of terrorism on modern society are hardly new: at the end of the nineteenth century, for example, anarchists assassinated a number of world leaders, including the U.S. president, William McKinley.

48. Sopko, "The Changing Proliferation Threat," 11–12.

49. Kennedy, *Preparing for the Twenty-First Century,* chapter 1.

50. Rodman, *America Adrift,* 50. For a fuller discussion of this topic, see Myran Weiner, "Security, Stability, and International Migration," *International Security* 17 (Winter 1992/93): 91–126.

51. Johnston, *Foreign Policy,* 147.

52. Robert D. Kaplan, "The Coming Anarchy," *The Atlantic Monthly* (February 1994).

53. Kennedy, *Preparing for the Twenty-First Century.*

54. Joyce Starr, "Water Wars," *Foreign Policy,* no. 82 (Spring 1991).

55. Eileen Claussen, "Environment and Security: The Challenge of Integration," in *Environmental Security and Security Debates,* 40.

56. Thomas F. Homer-Dixon, "Environmental Scarcity and Violent Conflict: Evidence from Cases," *International Security* 19 (Summer 1996): 36–39.

57. United Nations, Intergovernmental Panel on Climate Change, "Climate Change 1995: Economic and Social Dimensions of Climate Change," second assessment report (New York: Cambridge University Press, 1996).

58. Claussen, "Environment and Security," in *Environmental Security and Security Debates,* 42.

59. Gibbons (White House transcript).

60. Warren Christopher, "American Diplomacy and the Global Environmental Challenges of the 21st Century" (Address and question-and-answer session at Stanford University, Palo Alto, Calif., released by the Bureau of Public Affairs, U.S. Department of State, April 9, 1996).

61. INSS, *Strategic Assessment 1996.*

62. The growing importance of economics suggests a hierarchy of interests for the United States different from one dominated by geostrategic considerations. This obviously means that greater attention should be paid not only to large, well-established economies but also to what are often termed the Big Emerging Markets (BEM). Domestic policy successes in a few key nations—for example, China, South Korea, Turkey, Poland, Indonesia, Brazil, South Africa—could accelerate positive trends toward democracy, the promotion of human rights, environmental management, regional stability, and the like. (The BEMs also show a strong proclivity for buying products and services where the United States enjoys comparative advantages as an exporter.) In the case of Mexico, for example, the distinction between foreign and domestic affairs between Washington and Mexico City has practically disappeared—witness the peso crisis. See Jeffrey E. Garten, "The Big Emerging Markets: Changing American Interests in a Global Economy" (Remarks before the Foreign Policy Association, New York City, January 20, 1994). Garten was then Under Secretary of Commerce for International Trade. For background and analysis, see John Stremlau, "Clinton's Dollar Diplomacy," *Foreign Policy,* no. 97 (Winter 1994–95): 18–35.

63. Mathews, "Power Shift," 52. From a different perspective, Newt Gingrich has presented a similar analysis about the fate of hierarchical government; see Newt Gingrich, *To Renew America* (New York: HarperCollins, 1995).

64. The discussion is based on U.S. Congress, Joint Economic Committee, *The Great American Job Machine: The Proliferation of Low Wage Employment in the Economy* (Washington, D.C.: GPO, November 1986). See also Bennett Harrison and Barry Bluestone, *The Great U-Turn: Corporate Restruc-*

turing and the Polarizing of America (New York: Basic Books, 1988); U.S. Department of Commerce, Bureau of the Census, *Workers with Low Earnings: 1964 to 1990,* Current Population Reports, Consumer Income, series P-60, no. 178 (Washington, D.C.: GPO, March 1992); Lawrence Mishel and Jared Bernstein, *The State of Working America, 1992* (Armonk, N.Y.: Sharpe, 1993); Frank Levy and Richard Murnane, "U.S. Earnings Levels and Earnings Inequality: A Review of Recent Trends and Proposed Explanations," *Journal of Economic Literature* 30 (September 1992): 1333–1381.

65. The most prominent recent example of this kind of argument is that by Sheldon Danziger and Peter Gottschalk, *America Unequal* (Cambridge, Mass.: Harvard University Press, 1995). See also John Bound and George Johnson, "Changes in the Structure of Wages in the 1980s: An Evaluation of Alternative Explanations," *American Economic Review* 82 (1992): 371–392.

66. Strobe Talbott, "Democracy and the National Interest," *Foreign Affairs* 75 (November/December 1996): 50–52.

67. Samuel P. Huntington, *The Third Wave: Democratization in the Late Twentieth Century* (Norman, Okla.: University of Oklahoma Press, 1991).

68. Talbott, "Democracy and the National Interest," 51; Samuel P. Huntington, "Democracy for the Long Haul," *The Journal of Democracy* (April 1996); Mancur Olson, "Dictatorship, Democracy, and Development," *American Political Science Review* (September 1993). For a review of recent trends and developments, see Thomas Carothers, "Democracy Without Illusions," *Foreign Affairs* 76 (January/February 1995): 85–99.

69. Talbott, "Democracy and the National Interest," 57.

70. Ibid., 55–56.

71. David Held, *Democracy and the Global Order: From the Modern State to Cosmopolitan Governance* (Stanford, Calif.: Stanford University Press, 1995).

72. G. John Ikenberry, "The Myth of Post–Cold War Chaos," *Foreign Affairs* 75 (July/August 1996): 79–91.

73. Richard Rosecrance, "The Virtual State," *Foreign Affairs* 75 (July/August 1996): 45–61.

74. This is taken from INSS, *Strategic Assessment 1996.*

75. Fareed Zakaria, "The Post-Postal World," January 2, 1997 <http://www.IntellectualCapital.com>.

76. Mathews, "Power Shift," 58–62.

77. Ibid., 63–64.

78. William Kristol and Robert Kagan, "Toward a Neo-Reaganite Foreign Policy," *Foreign Affairs* 75 (July/August 1996): 18–32. See also Kagan, "American Power: A Guide for the Perplexed," *Commentary* (April 1996): 21–31.

79. Samuel P. Huntington, "America's Changing Strategic Interests," *Survival* 33, no. 1 (January 1991): 3–17.

80. Kim R. Holmes and Thomas G. Moore, eds., *Restoring American Leadership: A U.S. Foreign and Defense Policy Blueprint* (Washington, D.C.: Heritage Foundation, 1996), 7.

81. Charles William Maynes, "Bottom-Up Foreign Policy," *Foreign Policy,* no. 104 (Fall 1995): 47.

82. Chalmers Johnson, "Rethinking Asia," *The National Interest* (Summer 1993): 25–27.

83. See, for example, "Concerts, Collective Security, and the Future of Europe," *International Security* 16 (Summer 1991): 114–161.

84. Bob Dole, "Shaping America's Global Future," *Foreign Policy,* no. 98 (Spring 1995): 50–51.

85. Colin S. Gray, "Strategic Sense, Strategic Nonsense," *The National Interest,* no. 29 (Fall 1992): 11–20. For an argument for America as "holder of the balance," see Alberto S. Coll, "America as the Grand Facilitator," *Foreign Policy,* no. 87 (Summer 1992): 47–65.

86. See, for example, Owen Harries, "Madeleine Albright's Munich Mindset," *New York Times,* December 19, 1996.

87. Robert W. Tucker, "The Future of a Contradiction," *The National Interest* (Spring 1996): 20–27. For another defense of selectivity, see James Schlesinger, "Quest for a Post–Cold War Foreign Policy," *Foreign Affairs* 72 (America and the World 1992/93): 17–28.

88. Maynes, "Bottom-Up Foreign Policy," 42.

89. Ian Lesser, "Multilateral Security: Interdependence and U.S. Strategy," in *Prisms and Policy: U.S. Security Strategy after the Cold War,* ed. Norman D. Levin (Santa Monica, Calif.: RAND, 1995), 38.

90. Joseph Nye, "Soft Power," *Foreign Policy,* no. 80 (Fall 1990): 153–171. (Italics in original.) See also Nye, *Bound to Lead: The Changing Nature of American Power* (New York: Basic Books, 1990).

91. Mathews, "Power Shift," 50–51.

92. Clinton, "Remarks to the People of Detroit."

93. On this point, see Will Marshall, "U.S. Global Leadership for Democracy," in *Mandate for Change,* eds. Will Marshall and Martin Schram (New York: Berkeley Books, 1993).

94. Graham Fuller, "Democratic Internationalism: Toward a New Foreign Policy," in *Prisms and Policy,* 66.

95. Hoffmann, "In Defense of Mother Teresa," 175.

96. Zbigniew Brzezinski, "Selective Global Commitment," *Foreign Affairs* 70 (Fall 1991): 5–6.

97. Nolan, ed., *Global Engagement,* 591.

98. Ibid., 4–5, 8.

99. Ibid., 16.

100. William J. Perry, "Defense in the Age of Hope," *Foreign Affairs* 75 (November/December 1996): 64–72.

Appendix B

Evolution of Security Agencies and Departments

Alistair J. K. Shepherd

National Security Council

Before passage of the National Security Act of 1947 (NSA '47) no formal advisory body existed to which the president might turn for advice on national security issues. He usually acted on his own authority, taking advice from a small selection of unofficial advisers as he saw fit. The next several pages describe how the president dealt with on national security issues before and after 1947.

In the nineteenth century, Presidents Jefferson, Madison, Monroe, Polk, Lincoln, and McKinley (the most active presidents in foreign affairs) acted nearly alone. However, the industrialization of warfare and the experience of the Spanish-American War served to encourage increased consultation between the War Department and Navy Department.

In the two decades after the war with Spain, consultations on national security increasingly took place among the State, War, and Navy Departments through letters among the secretaries. No department, however, would reveal its military or political thinking and objectives to the others, and decisions were left exclusively to the president. The consultation process took a small step forward in 1903 when the Joint Board of the Army and Navy was established, but it left the State Department out of any joint discussions. During World War I, this board was joined by a permanent Joint State and Navy Neutrality Board, an advisory body on diplomacy and international law. The amount of correspondence among the three departments tripled from the prewar average as conferences, committees, and letters began to knit them together. The two boards had little effect on policy, however, as President Woodrow Wilson tended to make decisions without assistance from these three departments or the boards. Shortly after Franklin D. Roosevelt became president, the secretary of state named a high-level State Department official to sit in on the Army and Navy Joint Board's planning committee. Yet the president remained the sole coordinator of national security policy.

In 1938, as Europe slipped toward war, the secretary of state proposed an interdepartmental committee to consider matters of national policy. The Standing Liaison Committee was created, consisting of the Departments of State, War, and the Navy; but real questions of policy rarely came up and it was disbanded in 1943. The 1939 reorganization act established the Executive Office of the President and, within this, the Office for Emergency Management, which created many of the agencies established between 1939 and 1945. Almost all these new agencies reported directly to the president. In December 1940 the secretaries of state, war, and the navy started weekly conferences, and by the autumn of 1941 the president was holding the Council of War, attended by the three secretaries and the chiefs of staff of the army and navy. The Council of War, however, operated more as a platform for the president to announce his decisions than as a forum for open discussion. To coordinate the U.S. war effort the Joint Chiefs of Staff (JCS) was created in early 1942 and became the principal body the president consulted. In reality, the idea of coordinating strategy and policy seemed to die when war erupted, and the president really consulted only the JCS and personal advisers such as Harry Hopkins. As the war drew to an end the State–War–Navy Coordinating Committee was set up to draft military-government directives and surrender terms. This committee turned out to be the immediate predecessor of the National Security Council (NSC).

Directly after the war a number of plans emerged for reorganizing the entire national security apparatus. Several years of negotiation resulted in the NSA '47 (the full text of which appears as Appendix D on page 228). This was the act that created the NSC under the immediate direction of the president. Congress hoped that the NSC would harness the president to the advice of the uniformed military, reducing his capability to act unilaterally. The NSC initially consisted of the president, the secretaries of state and defense, the three service secretaries, the chairman of the newly created National Security Resources Board, and certain other officials whom the president could nominate with the advice and approval of the Senate.

A permanent staff would support the NSC in its function of assisting the president in integrating and implementing national security policy. The staff specifically would examine U.S. national security goals in relation to national power, study policies on areas of common interest to those departments and agencies concerned with national security, and suggest guidelines and courses of action for the president. The role of the NSC was purely advisory; it had no power of its own and was in reality an extension of the presidency. As such, the personality and individual desires of each president would determine its role and effectiveness.

By 1949–1950 it was evident that the NSC was not as prominent in policy advising as it might have been. President Harry S Truman did not use it with any regularity or purpose. In 1949, Truman added the vice president and the secretary of the treasury to the NSC, and the Central Intelligence Agency (CIA) director began to sit in as an observer and adviser. The National Security Act amendments, also passed in 1949, made changes to the composition of the NSC and stressed its advisory, as opposed to policymaking, nature by placing it in the Executive Office of the President. The three service secretaries were removed from the NSC; and the members of the JCS were designated as the principal military advisers to the NSC, initiating regular attendance by the chairman of the JCS. To assist with specific problems, the NSC began to establish standing committees, and the president appointed a nonpolitical executive secretary to head the NSC staff. The basic organizational structure of the NSC after these changes were implemented is shown in figure 1 on page 148. The executive secretary brokered ideas, carried NSC recommendations to the president, briefed him daily on NSC matters, and maintained his NSC files. In effect he was the president's administrative assistant for national security affairs.

Figure 1
The Truman National Security Council

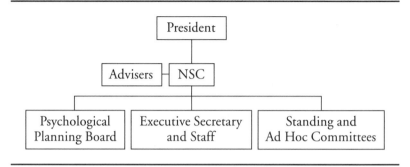

Soon after the outbreak of the Korean War in June 1950, Truman began to make far more use of the NSC and attend many more of its meetings. He directed that it would meet every Thursday and that the NSC and its staff would coordinate all major national security recommendations. In July, Truman ordered a reorganization and strengthening of the NSC, limiting attendance to the statutory members and enlarging the staff to give the NSC continuous support from a high-level interdepartmental staff.

The first administration of President Dwight D. Eisenhower saw major changes made to the NSC based on Robert Cutler's commissioned report. An interdepartmental planning board was created, along with the position of special assistant to the president for national security affairs (national security adviser). The planning board played a relatively active and independent role in catalyzing policy decisions and strategic planning. To improve operational planning and policy implementation, a new interagency committee, the Operations Coordinating Board (OCB), was formed. The OCB, which essentially replaced the Psychological Planning Board that Truman had established in 1951, coordinated psychological strategy with national strategy and, more important, was the coordinating and integrating arm of the NSC for all aspects of national security policy implementation. The OCB had a relatively large membership and an even larger supporting staff. The organizational structure of the NSC following Eisenhower's changes is illustrated in figure 2. This new structure seemed to work well but drew heavy

Figure 2
The Eisenhower National Security Council

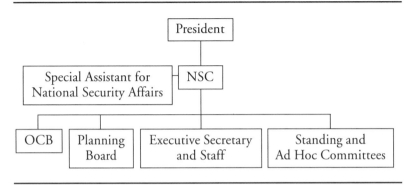

criticism during Eisenhower's last years in office. The principal complaints were its formalism and its domination by the views of the individual agencies, which prohibited the president from hearing the full range of policy options.

President John F. Kennedy came into office determined to replace the Eisenhower structure with a more open and fluid system. The State Department was directed to take the lead in foreign policy, but Kennedy's active involvement in this arena meant that he practically became his own secretary of state. As a result, the role of the special assistant for national security affairs was strengthened; the person holding this position directed a situation room from inside the White House. Kennedy believed that policy was affected by day-to-day events much more than by systematic or long-term planning. This belief led to the elimination in the NSC of the distinction between planning and operations.

Kennedy's active involvement in national security affairs often led him to deal with the agencies at the level of assistant secretary or below; he even disrupted the military chain of command during the 1961 Berlin crisis. The NSC under Kennedy was considerably reduced in size and was staffed primarily by people outside of government. Many of the NSC's functions were assumed by the smaller Standing Group or, in the case of crises such as the Cuban missile crisis, by very selective ad hoc committees. Yet overall its role was considerably enhanced owing to Kennedy's encouragement of an

Figure 3
The Kennedy National Security Council

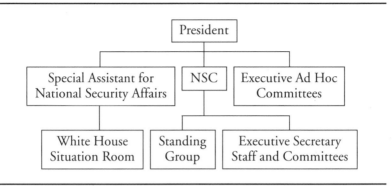

activist White House and the direct access he allowed his subordinates. The diminished structure of the NSC under President Kennedy is illustrated in figure 3.

President Lyndon B. Johnson continued Kennedy's informal approach to the management of national security policy but was personally less interested in foreign affairs and more inclined to delegate to the departments. Hence, the NSC declined in importance and became more a manager of the policy process than a source of policy advice. Johnson, effectively bypassing the NSC, established an informal Tuesday lunch with his secretaries of state and defense and his national security adviser. These lunches caused severe problems for the bureaucracy and for interagency coordination at lower levels because there were no records of decisions taken and the results were not widely dispersed. In 1966, Johnson made an effort to rectify this by trying to develop more systematic interagency procedures for dealing with national security issues. He established a Senior Interdepartmental Group (SIG on figure 4) and a variety of Interdepartmental Regional Groups (IRGs on figure 4) under the management of the State Department. This system, however, was never effectively supported by the president or secretary of state and achieved little. It is illustrated in figure 4.

Unlike his two predecessors, President Richard M. Nixon did not trust the State Department or the CIA and wanted a White House–centered mechanism for formulating foreign and national

Figure 4
The Johnson National Security Council

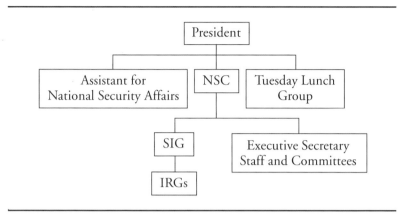

security policy, giving him a full range of options instead of a single interagency view. The National Decision Memorandum (NSDM 2) that reorganized the NSC can be found in Appendix C on page 190. (Beginning with Nixon's NSDM 2, it became the practice for each new administration to outline the new structure of the NSC in an early presidential directive; the key documents are reproduced in Appendix C beginning on page 190. The IRGs were renamed Interdepartmental Groups (IGs) and they now reported to an NSC review group chaired by the national security adviser (Henry Kissinger at that time).

The IGs had responsibility in the areas of contingency planning and policy development, while the Under Secretaries Committee took on some of the operational coordination functions of the old OCB. In addition, new senior-level committees were established for dealing with crisis management, covert action, and arms control, as well as an ad hoc committee for Vietnam. In the defense area, the Defense Program Review Committee was established with high-level representation from State, NSC, the Office of Management and Budget, and the Department of Defense (DOD) to review major defense fiscal policy and program issues in a broad strategic context. The basic organizational structure for President Nixon's NSC is shown in figure 5 on page 152.

Figure 5
The Nixon National Security Council

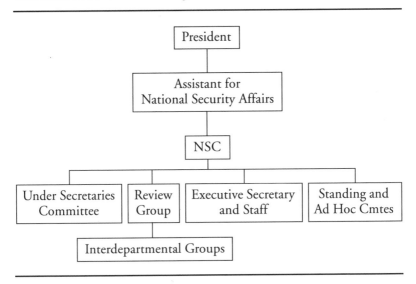

Effective power, however, was soon concentrated in the hands of Kissinger, who dominated the most critical areas of the formulation and execution of foreign policy. Kissinger was also the architect and principal spokesperson for a cohesive and strategic national security policy. As competition between State and the NSC grew, the original NSC system broke down and the national security adviser and his staff increasingly assumed operational responsibilities, to the complete exclusion of State. In 1973 Kissinger was appointed secretary of state while he retained his White House position, consolidating his control yet further. The elevation of Gerald R. Ford to the presidency saw Brent Scowcroft appointed as national security adviser, but there were no significant changes in the structure or procedures of the NSC.

President Jimmy Carter appointed Zbigniew Brzezinski as his national security adviser and between them they established a greatly simplified NSC structure: the Policy Review Committee (PRC) handled foreign policy, defense, and international economic issues, while the Special Coordinating Committee (SCC) handled sensitive functions such as arms control, crisis management, and covert action. Figure 6 illustrates the structure of the NSC outlined by

Figure 6
The Carter National Security Council

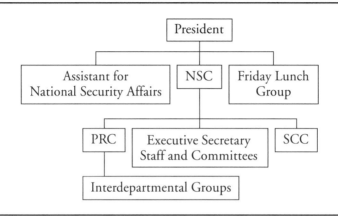

Carter's Presidential Directive/NSC-2 (text is on page 194). While he was simplifying the NSC, Carter showed his support for a stronger NSC by giving the position of national security adviser cabinet status and making the SCC a cabinet-level committee, including all NSC principals except the president. Carter tended to use his national security adviser as an alternate source of foreign policy advice on equal standing with the secretary of state, renewing the rivalry between the NSC and the State Department.

In contrast to Carter, President Ronald Reagan was committed to cabinet government and restoring the State Department to the position of primacy in foreign policy. His first national security adviser, Richard Allen, was convinced of the need for reducing the role of the NSC and supported a strong State Department; but when Secretary of State Alexander Haig claimed to function as a "vicar" for all U.S. policy concerns abroad—a declaration that triggered alarm and resistance in the White House—it derailed Haig's attempts to give State the central role in a restructured NSC.

After a year in office, President Reagan issued National Security Decision Directive (NSDD) 2 (see page 198) in January 1982, formally establishing the new NSC system. The NSC remained the principal forum for consideration of national security policy issues and the national security adviser was responsible for developing, coordinating, and implementing national security policy in the NSC.

The secretary of state was the primary foreign policy adviser, responsible for formulating, coordinating, and executing foreign policy. Separate Senior Interagency Groups (SIGs) were created to develop and implement policy for foreign policy, defense, and intelligence. In support of the SIGs a number of Interagency Groups (IGs) were permitted. State was required to establish five regional IGs and two functional ones in the areas of political-military affairs and international economic affairs. The regional IGs were specifically empowered to prepare contingency plans and create working groups to support NSC crisis-management operations. The CIA was to establish a counterintelligence IG and DOD was also required to establish IGs in functional areas. Other important structural innovations were undertaken early in the Reagan administration: the SCC was replaced by the Special Situation Group for crisis management, while covert action responsibilities were taken over by the National Security Planning Group (NSPG). The NSPG was a significant innovation. Its membership and precise charter details have not been revealed, but it clearly included the NSC principals and the president's senior White House advisers and it enabled a free exchange of views on all sensitive matters. In reality, however, these structures did not conform with the procedures laid out and the SIGs never got under way on a regular basis, while the regional IGs met irregularly at best.

A reorganization of the NSC in 1983 upgraded the status of senior staff, eight of whom became special assistants to the president, and revived the position of executive secretary to facilitate communication among the NSC, the agencies, and the White House. The next reorganization, in 1985, abolished the NSC's international economic policy SIG. Following the Iran-contra affair and the report of the president's Special Review Board, the NSC structure was again shaken up. New structures and practices were initiated to limit and rein in the proliferation of undersupervised, lower-level bodies. A Senior Review Group (SRG) and a Policy Review Group (PRG) were established to review unresolved issues from the IG-level committees in all regional and functional areas and to improve the preparation of these issues for presidential decision. The basic structure of the NSC at this point is illustrated in figure 7. The enduring problem in the management of national se-

Figure 7
The Reagan National Security Council

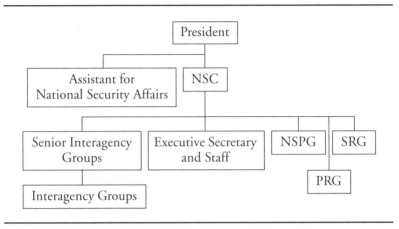

curity policy under Reagan was the tension between the national security adviser and the White House staff (illustrated by continuous White House resistance to a strong NSC role), coupled with the perennial tension between the State Department and the NSC.

On February 14, 1989, President George Bush issued National Security Directive (NSD) 1, reorganizing the NSC for his presidency (see press release on page 218). It restated that the NSC was the principal forum for discussing national security issues that required presidential decisions, that it was to advise and assist the president to integrate all aspects of national security, and that it was the principal means for coordinating the executive departments and agencies with respect to national security issues. In addition to the statutory members, the president's chief of staff and national security adviser would attend all meetings, as would the secretary of the treasury (except when asked not to); the attorney general would attend all meetings under Department of Justice jurisdiction (including covert action). Heads of other executive departments and agencies would be invited when appropriate.

NSD-1 also established three NSC subgroups: the NSC Principals Committee (NSC/PC), consisting of the national security adviser and the department secretaries; the NSC Deputies Committee (NSC/DC), consisting of the deputy national security adviser,

Figure 8
The Bush National Security Council

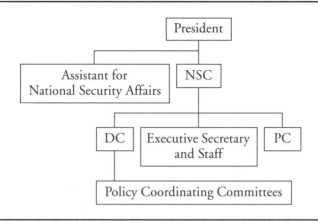

cabinet deputies, the vice chairman of the JCS, and the deputy director of the CIA; and the NSC Policy Coordinating Committees (NSC/PCCs), consisting of assistant secretary–level representatives from the appropriate departments. Initially there were six regional and four functional PCCs; nine more functional PCCs were added by NSD 10. This structure can be seen in figure 8. Overall, President Bush held very few formal NSC meetings, preferring to rely on the Principals and Deputies Committees to formulate and implement long-range strategy. Crisis situations tended to be handled by selected ad hoc groups or in one-on-one meetings.

When Bill Clinton was elected president, he kept the objectives and structure of his NSC very similar to Bush's NSC, as illustrated in figure 9 and proclaimed in his presidential directive, PDD 2 (see page 223). In addition to the statutory members, the following people were added to the NSC: the secretary of the treasury, the U.S. representative to the UN, the new assistant to the president for economic policy (the chair of a new National Economic Council), the national security adviser, and the chief of staff to the president. Others would be invited to attend when appropriate. The NSC/PC and NSC/DC were retained, and the NSC/PCCs were turned into Interagency Working Groups (NSC/IWGs). Some of these were to

Figure 9
The Clinton National Security Council

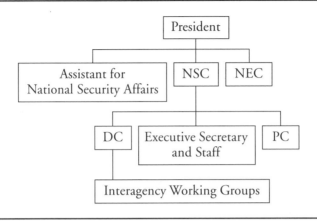

be ad hoc and others permanent, covering many issues ranging from economics to arms control.

Department of Defense

The Department of Defense was created by the National Security Act of 1947 (NSA'47), although it was referred to then as the National Military Establishment. Before its existence there was no single department handling military affairs. Most major decisions affecting the military services and their operations were made unilaterally by the president, who may or may not have consulted the chief of staff of the army or navy, the service secretaries, or perhaps one of his personal advisers in reaching his decision. The next several pages describe how the military was organized before and after passage of NSA'47 and how the president operated in relation to the military and national security.

Before 1947 the military services were completely separate organizations. The War Department was created in 1789 and the Department of the Navy in 1798. They both had clear-cut missions and operational areas that were separated by the coastline. Both departments were directly accountable to the president and each had a civilian secretary. At the beginning of the twentieth century, with

U.S. involvement in world affairs increasing, more centralized planning and advisory organizations came into use in both the army and navy. In 1903, the army created a general staff and the position of chief of staff, while the navy created a general board. Also in 1903, in an attempt to develop coordination and cooperation between the two services, the Joint Board of the Army and Navy was established. The navy finally created a counterpart to the army's chief of staff position with the position of chief of naval operations in 1914. The chief of staff of the army had direct access to the president while the civilian secretary relied entirely on the chief of staff for information and advice. The navy command structure tried to place the chief of staff under the general supervision of the civilian secretary; however, the chief of staff was commander of the fighting forces and as such would report directly to the president. This in effect gave the president direct control of defense affairs and policy, and so it remained until NSA '47.

A need to bring the War Department and the Navy Department closer together first became apparent during World War I and was driven by operational concerns. Virtually the entire U.S. war effort was directed by President Woodrow Wilson, who made unilateral decisions with little advice other than from the military chiefs of staff (separately). But the war introduced new concepts of joint operations and unity of command in the field, while the advent of air power cut across traditional service lines and raised questions of how air power should be handled and used. In the United States, the war effort was hampered by the fact that the army and the navy had separate organizations for supply and mobilization. This, too, indicated a need for greater cooperation and unity between the army and navy. Despite these indications, the army and navy remained bitterly opposed to unification throughout the interwar period. Their sole concession, in 1919, was to reconvene and enlarge the Joint Board.

World War II brought fundamental changes to the organization and operations of the armed services. The necessities of war fostered general agreement that unity of command had to replace mutual cooperation as the means for coordinating joint operations. This practice began to take hold in most theaters as unified commanders treated land, sea, and air forces as components of a full force capability. To help coordinate the military effort there was a rapid growth in joint organizations, with at least 75 interservice agencies creating a complex of boards, committees, and commissions. The most important of these, established in 1942, was the Joint Chiefs of Staff (JCS). With the exception of Harry Hopkins, President Roosevelt's personal adviser, the JCS became the president's principal advisers. The perceived need to increase coordination and cooperation in order to wage war in the industrial age led to several reports on reorganization that were issued before the war had even ended. These recommendations were prompted by several needs: to organize, mobilize, equip, and supply a large military force; for industrial mobilization in support of the military; and for the president to have access to strategic advice.

With respect to the military specifically, these plans for reorganization were bitterly opposed. The services remained determined to keep their separate identities. Once the war ended, however, the number of proposals on how to reorganize the armed services increased vastly—even the army and navy issued their own proposals in the hopes of achieving a reorganization on their terms. These proposals were put before Congress and the president and, by January 1947, a compromise agreement was reached, forming the basis for a new bill, the NSA '47.

The bill became law on July 26, 1947; the structure it created is illustrated in figure 10 on page 160. It replaced the traditional concept of national defense based primarily on military concerns with a broader concept of national security based on a close, interlocking relationship between military and civilian elements of government. NSA '47 created a federated agency called the National Military Establishment with a secretary of defense at its head to coordinate three separate executive departments (the army, navy, and newly created air force), each with its own secretary. The service secretaries were placed under the direction of the secretary of defense but would continue to handle their own administrative responsibilities. The three departments were linked together by a number of coordinating joint agencies such as the JCS. The secretary of defense was assigned as the principal assistant to the president on issues relating to national security and was in charge of establishing general policies and programs; exercising direction, authority, and control over

Figure 10
Structure Created by the National Security Act of 1947

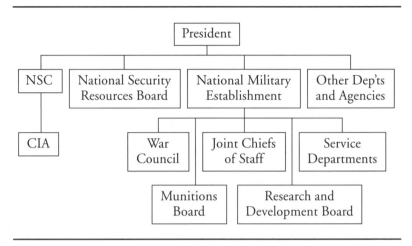

departments and agencies; and developing the budgets. The secretary of defense also was given responsibility for broad policy formulation and overall coordination, leaving operations to the individual armed services.

NSA '47 also created a number of other agencies (see appendixes A, C, and D) to coordinate national security, making U.S. security policy the collective responsibility of the government. Military defense, though still central, was to function in a wider framework of national security within which domestic, foreign, and military policies were to be coordinated. But it left the president, as had been the case in the past, with supreme authority as commander in chief.

Criticism of NSA '47 was immediate: it did not go far enough toward unification of the defense structure; the authority of the secretary of defense was not well founded, especially because the three service departments operated as independent entities; and ambiguities and overlaps remained in service roles and missions. These criticisms led to Public Law 216 of the 81st Congress; the National Security Act amendments of 1949 were approved on August 10, 1949. These amendments brought a number of structural changes: the National Military Establishment was converted into an executive department and renamed the Department of Defense (DOD); the army, navy, and air force lost their executive-branch status and were reclassified as military departments within the new DOD; and the JCS was given a nonvoting chairman (CJCS)—senior in rank to all military officers—who would preside over meetings, execute JCS business, and bring to the attention of the president or the secretary of defense matters upon which the JCS had a divided opinion. Perhaps most significant, the secretary of defense was given unqualified authority to direct and control DOD, including the military departments and field commands. The secretary of defense was also assigned a deputy and three assistants but was forbidden from having a military staff and for personnel had to rely on the Joint Staff (the staff that supports the JCS). These amendments strengthened the position of secretary of defense and marked a significant step away from the principle of federation represented by the National Military Establishment. The military departments continued to be separately administered by their respective secretaries, and Congress guaranteed their combat functions.

The continuing shortcomings and criticisms of the national security apparatus led President Eisenhower to request that a committee, the Rockefeller Commission, review the basic organization and procedures of DOD. A report was published in 1953; the president agreed with the committee's findings and submitted Reorganization Plan No. 6 to Congress on April 30, 1953. In it he stated three basic objectives: a clear and unchallenged civilian responsibility in the defense establishment, maximum defense at minimum cost, and the best possible military planning.

To accomplish the first objective, the line of authority within DOD was clarified so that there would be no question of the direction, authority, and control of the secretary of defense over the entire department. The doctrine of civilian control was confirmed with a single line of authority from the president through the secretary of defense—the national command authority. No function in any part of DOD was to be performed independent of the secretary of defense. The three service secretaries were seen as the secretary's operating managers and principal advisers on their departments. The JCS was excluded from the chain of command, thereby stressing its advisory role in national security policy development. The

Figure 11
Reorganization Plan No. 6, 1953

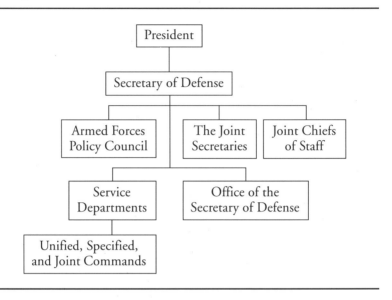

secretary of defense would in each case designate a military depart-ment to be the executive agent for a unified command. Under this arrangement the channel of responsibility and authority to a com-mander of a unified, specified, or joint command would unmistak-ably be from the president to the secretary of defense to the desig-nated civilian secretary of a military department, as illustrated in figure 11. In wartime or during an emergency, the military chiefs of the designated military departments were empowered to receive and transmit orders and act for their departments in their executive-agent capacity in the name and under the direction of the secretary of defense.

The second objective, cost reduction, was sought through the abolition of the Munitions Board, the Research and Development Board, and the Defense Supply Management Agency that had been created by the original NSA '47. Their functions were transferred to the secretary of defense for distribution among an augmented staff of six assistant secretaries and a general counsel of comparable rank. These assistant secretaries were to serve as staff and would be outside the direct line of administrative authority over the three departments; however, their linkage to the chain of command placed them in a strategic position with respect to the secretary of defense. He came to rely heavily on their advice, inevitably reducing the status of the service secretaries.

The third, and final, objective was sought through the strengthening of the JCS machinery to provide for the JCS to work more effectively as a unified planning agency, unrestricted by service positions or instructions, and to advise the secretary of defense based on the broadest conception of national security. The JCS was removed from the chain of command, which emphasized its basic planning and advisory role. Finally, the CJCS was given the responsibility for the management of the Joint Staff. It was hoped that JCS planning would encompass a wide range of views so that the secretary of defense would have a thorough knowledge of the background issues when making decisions.

Within five years a second Rockefeller Commission produced another report evaluating DOD's structure and procedures. The results greatly influenced the defense reorganization proposals Eisenhower presented to Congress in April 1958. His proposals covered five categories: unified commands, operational command channels, the JCS, defense administration, and research and development. Eisenhower's underlying belief was that the entire defense organization existed to make unified commands effective and, in 1958, the unified commands were not truly unified. As finally enacted on August 6, 1958, the Department of Defense Reorganization Act accepted with only small alterations most of the president's recommendations.

This act aimed to increase the effectiveness of the unified and specified commands. The forces assigned to unified or specified commands were put under the full operational command of the unified or specified commander and could be withdrawn from such commands only by authority of the secretary of defense, with the president's approval. The operational chain of command now ran from the president, to the secretary of defense, and on to the specified and unified commanders through the JCS, which also was to advise and assist the president and secretary of defense. The executive-agency system where departmental secretaries were in the operational chain of command was ended although they remained in the

Figure 12
Department of Defense Reorganization Act, 1958

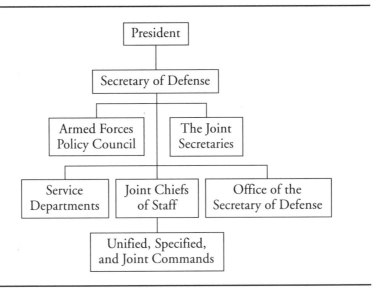

chain of command for support activities. These changes are illustrated in figure 12.

The act also brought significant changes to the JCS, tending to strengthen its overall role in the DOD decisionmaking process. Changes in defense administration were aimed at improving the support for combat forces, strengthening the authority of the secretary of defense, and eliminating interservice disputes and delays. The confusion over the status of military departments was clarified: the departments were separately organized under their own secretaries, who were responsible to the secretary of defense. Finally, the act tried to strengthen the research-and-development authority of the secretary of defense by creating a director of defense research and engineering who would be the principal adviser to the secretary of defense on scientific and technical matters.

This reorganization was expected to bring a number of significant benefits:

- Operational forces would be organized effectively into unified commands to achieve national objectives.

- Military command channels would be streamlined.

- The JCS would have a larger professional staff for unified strategic planning and would be in a better position to assist the secretary of defense in directing the unified commands.

- Clarification and strengthening of the authority of the secretary of defense would enable the secretary to function better as an agent of the president as commander in chief.

- The broadened powers of the secretary of defense over service roles and missions, and over military research and development, would promote an increase in the overall efficiency of DOD and curtail earlier tendencies toward interservice rivalry and controversy.

- The secretary of defense would have greater authority and flexibility in altering service combat missions, weapons development, and other logistic functions.

In essence, there was a vast increase in the authority of the secretary of defense, achieved by downgrading the powers of the service secretaries. The military departments were left to act primarily as agencies in support of unified and specified commands while they retained responsibilities for recruiting, training, equipping, and supporting the armed forces. They were also removed from the operational chain of command over combat units.

Between 1958 and 1978 there were a number of administrative and legislative modifications to DOD's organization, with the secretary of defense using the authority granted by the 1958 act to adjust DOD's structure. Changes were also made by Congress and the president; these mainly involved the addition of assistant secretaries and under secretaries for issues as diverse as health affairs and policy formulation. From July 1969 until July 1970 a blue-ribbon panel studied DOD's organization and management and made its recommendations. The final report on the implementation of the blue-ribbon panel recommendations, summarizing the steps taken, was published in 1975. In 1977 the secretary of defense, as an experiment, left vacant two of the nine authorized positions of assistant secretary of defense. He subsequently obtained congressional approval to abolish five statutory positions, two in the Office of the Secretary of Defense and one in each of the military departments, in the hope of streamlining the department and increasing efficiency.

The most recent restructuring of the functioning and structure of DOD originated in 1982. Between 1982 and 1986 there were severe criticisms of the JCS and numerous calls for sweeping organizational changes toward more "jointness" in the military. During this period a large number of studies were undertaken; all indicated the need for reform. On October 1, 1986, the Goldwater-Nichols Department of Defense Reorganization Act became law.

The act sought to increase greatly the jointness within DOD. The major provisions of the act can be put into five categories:

- The power and influence of the CJCS increased greatly. Among other things the CJCS was designated as the principal military adviser to the president and the secretary of defense.

- The CJCS's resources were affected. The CJCS was assigned a vice chairman and given control over the Joint Staff, which was to assist the CJCS, the vice chairman, and other members of the JCS while it operated under the CJCS's direction.

- There was a great increase in the authority of the unified commanders, who were given a range of subjects on which they had control over units assigned to them.

- The new classification—joint specialists—was created. The secretary of defense established an occupational category for officers whose primary responsibility was joint operations. Guidelines were established to prevent discrimination against officers of joint assignments, and they were to be promoted at the same rate as other officers.

- There was a consolidation of the two parallel (civilian and military) hierarchies at the top of the army, navy, and air force. Civilian staff were to take over certain functions and seven other functions were unified.

Joint Chiefs of Staff

Before enactment of the National Security Act of 1947 (NSA '47) no single military structure existed. The president, as commander in chief, consulted separately with the chiefs of staff of the army and the navy and with his personal advisers, and then took his own, unilateral decisions. There also was no formal cooperation or coordination in the advice that the two military departments (army and navy) gave to president, and joint decisions made on the battlefield depended on the personalities of the officers in command.

The first sign of cooperation between the Army Department and the Navy Department occurred in 1903 with the establishment of the Joint Army and Navy Board. The board consisted of the top military officers and chief planners of both the army and the navy. It was devised as a planning and discussion body and was limited to commenting on problems submitted to it by the two service secretaries. It had no decisionmaking powers. This, coupled with the way President Woodrow Wilson ran the U.S. war effort (making his own decisions and consulting others only when he chose), resulted in the board having little or no impact on the direction of the war. The board was revitalized in 1919; its membership expanded to six: the chiefs of the two armed services, their deputies, the chief of the war plans division for the army, and the director of the plans division for the navy. A working staff (Joint Planning Committee) made up of members of the plans divisions of both service staffs was also authorized. The 1919 board, however, was given no more legal authority or responsibility than its 1903 predecessor.

This remained the situation until July 1939 when President Franklin D. Roosevelt issued an executive order that reorganized the command system. This instructed the joint board to report on a routine basis directly to the president instead of through the service secretaries. At the Arcadia Conference, held in Washington after the United States had entered the war, President Roosevelt and Prime Minister Winston Churchill of the United Kingdom (UK) established the Combined Chiefs of Staff as the supreme military body for strategic direction of the U.S.–UK war effort. To create coordinated staff work on the U.S. side, President Roosevelt established the Joint Chiefs of Staff (JCS) as the U.S. equivalent to the Chiefs of Staff Committee in the UK.

The JCS initially consisted of the chief of naval operations (Admiral Ernest King), chief of staff of the army (General George C. Marshall), and the commanding general of the army air force (General Henry Arnold). At the departmental level General Marshall had just three principal subordinates and two major-theater commanders. Admiral King had a more decentralized, disorganized body: two naval force commanders, one theater commander, and numerous traditional and new offices and bureaus belonging to the shore establishment. In mid-1942, Admiral William D. Leahy, the military chief of staff to the president, became the de facto chairman of the JCS, but his responsibilities were primarily limited to serving as a liaison between the JCS and the president.

In 1942, the second element of the joint military structure was established: a supporting staff for the JCS. The supporting staff was composed of more than a dozen interlocking joint committees, boards, and agencies, consisting of service representatives who were temporarily assigned from the service staffs. The final element of the joint military structure was the establishment of unified and specified operational commands. By the end of the war the United States had five operational commands: unified European, Southwest Pacific (army), and Pacific Ocean (navy) commands and the two specified bomber commands of the army air force in Europe and in the Pacific.

Throughout the war the JCS functioned under the personal direction of the president, without any formal charter. The JCS synchronized the military effort with allies and coordinated operations worldwide for the U.S. armed forces. The president's reliance on the JCS for advice on the direction of the war left the civilian secretaries of the War Department and the Navy Department with little responsibility for strategic planning or operations. By the end of the war the need for a formal structure was apparent. The war had illustrated that the various military services had to cooperate and coordinate a great deal more in the age of "total war." It was recognized that the JCS machinery, or something similar for joint planning and strategic direction of operations, had come to stay.

The JCS was formally established by the NSA '47. It comprised the three service chiefs (army, navy, and the newly created air force) and the chief of staff of the president, as commander in chief. The JCS was to be the principal military adviser to the president and the secretary of defense. The JCS also was given a staff (the Joint Staff) of 100, divided among the services, that operated under a director appointed by the JCS. The director was to be an officer junior in rank to all members of the JCS. The Joint Staff was to perform duties as directed by the JCS.

NSA '47 was amended in 1949; the amendment created a nonvoting chairman (CJCS), senior in rank to all other military officers, whose duties were to include presiding over JCS meetings, expediting JCS business, and bringing to the attention of the secretary of defense or president matters on which the JCS had a divided opinion. The amendment also increased the size of the Joint Staff from 100 to 210 officers.

The Rockefeller Commission was established to study the organization of the entire national security apparatus and, in 1953, the committee made a number of recommendations that led to Reorganization Plan No. 6. With regard to the JCS, a number of structural and organizational changes again were made. The CJCS was assigned authority to manage the Joint Staff and to approve the JCS selection of officers to the Joint Staff. Second, the JCS appointment of the director of the Joint Staff was made subject to the approval of the secretary of defense. These reforms were to ensure that the CJCS had sufficient authority to organize and direct the staff system and other subordinate structures that supported the JCS, without detracting from the military advisory functions of the JCS.

Reforms attempted to reduce the workload of the JCS in two ways. First, the chiefs were encouraged to reduce their administrative burdens by delegating some of their service responsibilities to their subordinates. Second, the operational chain of command was revised to exclude the JCS. The new chain of command ran from the president to the secretary of defense, on to the military departments, and then to the operational commands. This change was more symbolic than substantive because the chiefs actually remained in the operational chain as representatives of their military departments. The objective was to emphasize planning and advising, not commanding, as the primary role of the JCS.

The Defense Reorganization Act in 1958 altered the JCS structure and procedures for a third time. The result was an increase in CJCS authority. The CJCS was given a vote equal with the other members of the JCS and was to manage the Joint Staff and director on behalf of the JCS, select the director in consultation with the JCS and with the approval of the secretary of defense, and control the work carried out by the Joint Staff. The members of the JCS were returned to the chain of operational command but were defined as operational staff to the secretary of defense, not as military commanders.

The Joint Staff was increased to 400 officers, still with approximately equal numbers from army, navy, air force, and marine corps. To prevent the emergence of an armed forces general staff, Joint Staff duty was limited to three years, except in wartime, with no reassignment to the JCS within three years of completing a tour. The traditional JCS system of committees, groups, and working teams—in existence since 1942—was abolished. It was replaced by a unified Joint Staff with directorates arranged along the lines of the unified commands. With the service secretaries no longer in the chain of operational command and with a Joint Staff that seemed adequate in size and organization, it was hoped that the JCS could deal more effectively with matters of command and higher strategic direction while the military departments were left with the job of rendering administrative and logistic support for combat units.

Minor amendments were passed during the 1960s. Changes in 1959–1960 led to the secretary of defense instituting a procedure whereby the secretary would sit with the JCS to consider disputed issues and either settle the matters or present them to the president for decision. In June 1967, Congress, on its own initiative, fixed the terms of the members of the JCS at four years.

The final major reorganization of the functioning and structure of the JCS came in 1986 with the Goldwater-Nichols Defense Reorganization Act. The process originated in 1982 when calls were made for sweeping organizational changes toward more "jointness" in the military. Criticism of the military structure in general, and the JCS in particular, led to a number of studies being undertaken between 1982 and 1986. Virtually all concluded that reform was needed. The result was passed into law on October 1, 1986, as the Goldwater-Nichols Department of Defense Reorganization Act.

The major provisions of the act can be classed in five categories. The first affected the CJCS, who was designated as the principal military adviser to the president, the NSC, and the secretary of defense (covering strategy, doctrine, operations, budget, and so forth). The CJCS was also given a number of other responsibilities and roles in the JCS structure that greatly increased the position's overall power and influence in national security planning.

The second category concerned the resources made available to the CJCS. The CJCS was assigned a vice chairman of four-star rank and from a different service who would be the nation's second-ranking officer, junior to the CJCS only. The vice chairman would not have a vote except when acting as chairman in the CJCS's absence.

The unified commands were the third category affected by the Goldwater-Nichols Act. The act strengthened the hand of the theater commanders in chief (CINCs) to encourage the army, navy, air force, and marine corps to cooperate more. The CINCs were given a range of areas in which they had control over units assigned to them and were given veto power over subordinates for the first time.

The fourth category of changes affected those officers serving as joint specialists, an occupational category established by the secretary of defense for officers in joint operations. These joint officers and specialists were to be promoted at the same rate as other officers assigned to the headquarters staff of each service. In addition, guidelines were established to prevent discrimination against officers in joint assignments. At least one officer with joint experience was to sit on the promotion board reviewing those officers in a joint assignment.

The final category of changes concerned the consolidation of military headquarters. The two parallel hierarchies (civilian and military) at the top of the army, navy, and air force were to be consolidated. Civilian staff were to assume certain functions and seven other functions were unified. By the end of 1988 the headquarters staff at DOD had been reduced by 10.8 percent.

Department of State

The State Department is one of the oldest departments in the U.S. government and its role in the development of national security policy has always been intensely debated. Circumstances have caused its influence to fluctuate between a position of prominence in the development of national security policy to marginalization or even neglect. The following pages attempt briefly to illustrate how the State Department has evolved and how its role in developing national security policy has fluctuated in line with changes in the presidency.

In 1775, the five-member Committee of Secret Correspondence was created by the Continental Congress; members corresponded with individuals abroad who were able to be of service to the colonies. The committee functioned intermittently and ineffectively as did its successor, the Committee for Foreign Affairs, which was formed in 1777. These shortcomings were mainly due to Congress's failure to give the committee jurisdiction over matters within Congress's sphere. In 1781 the committee gained a secretary and was renamed the Department of Foreign Affairs.

The government under the new constitution of 1789 retained a department of foreign affairs but quickly changed its name to the Department of State and augmented its functions and staff. The principal officer was the secretary of state. The years 1818 and 1826 saw the first attempts to reorganize the State Department, but the first effective reorganization did not occur until 1833 under Louis McLane. The reform established clear lines of responsibility and specific duties for individuals while it allowed for flexibility to meet future changes. Seven bureaus were established initially, including offices responsible for some domestic functions that were gradually transferred to other departments. In 1870, a restructuring led to an increase to nine bureaus; they were reduced to six by a consolidation in 1873.

The next major reorganization did not take place until 1909. The changes gave additional funds to the State Department; new positions were created, functions reassigned, and—of greatest importance—three new political–geographic divisions and a Division of Information were created. The number of staff increased to

210. During World War I this rose to 350, with an additional 450 temporary staff. The State Department played only a small role in World War I, however, because President Woodrow Wilson acted primarily on this own, taking advice almost exclusively from his personal advisers.

Important changes to the foreign-service arm of the State Department were made in 1924 with the adoption of the Rogers Act. Foreign-service officials were appointed and promoted solely on the basis of merit, thus providing a permanent career service in the State Department. The separate diplomatic and consular services were amalgamated, creating a unified foreign service for the first time. A reorganization of the State Department to streamline it and increase efficiency, consolidating some divisions and creating others, was undertaken in 1936 by Administrator of the State Department George Messersmith. Messersmith carried out a further reorganization in 1939, merging the foreign services of the Departments of Agriculture and Commerce with the foreign service of the State Department.

The outbreak of World War II in Europe necessitated the creation of a special division to carry out tasks that came from the inescapable involvement of the neutral United States. When the United States entered the war, the traditional dichotomy between military and civilian elements of the executive branch prevented the State Department's participation in deliberations over the conduct of the war. The secretary of state was often unaware of major military plans affecting diplomatic relations during and after the war. President Franklin D. Roosevelt acted essentially as his own secretary of state, depending for advice on his personal adviser, Harry Hopkins, and the Joint Chiefs of Staff.

In December 1944, a major reorganization plan for the State Department was issued. It refined the concept of grouping similar operations together, continued the primacy of the political–geographic areas, and concentrated administrative matters under the jurisdiction of a single, qualified, and experienced official. The restructuring continued in 1946 with the Foreign Service Act that merged the home and field services and the Manpower Act that authorized the entry of 250 officers into the foreign service at levels other than the entrance level. Opposition by some senior staff meant that only 166 eventually entered.

Between 1947 and 1949, Secretary of State George C. Marshall greatly improved procedures within the State Department and established the Policy Planning Staff. The staff was supposed to deal with long-term policy planning but tended to become involved in more current and pressing problems. He also introduced an executive secretariat to centralize document control and other services. In 1949, the Hoover Commission published a report on its two-year study of restructuring the executive branch. Its recommendations were adopted by Public Law 73 in May 1949.

The State Department took responsibility for defining foreign-policy objectives and for formulating and executing these objectives through five bureaus: four geographic bureaus and a fifth dealing with international organizations. Functional units for public affairs, legal services, congressional relations, and economic and social problems were also established. The secretary of state was given clear authority and responsibility for administering both the State Department and the foreign service. Contrary to the commission recommendations, however, the civil and foreign services were not fully combined, and the office of personnel still consisted of two separate divisions for the administration of foreign- and civil-service personnel.

The 1950–1951 Rowe Committee reported that the State Department's responsibilities and primary role in the conduct of foreign affairs demanded a large, highly qualified staff with a wide variety of professional skills. Hence, the personnel system was to provide for closer integration of the home and field services, greater flexibility, better methods of recruitment, and the means for relatively easy expansion and contraction. The committee essentially advocated a single service under the secretary of state.

In an attempt to achieve this recommendation the "Directive to Improve the Personnel Program of the Department of State and the Unified Foreign Service of the U.S." was issued in March 1951. It provided for a liberalized procedure for entry into the foreign service and an increased exchange of assignments between State Department and foreign-service officers. Lateral entry was encouraged, specialists were recognized, and dual-service positions were identi-

fied for exchange purposes. Despite its good intentions, the directive generally failed to meet its objective.

Reorganization Plan No. 8 in 1953 was the start of President
Dwight D. Eisenhower's attempts to dilute the principle of a single
unified foreign service. The reorganization created the U.S. Information Agency (USIA) and caused personnel and information activities to be transferred from the State Department to USIA and its
overseas service, USIS, although they remained subject to State Department policy guidance. The mission established for USIA was to
inform and influence foreign publics in promotion of the U.S. national interest, essentially the coordination of public diplomacy.
Through the years the organization and policy emphases of the
agency have changed significantly, but the core purposes have remained constant.

The dilution continued with the passage in 1954 of the Agriculture Act that reestablished a separate Foreign Agricultural Service
and the negotiation of a new Agriculture Department–State
Department agreement. There were also efforts to reestablish a separate foreign service for the Commerce Department, but this was
averted with the policy of using businessmen as commercial at-
taches. Finally, the Foreign Operations Administration was established
through the consolidation of numerous existing foreign aid programs.

Still more changes were brought in by the 1954 Wriston Committee that was appointed to recommend measures toward the
amalgamation and interchangeability of the State Department and
the field services. It praised the personnel of the State Department
and the foreign service but was highly critical of the way the foreign
service had been administered since 1946. It recommended a single
foreign-service system for the officer personnel of the State Department and the foreign service who had comparable functions (3,700
positions) and the correction of administrative shortcomings. The
secretary of state agreed and a crash program to implement these
changes followed.

The philosophy behind all these changes in the early 1950s reflected the Hoover Commission's belief that the State Department
should not be directly involved in program operations but instead
confine itself to formulating foreign policy and negotiating treaties.
The State Department's role was to ensure that the multiplicity of

agencies now involved in foreign affairs spoke with one voice for the United States.

After the turmoil of the 1950s a large measure of stability, efficiency, and optimism returned in the early 1960s. In contrast with the previous administration, President John F. Kennedy wanted the State Department to take the lead in coordinating both foreign policy and operations abroad. He wanted the State Department to respond more quickly to White House requests for information and directives for action. In November 1961, a major reorganization of personnel moved many people from the White House to the State Department in a further attempt to make it take charge of foreign affairs. State Department response to the White House improved and the National Policy Papers—systematic plans setting out goals for a complete range of foreign affairs operations on a country-by-country basis—were created. The department's effectiveness, however, was still poor and further hampered by President Kennedy acting somewhat as his own secretary of state.

The Arms Control and Disarmament Agency (ACDA) was created in 1961 to advance the U.S. foreign policy objective of shaping a more secure world. It was established to deal with the diplomatic, military, technical, economic, and information aspects of arms control, disarmament, and nonproliferation policies. It managed, and continues to manage, U.S. participation in international negotiations on the aforementioned issues and has led all the U.S. delegations to the Conference on Disarmament. It also led or actively participated in all the U.S.-Soviet arms negotiations since 1961. The director of ACDA reports directly to the president, the national security adviser, and the secretary of state and serves as their principal adviser on arms control, disarmament, and nonproliferation issues.

In March 1966, National Security Action Memorandum (NSAM) 341 assigned the secretary of state authority and responsibility for the overall direction, coordination, and supervision of interdepartmental activities of the U.S. government overseas, excluding the military. This had been the case previously but during the Eisenhower administration the State Department Policy Planning Staff had become almost an adjunct of the National Security Council (NSC). President Lyndon B. Johnson was merely reasserting the position of the State Department as his predecessor, President

Kennedy, had done. Interdepartmental activities were defined and mechanisms to assist the secretary were established. The mechanisms consisted of a Senior Interdepartmental Group (SIG) and a number of Interdepartmental Regional Groups (IRGs). The SIG was created to assist the secretary of state in carrying out the interdepartmental responsibilities that could not be dealt with at the IRG level. Both groups had permanent members from the State Department, Department of Defense (DOD), Joint Chiefs of Staff (JCS), Central Intelligence Agency (CIA), USIA, and the Agency for International Development (AID).

The SIG–IRG system was, however, given a low priority by most and by the time its potential was realized it was too late. Richard M. Nixon's election in 1969 signaled the end for the SIG–IRG mechanism. A Nixon presidential directive in January 1969 moved the focus of power from the State Department back to the NSC, which remained the principal forum for the consideration of national security policy issues requiring presidential decisions until late 1973 when Henry Kissinger became secretary of state.

An attempt to modernize internal procedures, particularly regarding personnel, was made in December 1970 in a report entitled "Diplomacy in the 70s." It contained 500 recommendations for establishing modern management procedures and improving personnel administration. The reform program that emerged was designed to provide the State Department with a strengthened capacity for managing foreign affairs. The program was based on the principle that the State Department should be the point at which the diverse special interests of the various agencies could be turned into national policy under the guidance of the president, consistent with the responsibility of the NSC. Among the reforms was a new system to improve functional specialization in the foreign service. Applicants had to choose their areas of specialization (administrative, economic, consular, or political) before they gained any foreign-service experience. In mid-1974 several modifications were made to the system, making it less rigid by allowing officers to change their specialization while still in the junior grades. At the top levels there was strong emphasis on broadening the viewpoints of specialists by assigning them outside their areas of expertise.

The secretary of state established the Priorities Policy Group in June 1975 to provide a mechanism for linking resource allocation decisions to policy decisions. This was followed in January 1978 by President Jimmy Carter's Reorganization Plan No. 2 that consolidated various parts of the department. In 1983, Secretary of State George Shultz created a five-member, long-range foreign policy planning council.

Soon after President Bill Clinton took office in February 1993 he ordered a reorganization of the State Department aimed at streamlining the bureaucracy; it combined some functions, eliminated up to 40 jobs from the department's supervisory ranks, and cut 40 percent of the deputy assistant secretaries. The reorganization called for the State Department's functions to be grouped into five main areas, each headed by an under secretary who reported to the secretary of state. The plan grouped some previously independent functions and created two additional senior-level jobs, an under secretary for global affairs and an ambassador-at-large who was to direct U.S. relations with the states of the former Soviet Union. The under secretary for global affairs had oversight for promoting democracy and human rights; combating narcotics, terrorism, population, and refugee problems; and addressing oceanic, scientific, and environmental affairs. Figure 13 provides the organizational structure of the State Department in mid-1998.

In 1995, the Senate's State Department Reorganization Bill called for $1.7 billion in spending cuts over a five-year period. Clinton followed this cutback in April 1997 with another reorganization proposal that incorporated more fully into the department those agencies within its orbit. ACDA will become completely integrated with the State Department after a brief transition during which ACDA's director will be dual-hatted as under secretary of state for arms control and international security affairs. In exchange for relinquishing the directorship, the under secretary will then receive the additional title of senior adviser to the president and secretary of state. USIA will be integrated along similar lines, with its director dual-hatted as a new under secretary of state for public diplomacy. AID will remain a distinct agency but many of its administrative functions will be merged with the State Department.

Figure 13
Department of State, 1998

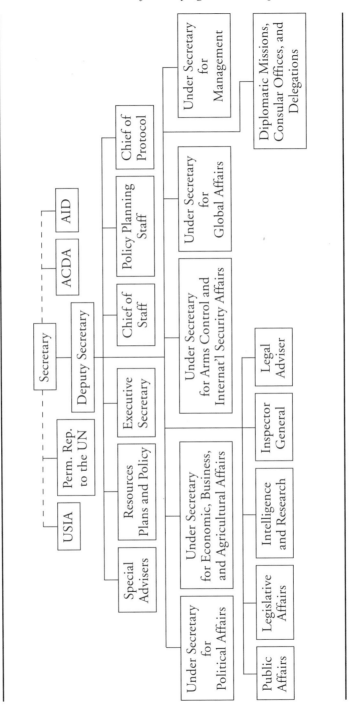

Central Intelligence Agency

Before the creation of the Central Intelligence Agency (CIA) there was no central intelligence-gathering mechanism in the United States. Although during times of war the army and navy had set up information-gathering and investigative offices, these offices were dissolved soon after fighting ended.

The first intelligence agency to be established was the Office of Naval Intelligence (ONI), created in 1882. This was followed promptly by the army's Military Intelligence Division (MID) in 1885. The ONI initially collected data centered on detailed, technical information about foreign navies. It concentrated on the ships and weapons more than on the movements and intentions of those navies. By the 1930s the type of information collected had expanded to many other issues, ranging from the war capacities to the commercial interests of foreign navies. Evaluation of information, however, was not undertaken by the ONI until 1937. This part of the process was usually left to the final consumer of the information.

The development of the MID was hampered from the outset by internal opposition. The MID was often incorporated into other divisions and its director was usually subordinate to the heads of other departments within the army. World War I finally brought greater, albeit temporary, prominence to the MID because of an increase in the number of its staff and the size of its budget. After 1921, however, its position again declined in importance, its staff was cut, and its budget was reduced. This downward trend continued until the onset of World War II.

These two intelligence-gathering operations remained entirely separate and did not share information with each other. Strategic use of the intelligence to assist in developing the concept of national security usually was made only by the end user of the gathered information, who often was the president himself. There was no coordination or real evaluation of information within the intelligence agencies, and this played a role in the element of surprise achieved by the Japanese at Pearl Harbor.

It was in the lead-up to World War II that the president first made an attempt to coordinate intelligence gathering. In July 1941, President Franklin D. Roosevelt attempted to bring together the uncoordinated strands of U.S. intelligence gathering by setting up the office of the Coordinator of Intelligence (COI); William Donovan was its director. This was the first time in U.S. history that there had been a peacetime, civilian, centralized intelligence agency incorporating military concerns. It was not, however, a centralized repository for intelligence. Knowledge was centered in the ONI and the MID and the office foundered within a year. In June 1942, the COI was incorporated into the military and became the Office of Strategic Services (OSS), under the jurisdiction of the newly created Joint Chiefs of Staff (JCS). The OSS was responsible for collecting and analyzing foreign intelligence concerning areas in which U.S. military forces operated. In December 1942 the JCS agreed on a directive for the OSS: sabotage, espionage, counterespionage, and covert action. This was extended in October 1943 when the OSS was given responsibility for all forms of morale subversion, including disinformation and propaganda. At its height the OSS had a staff of approximately 12,000. The structure of the OSS is provided in figure 14 at the top of page 182. After the war ended the OSS was disbanded by executive order in September 1945.

The disbanding of the OSS sparked a fierce bureaucratic battle, which raged until January 1946, over who would control intelligence. President Harry S Truman recognized the need for a coordinated postwar intelligence establishment; and in January 1946 he issued a directive establishing the Central Intelligence Group (CIG) and a National Intelligence Authority (NIA), jointly funded by the army, the navy, and the State Department although the military maintained its own independent intelligence services. The CIG and NIA were under the overall control of the president and under the authority of a director of central intelligence (DCI) appointed by the president. As with all other national security issues before 1947, the president had direct control over the agencies and their operations. The NIA consisted of the secretaries of the War Department, the Navy Department, and the State Department and a presidential representative.

These two agencies lasted approximately 18 months. The National Security Act of July 1947 abolished them and replaced them with the Central Intelligence Agency (CIA), headed by the DCI. The CIA was directly responsible to the president under the direction

Figure 14
Office of Strategic Services, 1945

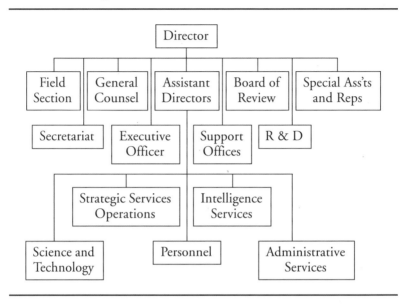

of the National Security Council (NSC). Figure 15 shows the organizational structure of the CIA at its founding. Many of the features of the OSS and CIG were incorporated, and many lessons were taken aboard. It was made clear that the CIA was to be an intelligence agency, not a covert action agency. It was to advise the NSC on intelligence matters related to national security, make recommendations on coordinating intelligence activities of government agencies generally, correlate and evaluate intelligence and see to its proper communication within government, and carry out other national security intelligence functions as the NSC might direct.

The mandate of the CIA was broadened by the 1949 Central Intelligence Act that empowered the DCI to spend agency funds "without regard to the provisions of law and regulation," which essentially provided legal authority for covert operations and actions. As the CIA developed and adapted to the changing world, its structure altered with the addition, consolidation, and expansion of various directorates and positions. On its establishment the CIA had four offices under the guidance of the executive director: the Office of Collection and Dissemination, the Office of Reports and Esti-

Figure 15
Central Intelligence Agency, 1947

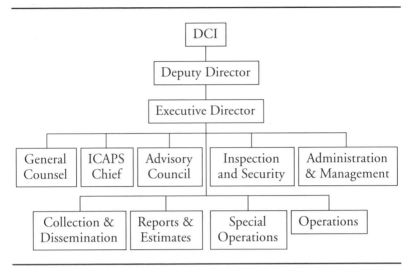

mates, the Office of Special Operations, and the Office of Operations. By 1950 this had been increased to six offices with the addition of the Office of Scientific Intelligence and the Office of Policy Coordination. In 1953, a major reorganization restructured the CIA into three directorates, each headed by a deputy director. There were directorates for plans, intelligence, and administration, each with a number of separate offices covering a broad area of issues relevant to each directorate. By 1964 the number of directorates had increased to four with the addition of the directorate for science and technology. The administration directorate had been renamed "support." These continued to be headed by deputy directors under the overall leadership of the DCI and the deputy director. In the mid-1980s the structure was largely the same, with one deputy director each for operations, science and technology, intelligence, and administration. Naturally, as the world developed and changed, as the structure of the CIA evolved, and as presidents came and went, the activities that the CIA was engaged in also changed.

It is important to note that the DCI is not only the administrative head of the CIA but is also the president's principal adviser on intelligence matters and holds the concurrent position of head of

Figure 16
The Intelligence Community, 1998

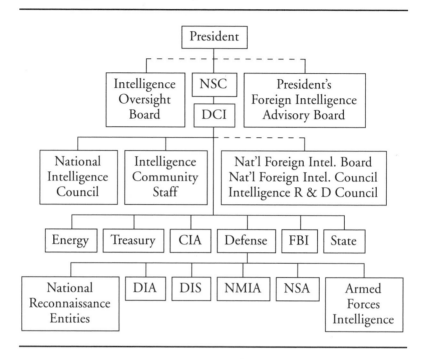

the entire U.S. intelligence community. The DCI does not, however, have direct command authority over the other intelligence agencies. These agencies are numerous and it is the DCI's job to collect and coordinate all the information and present it to the president when it is needed. To do this, the DCI is aided by the National Intelligence Council (NIC).

The NIC is composed of approximately 20 functional and regional National Intelligence Officers (NIO), who are drawn from all the agencies and offices in the intelligence community, and a similar number of support analysts. The members of the NIC work directly for the DCI and produce national intelligence estimates (NIE), special national intelligence estimates (SNIE), and interagency intelligence memoranda, which are used by the DCI directly to inform the president of intelligence issues. This relationship between the DCI and the president is the key element to the agency's influence. Figure 16 shows the other intelligence agencies that the DCI must work with.

The activities that the CIA was entitled to undertake were supposed to be kept in check by individual congressional leaders, not by congressional committees. It remained this way until the mid-1970s when events in Vietnam and the Watergate scandal made intelligence gathering in a democratic society a political issue. The 1974 Hughes-Ryan Act required Congress to be informed in a timely manner of CIA covert action programs or, if the operations were sensitive, the chairmen of various committees were to be informed. This system was ensured by Congress, which made funding available for operations in foreign states if the activities were solely for obtaining necessary intelligence, unless the president sanctioned an operation important to national security.

The significant change in the oversight of the CIA came after 1975 with the establishment of three new commissions to investigate allegations against the CIA. These commissions (the Rockefeller Commission, the Senate commission led by Frank Church, and the House select committee led by Otis Pike) had differing levels of success, but they all reached the same general conclusions regarding the CIA. The investigations revealed assassination plots against foreign leaders, domestic surveillance of U.S. citizens and journalists, mail opening, and possession of lethal toxins and devices. They concluded, however, that the CIA was not a rogue monster but simply needed stricter authority and control. The Senate Select Committee on Intelligence was established in 1976 and the House Permanent Select Committee on Intelligence followed in 1977. The addition of controls continued in 1976 when President Gerald R. Ford signed Executive Order 11095 that prohibited the CIA from carrying out assassinations. The CIA began reporting not only to the NSC and the president but also to the House and Senate intelligence oversight and appropriations committees.

Controls were again added in 1978, when President Jimmy Carter signed Executive Order 12036 that established roles, missions, and restrictions on U.S. intelligence activities that, among other things, established a remodeled and much more rigorous decisionmaking cycle for covert action. A new understanding developed among the CIA, the presidency, and the Congress that

Figure 17
Central Intelligence Agency, 1998

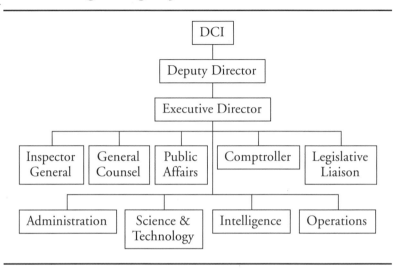

acknowledged a role and need for secrets. The process of reporting to Congress was emphasized yet again in the 1980 Intelligence Oversight Act; it mandated that the intelligence committees of the House and Senate be given prior notice of CIA activities, but it reduced the number of committees that needed to be informed of covert action to just those two.

The pendulum appeared to swing the other way in 1981 when President Ronald Reagan signed Executive Order 12333, which sought to reinvigorate the U.S. intelligence community to deal with a wide range of national security threats. It authorized the CIA to operate in the United States to collect "significant foreign intelligence as long as surveillance of the domestic operations of U.S. citizens and corporations is not involved." Controls returned the following year, however, when the first of the Boland amendments passed, banning the CIA from participating in or funding the overthrow of the Sandinistas in Nicaragua. A congressional inspector general was appointed in 1990 in yet another step that increased oversight of the CIA.

In 1991, the newly appointed DCI, Robert Gates, undertook a comprehensive reexamination of the intelligence community. The recommendations of 14 separate tasks forces produced significant proposals for changes in the broader intelligence community. The Intelligence Organization Act of 1992 defined, for the first time by law, the "intelligence community" and listed the three roles of the DCI. In 1996 the results of a review of the U.S. intelligence community were published. The review commission was chaired by former secretary of defense Harold Brown and concluded the CIA and other intelligence agencies should act more closely as a community and that intelligence for the policy community should improve in quality and utility. The need for a strong intelligence community was reaffirmed.

Currently the CIA is organized into four separate directorates— Operations (DO), the clandestine service; Science and Technology (DS&T), which comes up with intelligence tools and technology; Intelligence (DI), the analysts; and Administration (DA), the support personnel—reporting through an executive director and deputy director to the DCI. A public affairs office and a comptroller report in a similar way. A general counsel, CIA inspector general, legislative liaison, and director of intelligence community staff, as well as national intelligence officers, report directly to the DCI. Figure 17 illustrates the organization of the CIA in 1998.

Sources

National Security Council

Lord, Carnes. *The Presidency and the Management of National Security.* New York: The Free Press, 1988.

Lowenthal, Mark. *The National Security Council: Organizational History.* Washington, D.C.: CRS, 1978.

Office of the State Department Historian. "The History of the National Security Council 1947–1997." 1997 <www2.whitehouse.gov/WH/EOP/ NCS/html/NSChistory/gtml#history>.

Prados, John. *Keepers of the Keys: A History of the National Security Council from Truman to Bush.* New York: William Morrow and Company, 1991.

Sarkesian, Sam C. *U.S. National Security: Policymakers, Processes, and Politics.* Boulder, Colo.: Lynne Rienner Publishers, Inc., 1995.

Shoemaker, Christopher C. *Structure, Function and the NSC Staff: An Officer's Guide to the National Security Council.* Carlisle, Pa.: Strategic Studies Institute, U.S. Army War College, 1989.

Yoshpe, Harry B. *Organization of National Security.* Washington, D.C.: Industrial College of the Armed Forces, 1963.

Department of Defense

Cole, Alice C., Alfred Goldberg, Samuel A. Tucker, Rudolph A. Winnacker. *The Department of Defense: Documents on Establishment and Organization 1944–1978.* Washington, D.C.: Office of the secretary of Defense Historical Office, 1978.

Defense Organization: The Need for Change. Staff Report to the Committee on Armed Services, United States Senate. Washington, D.C.: GPO, 1985.

Furer, Julius Augustus. *Administration of the Navy Department in World War II.* Washington, D.C.: Department of the Navy, 1959.

Hammond, Paul Y. *Organizing for Defense: The American Military Establishment in the Twentieth Century.* Princeton: Princeton University Press, 1961.

Hooper, Edwin Bickford. *United States Naval Power in a Changing World.* New York: Praeger, 1988.

Krulak, Victor H. *Organization for National Security: A Study.* Washington, D.C.: United States Strategic Institute, 1983.

Nelson, Otto L., Jr. *National Security and the General Staff.* Washington, D.C.: Washington Infantry Journal Press, 1946.

Yoshpe, Harry B. and Stanley L. Falk. *Organization for National Security.* Washington, D.C.: Industrial College of the Armed Forces, 1963.

Joint Chiefs of Staff

Hammond, Paul Y. *Organizing for Defense: The American Military Establishment in the Twentieth Century.* Princeton: Princeton University Press, 1961.

Defense Organization: The Need for Change. Staff Report to the Committee on Armed Services, United States Senate. Washington, D.C.: GPO, 1985.

Millett, Allan R., Mackubin Thomas Owens, Bernard E. Trainor, Edward C. Meyer, and Robert Murray. *The Reorganization of the Joint Chiefs of Staff: A Critical Analysis.* Washington, D.C.: Pergamon-Brassey's, 1986.

Yoshpe, Harry B. and Stanley L. Falk. *Organization for National Security.* Washington, D.C.: Industrial College of the Armed Forces, 1963.

Department of State

Estes, Thomas S. and E. Allen Lighter Jr. *The Department of State.* New York: Praeger, 1976.

National Archives and Records Administration, Office of the Federal Register. *The United States Government Manual 1996/1997.* Washington, D.C.: GPO, May 1996.

Stuart, Graham H. *The Department of State: A History of Its Organization, Procedure, and Personnel.* New York: Macmillan, 1949.

Central Intelligence Agency

Brown Commission Report. *Preparing for the 21st Century: An Appraisal of U.S. Intelligence.* Washington, D.C.: GPO, 1996.

Johnson, Loch K. *America's Secret Power: The CIA in a Democratic Society.* New York: Oxford University Press, 1986.

Jordan, Amos A., Lawrence J. Korb, and William J. Taylor Jr. *American National Security: Policy and Process.* Baltimore, Md.: The Johns Hopkins University Press, 1993.

Leary, William M. *The Central Intelligence Agency: History and Documents.* Tuscaloosa, Ala.: University of Alabama Press, 1984.

Ranelagh, John. *The Agency: The Rise and Decline of the CIA.* New York: Simon & Schuster, 1986.

Troy, Thomas F. *Donovan and the CIA: A History of the Establishment of the Central Intelligence Agency.* Washington, D.C.: Central Intelligence Agency Center for the Study of Intelligence, 1981.

Victory, Bernard C., ed. *Modernizing Intelligence: Structure and Change for the 21st Century.* Fairfax, Va.: National Institute for Public Policy, 1997.

Appendix C

Presidential Directives

*Compiled by Lesley S. Young, Alistair J. K. Shepherd,
and John E. Kreul*

The following presidential directives on the restructuring of the National Security Council are reproduced verbatim.

National Security Decision Memorandum 2

THE WHITE HOUSE
WASHINGTON

January 20, 1969

National Security Decision Memorandum 2

TO: The Vice President
The Secretary of State
The Secretary of Defense
The Assistant to the President for National Security
     Affairs
The Director of Central Intelligence
The Chairman, Joint Chiefs of Staff
The Director of the U.S. Information Agency
The Director of the Office of Emergency
     Preparedness

SUBJECT: Reorganization of the National Security Council
System

To assist me in carrying out my responsibilities for the conduct of national security affairs, I hereby direct that the National Security Council system be reorganized as follows:

A. *The National Security Council (NSC)*

The functions, membership and responsibilities of the National Security Council shall be as set forth in the National Security Act of 1947, as amended.

The National Security Council shall be the principal forum for consideration of policy issues requiring Presidential determination. The nature of the issues to be considered may range from current crises and immediate operational problems to middle and long-range planning.

The Council shall meet regularly, and discussion will—except in unusual circumstances—be limited to agenda subjects.[1] The Assistant to the President for National Security Affairs, at my direction and in consultation with the Secretaries of State and Defense, shall be responsible for determining the agenda and ensuring that the necessary papers are prepared. Other members of the NSC may propose items for inclusion on the agenda. The Assistant to the President shall be assisted by a National Security Council Staff, as provided by law.

B. *The National Security Council Review Group*

An NSC Review Group is hereby established to examine papers prior to their submission to the NSC. These papers may be received from NSC Interdepartmental Groups,[2] from NSC *Ad Hoc* Groups,[2] or from Departments (at their discretion).

The role of the Review Group shall be to review papers to be discussed by the NSC to assure that: 1) the issue under consideration is worthy of NSC attention; 2) all realistic alternatives are presented; 3) the facts, including cost implications, and all department and agency views are fairly and adequately set out. The Review

---

1. The Director of Central Intelligence will brief the NSC on each agenda item prior to its consideration.

2. Discussed below.

Group shall also be empowered to assign action to the NSC Interdepartmental Groups or NSC *Ad Hoc* Groups, as appropriate.

The membership of the Review Group shall include:

— The Assistant to the President for National Security Affairs (Chairman);

— The representative of the Secretary of State;

— The representative of the Secretary of Defense;

— The representative of the Director of Central Intelligence;

— The representative of the Chairman, Joint Chiefs of Staff

Depending on the issue under consideration, other agencies shall be represented at the discretion of the Chairman.

C. *The National Security Council Under Secretaries Committee*

The NSC Under Secretaries Committee shall consider:

1. Issues which are referred to it by the NSC Review Group.

2. Matters pertaining to interdepartmental activities of the U.S. Government overseas:

— which are of an operational nature[3] (in distinction to matters involving a substantial security policy question); *and*

— on which NSC Interdepartmental Groups have been unable to reach agreement, or which are of a broader nature than is suitable to any such group; *and*

— which do not require consideration at Presidential or NSC level; *and*

— which are then referred to it by the Secretary of State.

The results of NSC Under Secretaries Committee consideration of the matters listed in 2. above, will be submitted to the Secretary of State.

---

3. Determination shall be made jointly by the Secretary of State and the Assistant to the President for National Security Affairs.

3. Other operational matters referred to it jointly by the Under Secretary of State and the Assistant to the President for National Security Affairs.

The membership of the Under Secretaries Committee shall include:

— The Under Secretary of State (Chairman);

— The Deputy Secretary of Defense;

— The Assistant to the President for National Security Affairs;

— The Director of Central Intelligence

— The Chairman, Joint Chiefs of Staff

Depending on the issue under consideration, other agencies shall be represented at the discretion of the Chairman.

D. *National Security Council Interdepartmental Groups*

Existing Interdepartmental Regional Groups and the existing Political-Military Interdepartmental Group, chaired by the appropriate Assistant Secretary of State, are hereby reconstituted as part of the National Security Council structure. The Interdepartmental Groups shall perform the following functions: 1) discussion and decision on interdepartmental issues which can be settled at the Assistant Secretary level, including issues arising out of the implementation of NSC decision; 2) preparation of policy papers for consideration by the NSC; 3) preparation of contingency papers on potential crisis areas for review by the NSC.

The membership of the interdepartmental regional groups shall include the agencies represented on the NSC Review Group. Depending on the issue under consideration, other agencies shall be represented at the discretion of the Chairman.

E. *National Security Ad Hoc Groups*

When appropriate, I intend to appoint NSC *Ad Hoc* Groups to deal with particular problems, including those which transcend regional boundaries.

* * * * *

The operational responsibility or authority of a Secretary over personnel from his Department serving on interdepartmental committees—in the performance of interdepartmental group duties—is not limited by this NSDM. Nor does this NSDM limit the authority and responsibility of the Secretary of State for those interdepartmental matters assigned to him by NSDM 3.

Copies of reports of the interdepartmental groups shall be transmitted to the heads of Departments and Agencies simultaneously with their submission to the NSC Review Group.

NSAM 341 is hereby rescinded.

/s/ Richard Nixon

Presidential Directive/NSC-2

THE WHITE HOUSE
WASHINGTON

January 20, 1977

Presidential Directive/NSC-2

TO: The Vice President
        The Secretary of State
        The Secretary of Defense

ALSO:
The Secretary of the Treasury
The Attorney General
The United States Representative to the United
    Nations
The Director, Office of Management and Budget
The Assistant to the President for National Security
    Affairs
The Chairman, Council of Economic Advisors
The Administrator, Agency for International
    Development

The Director, Arms Control and Disarmament
    Agency
The Chairman, Joint Chiefs of Staff
The Director of Central Intelligence
The Administrator, Energy Research and
    Development Administration

SUBJECT: The National Security Council System

To assist me in carrying out my responsibilities for the conduct of national security affairs, I hereby direct the reorganization of the National Security Council system. The reorganization is intended to place more responsibility in the departments and agencies while insuring that the NSC, with my Assistant for National Security Affairs, continues to integrate and facilitate foreign and defense policy decisions.

a. *The National Security Council (NSC)*

The functions, membership, and responsibilities of the National Security Council shall be as set forth in the National Security Act of 1947, as amended. In addition, other senior officials, including the Secretary of the Treasury, the Attorney General, the United States Representative to the United Nations, the Director of the Office of Management and Budget, the Assistant to the President for National Security Affairs, the Chairman of the Council of Economic Advisors, the Director of the Arms Control and Disarmament Agency, the Chairman of the Joint Chiefs of Staff, the Director of Central Intelligence, and the Administrator of the Energy Research and Development Administration shall attend appropriate NSC meetings.

The National Security Council shall be the principal forum for international security issues requiring Presidential consideration. The NSC shall assist me in analyzing, integrating and facilitating foreign, defense, and intelligence policy decisions. International economic and other interdependence issues which are pertinent to national security shall also be considered by the NSC.

The Council shall meet regularly. The Assistant to the President for National Security Affairs, at my direction and in consultation with the Secretaries of State and Defense and, when appropriate, the Secretary of the Treasury and Chairman, Council of Economic Advisers, shall be responsible for determining the agenda and insuring that the necessary papers are prepared. Other members of the NSC may propose items for inclusion on the agenda. The Assistant to the President shall be assisted by a National Security Council staff, as provided by law.

b. *NSC Policy Review Committee*

An NSC Policy Review Committee is hereby established to develop national security policy for Presidential decision in those cases where the basic responsibilities fall primarily within a given department but where the subject also has important implications for other departments and agencies. This Committee shall deal with such matters as:

— foreign policy issues that contain significant military or other interagency aspects;

— defense policy issues having international implications and the coordination of the annual Defense budget with foreign policy objectives;

— the preparation of a consolidated national intelligence budget and resource allocation for the Intelligence Community (thus assuming under the chairmanship of the Director of Central Intelligence the functions and responsibilities of the Committee on Foreign Intelligence); and

— those international economic issues pertinent to U.S. foreign policy and security, with staffing of the underlying economic issues through the Economic Policy Group.

I shall designate for each meeting the appropriate Chairman of the Policy Review Committee and attendance, depending on the subject matter being considered. Membership, in addition to the statutory members of the NSC and the Assistant for National Security Affairs, shall include, as appropriate, other senior officials.

c. *The NSC Special Coordination Committee*

A second NSC Committee, the Special Coordination Committee, is hereby established to deal with specific cross-cutting issue requiring coordination in the development of options and the implementation of Presidential decisions. The Committee shall deal with such matters as: the oversight of sensitive intelligence activities, such as covert operations, which are undertaken on Presidential authority; arms control evaluation; and it will assist me in crisis management.

The Special Coordination Committee shall be chaired by the Assistant for National Security Affairs. Membership shall include the statutory members of the NSC, or their representatives, and other senior officials, as appropriate.

d. *NSC Interdepartmental Groups*

Existing NSC Interdepartmental Groups, chaired by a designated senior departmental official, are to continue as needed under the direction of the NSC Policy Review Committee.

The membership of the Interdepartmental Groups shall include the agencies represented on the NSC Policy Review Committee. Depending on the issue under consideration, other agencies shall be represented at the discretion of the Policy Review Committee.

e. *National Security Council Ad Hoc Groups*

When appropriate, I intend to appoint NSC Ad Hoc Groups to deal with particular problems, including those which transcend departmental boundaries.

/s/ Jimmy Carter

National Security Decision Directive 2

THE WHITE HOUSE
WASHINGTON
January 12, 1982
NATIONAL SECURITY COUNCIL STRUCTURE

I. *National Security Council*

The National Security Council (NSC) shall be the principal forum for consideration of national security policy issues requiring Presidential decision.

The functions and responsibilities of the NSC shall be as set forth in the National Security Act of 1947, as amended.

The NSC shall meet regularly. Those heads of Departments and Agencies who are not regular members shall participate as appropriate, when matters affecting their Departments or Agencies are considered.

The Assistants to the President for National Security Affairs, in consultation with the regular members of the NSC, shall be responsible for developing, coordination and implementing national security policy as approved by me. He shall determine and publish the agenda of NSC meetings. He shall ensure that the necessary papers are prepared and—except in unusual circumstances—distributed in advance to Council members. He shall staff and administer the National Security Council.

Decision documents shall be prepared by the Assistant to the President for National Security Affairs, and disseminated by him after approval by the President.

II. *NSC Responsibilities of the Secretary of State*

The Secretary of State is my principal foreign policy advisor. As such, he is responsible for the formulation of foreign policy and for the execution of approved policy.

I have assigned to the Secretary of State authority and responsibility, to the extent permitted by law, for the overall direction, coordination, and supervision of the interdepartmental activities incident to foreign policy formulation, and the activities of Executive Departments and Agencies of the United States overseas. Such activities do not include those of United States military forces operating in the field under the command of a United States area military commander, and such other military activities as I elect, as Commander-in-Chief, to conduct exclusively through military or other channels. Activities that are internal to the execution and administration of the approved programs of a single Department or Agency and which are not of such nature as to affect significantly the overall US overseas program in a country or region are not considered to be activities covered within the meaning of this directive.

The Secretary of State is responsible for preparation of those papers addressing matters affecting the foreign policy and foreign relations of the United States for consideration by the NSC.

III. *NSC Responsibilities of the Secretary of Defense*

The Secretary of Defense is my principal defense policy advisor. As such, he is responsible for the formulation of general defense policy, policy related to all matters of direct and primary concern to the Department of Defense, and for the execution of approved policy. The Joint Chiefs of Staff are the principal military advisors to me, the Secretary of Defense, and the NSC.

I have assigned to the Secretary of Defense authority and responsibility, to the extend permitted by law, for the overall direction, coordination, and the supervision of the interdepartmental activities incident to defense policy formulation.

The Secretary of Defense is responsible for preparation of those papers addressing matters affecting the defense policy of the United States for consideration by the NSC.

IV. *NSC Responsibilities of the Director of Central Intelligence*

The Director of Central Intelligence is my personal advisor on intelligence matters. As such, he is responsible for the formulation of intelligence activities, policy, and proposals, as set forth in relevant Executive Orders. I have assigned to the Director of Central Intelligence authority and responsibility, to the extent permitted by law and Executive Order, for the overall direction, coordination, and supervision of the interdepartmental activities incident to intelligence matters.

The Director of Central Intelligence is responsible for the preparation of those papers addressing matters affecting the intelligence activities, policy, and proposals of the United States for consideration by the NSC.

V. *Interagency Groups*

To assist the NSC at large and its individual members in fulfilling their responsibilities, interagency groups are established as described herein. The focus of these interagency groups is to establish policy objectives, develop policy options, make appropriate recommendations, consider the implications of agency programs for foreign policy or overall national security policy, and undertake such other activities as may be assigned by the NSC.

A. *The Senior Interagency Group—Foreign Policy (SIG-FP)*

To advise and assist the NSC in exercising its authority and discharging its responsibility for foreign policy and foreign affairs matters, the SIG-FP is established. The SIG-FP shall be composed of the Director of Central Intelligence; the Assistant to the President for National Security Affairs; the Deputy Secretary of State (Chairman); the Deputy Secretary of Defense of Under Secretary of Defense for Policy; and Chairman, Joint Chiefs of Staff. Representatives of other Departments and Agencies with responsibility for specific matters to be considered will attend on invitation by the Chairman.

When meeting to consider arms control matters, the Group will be augmented by the Director, Arms Control and Disarmament Agency.

The SIG-FP will:

1. Ensure that important foreign policy issues requiring interagency attention receive full, prompt, and systematic consideration;

2. Deal with interdepartmental matters raised by any member or referred to it by subordinate interagency groups, or, if such matters require higher-level consideration, report them to the Secretary of State for decision or referral to the NSC;

3. Assure a proper selectivity of the foreign policy/foreign affairs areas and issues to which the United States applies its efforts;

4. Monitor the execution of approved policies and decisions; and

5. Evaluate the adequacy and effectiveness of interdepartmental overseas programs and activities.

A permanent secretariat, composed of personnel of the State Department augmented as necessary by personnel provided in response to the Chairman's request by the Departments and Agencies represented on the SIG-FP, shall be established.

B. *The Senior Interagency Group—Defense Policy (SIG-DP)*

To advise and assist the NSC in exercising its authority and discharging its responsibility for defense policy and defense matters, the SIG-DP is established. The SIG-DP shall consist of the Director of Central Intelligence; the Assistant to the President for National Security Affairs; the Deputy of an Under Secretary of State; the Deputy Secretary of Defense (Chairman); and the chairman, Joint Chiefs of Staff. Representatives of other Departments and Agencies with responsibility for specific matters to be considered will attend on invitation by the Chairman.

The SIG-DP will:

1. Ensure that important defense policy issues requiring interagency attention receive full, prompt, and systematic consideration;

2. Deal with interdepartmental matters raised by and member or referred to it by subordinate interagency groups, or if such matters require higher-level consideration, report them to the Secretary of Defense for decision or referral to the NSC; and

3. Monitor the execution of approved policies and decisions.

A permanent secretariat, composed of personnel of the Department of Defense augmented as necessary by personnel provided in response to the Chairman's request by the Departments and Agencies represented on the SIG-DP, shall be established.

C. *The Senior Interagency Group—Intelligence (SIG-I)*

To advise and assist the NSC in exercising its authority and discharging its responsibility for intelligence policy and intelligence matters, the SIG-I is established. The SIG-I shall consist of the Director of Central Intelligence (Chairman); the Assistant to the President for National Security Affairs; the Deputy Secretary of State; the Deputy Secretary of Defense; and Chairman, Joint Chiefs of Staff. Representatives of other Departments and Agencies will attend on invitation by the Chairman when such Departments and agencies have a direct interest in intelligence activities.

When meeting to consider sensitive intelligence collection activities referred by the Director of Central Intelligence, the membership of the Group shall be augmented, as necessary, by the head of each organization within the Intelligence Community directly involved in the activity in question. When meeting to consider counterintelligence activities, the Group shall be augmented by the Director, Federal Bureau of Investigation and the Director, National Security Agency.

The SIG-I will:

(1) Establish requirements and priorities for national foreign intelligence;

(2) Review such National Foreign Intelligence Program and budget proposals and other matters as are referred to it by the Director of Central Intelligence;

(3) Review proposals for sensitive foreign intelligence collection operations referred by the Director of Central Intelligence;

(4) Develop standards and doctrine for the counterintelligence activities of the United States; resolve interagency differences concerning the implementation of counterintelligence policy; and develop and monitor guidelines, consistent with applicable law and

Executive orders, for the maintenance of central counterintelligence records;

(5) Consider and approve any counterintelligence activity referred to the Group by the head of any organization in the Intelligence Community;

(6) Submit to the NSC an overall annual assessment of the relative threat to United States interests from intelligence and security services of foreign powers and from international terrorist activities, including an assessment of the effectiveness of the United States counterintelligence activities;

(7) Conduct an annual review of ongoing sensitive national foreign intelligence collection operations and sensitive counterintelligence activities and report thereon to the NSC; and

(8) Carry out such additional coordination review and approval of intelligence activities as the President may direct.

A permanent secretariat, composed of personnel of the Central Intelligence Agency augmented as necessary by the personnel provided in response to the Chairman's request by the Departments and Agencies represented on the SIG-I, shall be established.

D. *Regional and Functional Interagency Groups*

To assist the SIG-FP, Interagency Groups (IGs) shall be established by the Secretary of State for each geographic region corresponding to the jurisdiction of the geographic bureaus in the Department of State, for Political-Military Affairs, and for International Economic Affairs. Each IG shall be comprised of the Director of Central Intelligence; the Assistant to the President for National Security Affairs; The Chairman, Joint Chiefs of Staff; the appropriate Assistant Secretary of State (Chairman); and a designated representative of the Secretary of Defense. Representatives of other Departments and Agencies with responsibility for specific matters to be considered will attend on invitation by the Chairman. The IG for International Economic Affairs will, in addition to the above membership, include representatives of the Secretary of the Treasury, the Secretary of Commerce, and the U.S. Trade Representative.

The IG for arms control matters will, in addition to the above membership, include a representative of the Director, Arms Control and Disarmament Agency. Arms control IGs will be chaired by the representative of the Secretary of State or the representative of the Director, Arms Control and Disarmament Agency in accordance with guidelines to be provided by the SIG-FP.

To assist the Sig-DP, IGs shall be established by the Secretary of Defense corresponding to the functional areas within the Department of Defense. Each IG shall be comprised of the appropriate Under or Assistant Secretary of Defense (Chairman); a representative of the Secretary of State; the Director of Central Intelligence; the Assistant to the President for National Security Affairs; and Chairman, Joint Chiefs of Staff. Representatives of other Departments and Agencies will attend on invitation by the Chairman.

Under and Assistant Secretaries, in their capacities as Chairmen of the IGs, will assure the adequacy of United States policy in the areas of their responsibility and of the plans, programs, resources, and performance for implementing that policy. They will be responsible for the conduct of interagency policy studies within the areas of their responsibility for consideration by the SIGs.

The Regional IGs also shall prepare contingency plans pertaining to potential crises in their respective areas of responsibility. Contingency planning will be conducted in coordination with the Chairman of the Political-Military IG, with the exception of the military response option for employment of forces in potential crises, which will remain within the purview of the Department of Defense and will be developed by the Joint Chiefs of Staff.

To deal with specific contingencies, the IGs will establish full-time working groups, which will provide support to the crisis management operations of the NSC. These groups will reflect the institutional membership of the parent body, together with such additional members as may be required to respond to the contingency with the full weight of available expertise.

To assist the SIG-I, IGs shall be established by the Director of Central Intelligence. The IG for Counterintelligence shall consist of representatives of the Secretary of State; Secretary of Defense; the

Director of Central Intelligence; the Director, Federal Bureau of Investigation; Chairman, Joint Chiefs of Staff; the Director, National Security Agency; and a representative of the head of any other Intelligence Community organization directly involved in the activities under discussion. The IG for Counterintelligence will be under the chairmanship of the representative of the Director of Central Intelligence of the Director, Federal Bureau of Investigation in accordance with guidelines to be provided by the SIG-I.

The operational responsibility or authority of a Secretary of other Agency head over personnel from the Department of Agency concerned serving on IGs—including the authority to give necessary guidance to the representatives in the performance of IG duties—is not limited by this Directive.

Distribution:
A, B

National Security Decision Directive 266

THE WHITE HOUSE
WASHINGTON

March 31, 1987

IMPLEMENTATION OF THE RECOMMENDATIONS OF THE PRESIDENT'S SPECIAL REVIEW BOARD

The President's Special Review Board submitted its Report on February 26, 1987. I addressed the Nation on March 4 and announced first, that I endorse the Board's recommendations; and second, that I intend to go beyond the Board's recommendations to put the National Security Council (NSC) process in even better order. This Directive spells out the specific steps I have approved to implement the letter and spirit of the Board's recommendations.

Many steps were taken even prior to the issuance of the Board's Report. The NSC staff was rebuilt and made subject to proper management discipline. A directive was issued on my instruction to prohibit the NSC staff itself from undertaking covert operations. A comprehensive legal and policy review of such operations, ordered by me, was already far advanced. Proper procedures for consultation with the Congress were reaffirmed and are being observed.

In light of the Board's Report, additional measures are required. This Directive sets forth the specific timetable according to which I expect all such measures to be completed. It is of utmost importance that the NSC—including all members of, and advisors to, the NSC, the Assistant to the President for National Security Affairs, the NSC staff, and all other participants in the NSC process act decisively to accomplish my objectives fully.

I shall inform Congress of the nature and progress of these Executive branch efforts prior to the end of March; I also shall call upon Congress to heed the balance of the Board's recommendations, namely:

— that no substantive change be made in the provisions of the National Security Act dealing with the structure and operation of the NSC system;

— that the position of Assistant to the President for National Security Affairs not be made subject to Senate confirmation; and

— that Congress replace the existing Intelligence Committees of the Senate and House of Representatives with a new joint committee with a restricted staff to oversee the intelligence community.

These recommendations of the Board, which are addressed to Congress I also strongly endorse.

I.   Model for the National Security Council System

The structure and procedures of the National Security Council shall incorporate all aspects of the model of the NSC system described in the Report of the President's Special Review Board as the Board's principal recommendation. This directive implements that recommendation in each of the following respects:

— organizing for national security, including provision of appropriate guidelines to participants in the NSC process;

— the role and functions of the Assistant to the President for National Security Affairs;

— the nature and responsibilities of the NSC staff; and

— the NSC and interagency process.

A. Organizing for National Security

The National Security Council shall be the principal forum for consideration of national security policy issues requiring presidential decision. The function of the NSC shall be as set forth in the National Security Act of 1947, as amended. Broadly speaking, the NSC shall advise the President with respect to the integration of domestic, foreign, and military policies relating to the national security so as to enable Executive departments and agencies to cooperate more effectively in matters involving the national security.

Participation in the NSC shall be as provided by law and this Directive. Statutory members of the NSC are the President, the Vice President, the Secretary of State, and the Secretary of Defense. Other heads of Executive departments and agencies and senior officials within the Executive Office of the President shall participate in the NSC as provided in this Directive.

The Director of Central Intelligence and the Chairman of the Joint Chiefs of Staff are statutory advisors to the NSC. The Director of Central Intelligence shall advise the NSC with respect to coordinating intelligence activities of Executive departments and agencies in the interest of national security and as otherwise provided by law. The Chairman of the Joint Chiefs of Staff shall be principal military advisor to the President, the Secretary of Defense, and the NSC.

The Directors of the United States Arms Control and Disarmament Agency and United States Information Agency are special statutory advisors to the NSC. The Director of the Arms Control and Disarmament Agency shall be principal advisor to the President, the Secretary of State, and the NSC on arms control and disarmament matters. The Director of the United States Information Agency shall be principal advisor to the President, the Secretary of State, and the NSC on international informational, educational, and cultural matters.

The Secretary of State shall be the President's principal foreign policy advisor. As such, the Secretary shall be responsible for the formulation of foreign policy, subject to review within the NSC process and the President's guidance as appropriate, and for the execution of approved policy. I assign to the Secretary of State authority and responsibility, to the extent permitted by law and this Directive, for the overall direction, coordination, and supervision of the interdepartmental activities incident to foreign policy formulation, and the activities of Executive departments and agencies of the United States overseas. Such activities shall not include those of United States military forces operating in the field under the command of a United States area military commander, and such other military activities as I elect, as Commander in Chief, to conduct exclusively through military or other channels. Activities that are internal to the execution and administration of the approved programs of a single department or agency and that are not of such nature as to affect significantly the overall United States overseas program in a country or region are not considered to be activities covered within the meaning of this Directive.

The Secretary of Defense shall be the President's principal defense policy advisor. As such, the Secretary shall be responsible for the formulation of general defense policy, subject to review, within the NSC process and the President's guidance as appropriate, for policy related to all matters of direct and primary concern to the Department of Defense, and for the execution of approved policy. I assign to the Secretary of Defense authority and responsibility, to the extent permitted by law and this Directive, for the overall direction, coordination, and supervision of the interdepartmental activities incident to defense policy formulation.

The Director of Central Intelligence shall be the President's principal advisor on intelligence matters. As such, the Director shall be responsible for the formulation of intelligence activities, policy and proposals, subject to review within the NSC process and the President's guidance as appropriate, as set forth in law and relevant Executive orders. I assign to the Director of Central Intelligence authority and responsibility, to the extent permitted by law, Executive order, and this Directive, for the overall direction, coordination, and supervision of the interdepartmental activities incident to intelligence matters.

Although taking part in the NSC system by virtue of official positions as heads of Executive departments or agencies or as senior officials within the Executive Office of the President, all NSC participants shall sit as advisors to the President in connection with the President's exercise of authority under the Constitution and laws of the United States. In their capacity as department and agency heads, NSC participants shall ensure the effective and expeditious execution and implementation of overall national security policies established by the President. Execution and implementation of such policies shall not be the responsibility of the Assistant to the President for National Security Affairs or of the NSC staff except as the President specifically directs.

B. The Assistant to the President for National Security Affairs

The Assistant to the President for National Security Affairs ("National Security Advisor") shall have primary responsibility for day-to-day management of the National Security Council process, and shall serve as principal advisor on the President's staff with respect to all national security affairs. The National Security Advisor shall have access and report direct to the President, and shall keep the President and the Chief Staff to the President fully and currently informed on all matters of substance.

As manager of the NSC process, the National Security Advisor shall ensure the following: that matters submitted for consideration by the NSC cover the full range of issues on which review is required; that those issues are fully analyzed; that a full range of options is considered; that the prospects and risk of each are examined; that all relevant intelligence and other information is available to NSC participants; that legal matters are addressed; and that difficulties in implementation are confronted. The National Security Advisor shall monitor policy implementation to ensure that policies are executed in conformity with the intent of presidential decisions. He shall initiate periodic reassessments of policies and operations, in light of changed circumstances or United States interests. The National Security Advisor shall keep NSC participants currently informed of presidential decisions. He shall ensure that NSC consultations and presidential decisions are adequately recorded, and that appropriate and timely preparations are made with respect to meetings convened under NSC auspices.

As the President's principal staff advisor on national security affairs, the National Security Advisor shall present his own views and advice and, at the same time, faithfully represent the views of other NSC participants.

C. The National Security Council Staff

The functions and responsibilities of the Executive Secretary of the National Security Council shall be as provided by the National Security Act of 1947, as amended. The Executive Secretary heads the NSC staff and, in accordance with applicable laws and regulations, appoints and fixes the compensation of personnel required to perform such duties as may be prescribed by the President, the NSC, or the National Security Advisor. The Executive Secretary shall establish procedures within the NSC Executive Secretariat for maximum effective support of the NSC and the National Security Advisor in performance of responsibilities assigned by the President. With the guidance and under the instruction of the National Security Advisor, the Executive Secretary shall develop and implement appropriate policies with respect to the overall size of the NSC staff, the background and experience of its members, the duration of their service, and the organization of staff offices. The objectives shall be twofold: first, an NSC staff that is small, highly competent, broadly experienced in the making of national security policy, and properly balanced from among Executive departments and agencies and persons drawn from within and outside government; and second, an NSC staff organization that imposes clear vertical lines of control and accountability.

The Executive Secretary, through the National Security Advisor, shall recommend for my consideration specific measures designed to enhance the continuity of the functioning of the NSC, including measures to ensure adequate institutional record keeping from administration to administration. Specific recommendation for these purposes shall be made not later than June 30, 1987.

The NSC staff, through the Executive Secretary, shall assist the National Security Advisor in each aspect of his roles both as manager of the NSC process and as my principal staff advisor on national security affairs.

The NSC staff shall include a Legal Advisor whose particular responsibility it will be to provide legal counsel to the National Security Advisor, the Executive Secretary, and the NSC staff with respect to the full range of their activities, and to assist the National Security Advisor in ensuring that legal considerations are fully addressed in the NSC process and in interagency deliberations. The NSC Legal Advisor shall be accorded access to all information and deliberations as may be required for these purposes, and shall advise the National Security Advisor and Executive Secretary as appropriate on all matters within his responsibility. He shall work cooperatively with the Counsel to the President, the Legal Adviser of the Department of State, and with senior counsel to another NSC members, advisors, and participants.

D. The National Security Council and Interagency Process

1. National Security Council Meetings

The National Security Council shall meet regularly to consider matters directed by the President or recommended by the National Security Advisor or by the other NSC members. The National Security Advisor shall attend all NSC meetings and shall be responsible for the agenda and conduct of such meetings under my direction. The statutory members of the NSC, and the Director of Central Intelligence and Chairman of the Joint Chiefs of Staff, as statutory advisors to the NSC, shall attend NSC meetings. In addition, the Attorney General, the Secretary of the Treasury, and the Chief of Staff to the President at my invitation shall attend NSC meetings. The special statutory advisors to the NSC, the Director of the Office of Management and Budget, and the heads of other Executive departments and agencies shall be invited to attend such NSC meetings as relate to matters vested under their authority .

The National Security Advisor shall provide NSC participants advance notice of all NSC meetings and agenda therefor. To the extent practicable, the National Security Advisor shall circulate decision documents in advance of such meetings. The Executive Secretary of the NSC and the NSC staff shall assist the National Security Advisor in connection with appropriate preparations for, and follow-up to, NSC meetings, as directed by the President. Such assistance shall include preparation of meeting minutes and the development and dissemination of decision documents and, as appropriate, study directives. All decision documents shall be submitted for the President's review and action by the National Security Advisor. The National Security Advisor shall transmit decision documents to the President through the Chief of Staff to the President. National Security Decision Directives, intelligence findings, and similar decision documents shall be coordinated, in advance of their submission to the President, by the NSC Legal Advisor with the Counsel to the President.

2. The Interagency Process

To assist the NSC at large and its individual members and advisors in fulfilling their responsibilities, I previously directed or authorized the establishment of senior interagency groups and regional and functional interagency groups. The purpose of such groups was to establish policy objectives, develop policy options, make appropriate recommendations, consider the implications of agency programs for foreign policy or overall national security policy, and undertake such other activities as may be assigned by the NSC.

The NSC, through the National Security Advisor, shall review the structure of senior interagency groups and regional and functional interagency groups established pursuant to, or under authority of, presidential directives or applicable memoranda, and shall recommend all such changes thereto as may be necessary or desirable to realize fully and promptly in practice the Special Review Board's recommended model for the NSC system, as well as all of the Board's other recommendations. These include establishment of an interagency process in which the National Security Advisor chairs the senior level committees of the NSC. The National Security Advisor shall present, for consideration by the NSC, a draft National Security Decision Directive for this purpose not later than April 30, 1987.

II. Covert Actions and Use of Non-Government Personnel

I have directed the National Security Council's Planning and Coordination Group (PCG) to review all covert action programs. This review is designed to ensure that such programs are commenced and pursued in accordance with law and are consistent with United States policy. The PCG shall complete this review on an expedited basis. It shall report its findings to the NSC on or before April 30, 1987. The NSC promptly shall review all such programs and seek my concurrence in their continuation as appropriate. The NSC, through the National Security Advisor, shall review current procedures for covert action policy approval and coordination and shall recommend such changes as may be necessary or desirable to ensure, among other things, the following:

— that proposed covert actions will be coordinated with NSC participants, including the Attorney General, and their respective recommendations communicated to the President;

— that all requirements of law concerning covert activities, including those requirements relating to presidential authorization and congressional notification, will be addressed in a timely manner and complied with fully;

— consistent with the foregoing, that covert activities will be subject to tightly restricted consideration, and measures to protect the security of all information concerning such activities will be enhanced;

— that the NSC staff itself will not undertake the conduct of covert activities;

and

— that the use of private individuals and organizations as intermediaries to conduct covert activities will be appropriately limited and subject in every case to close observation and supervision by appropriate Executive departments and agencies.

This review shall take fully into account such changes as I have authorized by this Directive to the structure of the NSC. The National Security Advisor shall presents for consideration by the NSC, a revised National Security Decision Directive on procedures for covert

214 A New Structure for National Security Policy Planning

action policy approval and coordination not later than April 30, 1987.

III. Intelligence Process

Maintaining the integrity and objectivity of the intelligence process is an important goal of the United States intelligence efforts. It demands, as the President's Special Review Board has stated, careful differentiation between the respective roles of foreign intelligence, on the one hand, and policy advocacy, on the other. The Director of Central Intelligence shall provide such additional review of, guidance for, and direction to, the conduct of national foreign intelligence estimates as may be required to accomplish fully this objective. The Director of Central Intelligence shall review established procedures for the production of national foreign intelligence estimates and, not later than July 31, 1987, shall inform the NSC, through the National Security Advisor, of any modifications or additions thereto he may deem appropriate for this purpose.

IV. Reporting

The National Security Advisor shall keep me fully informed of progress on all aspects of the implementation of the recommendations of the President's Special Review Board.

National Security Decision Directive 276

THE WHITE HOUSE
WASHINGTON
June 9, 1987

National Security Council Interagency Process

Introduction

In National Security Decision Directive (NSDD) 266, I directed that the recommendations of the President's Special Review Board, including the model for the National Security Council (NSC) system, be implemented in full. To that end, I chartered a review of the structure of senior interagency groups and regional and functional interagency groups established pursuant to, or under the authority of, presidential Directives or applicable memoranda. This review was designed to identify such changes in the interagency process as might be necessary or desirable to realize fully and promptly in practice the Special Review Board's recommendations, including the specific recommendation that the Assistant to the President for National Security Affairs (the "National Security Advisor") chair the senior committees of the NSC. The present Directive reflects changes in the interagency process I have authorized as a result of that review.

Interagency Groups

Interagency groups can provide an effective medium for the development of advice and policy for consideration by the President. They achieve their goal when they provide thorough and clear analyses of all policy choices, coordinate policy implementation, and review policy in light of experience.

NSDD 2, dated January 12, 1982, established the senior interagency structure. It created three functional senior interagency groups (SIGs)—one on foreign policy, chaired by the Secretary of State; one on defense policy, chaired by the Secretary of Defense; and one on intelligence policy, chaired by the Director of Central Intelligence. Subsequent Directives and memoranda established some 22 additional SIGs and 55 interagency groups (IGs), including certain groups chaired by the National Security Advisor or members of the NSC staff. IGs in turn typically have established working groups and task forces to assist in, and support, their work.

After five years' experience, a review of the interagency process was due, even without the impetus of the Special Review Board's report. This review revealed that many interagency groups, although formally established, have not met or ceased to meet when the circumstances that brought them into being changes; and that new interagency groups have come into being to deal with contingencies as they have arisen. As the Special Review Board noted, these groups have not, in every case, served the goal of effective policy deliberation.

To improve the interagency process at large, and to implement the Special Review Board's recommendations, I therefore am directing or authorizing the following:

1. *National Security Council.* As specified in NSDD 266, the NSC shall be the principal forum for consideration of national security issues requiring presidential decision. The functions of, and participant in, the NSC shall be as set forth in the National Security Act of 1947, as amended, and NSDD 266. The NSC shall meet at the direction of the President.

2. *National Security Planning Group.* The National Security Planning Group (NSPG) shall be a committee of the NSC. The President, the Vice President, the Secretary of State, the Secretary of Defense, the Attorney General, the Secretary of the Treasury, the National Security Advisor, the Chief of Staff to the President, the Director of Central Intelligence, the Chairman of the Joint Chiefs of Staff, and the Director of the Office of Management and Budget shall attend NSPG meetings. The NSPG shall meet, as circumstances warrant, to monitor and review the development and implementation of national security policy on behalf of the NSC. The responsibilities of the NSPG with regard to covert action shall be as provided in a separate presidential Directive revising NSDD 159.

The National Security Advisor or the Deputy Assistant to the President for National Security Affairs (the "Deputy National Security Advisor") shall be responsible for the attendance, agenda, and conduct of such meetings at my direction. The Directors of the United States Information Agency and the United States Arms Control and Disarmament Agency, the heads of other Executive departments and agencies, and other advisors to the President shall be invited by the National Security Advisor, acting at my direction, to attend NSPG meetings as matters on the agenda of such meetings shall dictate.

3. *Senior Review Group.* A Senior Review Group (SRG) shall be the Cabinet level interagency group for the consideration of national security issues. The SRG shall be comprised of the National

Security Advisor, the Secretary of State, the Secretary of Defense, the Chief of Staff to the President, the Director of Central Intelligence, and the Chairman of the Joint Chiefs of Staff. The National Security Advisor shall invite the attendance of heads of such other Executive departments or agencies, and of such senior officials within the Executive Office of the President, as matters on the agenda of SRG meetings shall dictate. The National Security Advisor shall chair the SRG, which shall meet at his request or the request of its standing members, to review, coordinate, and monitor the implementation of national security policy on behalf of the NSC.

4. *The Policy Review Group.* The Policy Review Group (PRG) shall be the senior sub-Cabinet level interagency group. The PRG shall be comprised of the Deputy National Security Advisor, a representative of the Office of the Vice President, and an Under or Assistant Secretary or other senior official of equivalent rank of the Department of State, the Department of Defense, the Central Intelligence Agency, the Organization of the Joint Chiefs of Staff, the Office of Management and Budget, and, as matters on the agenda of the PRG dictate, of the Executive Office of the President and other interested Executive departments and agencies. The Deputy National Security Advisor shall chair the PRG, which shall meet regularly at his request or the request of its standing members, The PRG's primary responsibility shall be to review and make recommendations concerning national security policy developed through the day-to-day functioning of the interagency process, including such senior interagency groups and regional and functional interagency groups as may hereafter be formed or authorized to continue in existence as provide in paragraph 5 hereof. The PRG shall assume the functions described in NSDD 30 and previously exercised by the Crisis Pre-Planning Group and those described in NSDD 207 and previously exercised by the Terrorist Incident Working Group. The Planning and Coordination Group (PCG), as provided in a separate presidential Directive revising NSDD 159, shall continue to be the senior sub-Cabinet level interagency group responsible for covert action.

Matters considered and recommendations for follow-on action made by the PRG shall be referred to responsible Executive departments and agencies. Recommendations made by the PRG shall be submitted for consideration by the SRG, NSPG, or NSC, as appropriate.

5. *Other Interagency Groups.* Within their respective areas of authority as set forth in NSDD 266, the Secretary of State, the Secretary of Defense, the Director of Central Intelligence, the Director of the United States Arms Control and Disarmament Agency, and the Director of the United States Information Agency may approve the continuation of existing senior interagency groups and regional or functional interagency groups to the extent necessary or desirable to promote an effective NSC process; by June 30, 1987, the National Security Advisor shall be notified of those interagency groups they have determined shall continue to function.

The National Security Advisor is authorized to approve or direct the formal establishment of additional senior interagency groups to the extent required for an effective NSC process, and to approve the continuation of such existing senior interagency groups as may be chaired by members of the NSC staff.

NSDD 2 and other presidential Directives and applicable memoranda, to the extent inconsistent with this Directive or with NSDD 266, are rescinded.

National Security Directive-1 Press Release, April 17, 1989

National Security Council Organization

The President has issued National Security Directive 1 (NSD-1) establishing the organization of the National Security Council system for his Administration to assist him in carrying out his responsibilities in the area of national security.

— The National Security Council (NSC) shall be the principal forum for consideration of national security policy issues requiring presidential determination.

— The functions of the NSC shall be as set forth in the National Security Act of 1947, as amended, and by NSD-1.

— The NSC shall advise and assist the President in integrating all aspects of national security policy as it affects the United States— domestic, foreign, military, intelligence, and economic.

— Along with its subordinate bodies, the NSC will be the President's principal means for coordinating Executive departments and agencies in the development and implementation of national security policy.

— In addition to its statutory members and statutory advisors, the Chief of Staff to the President and the Assistant to the President for National Security Affairs shall attend NSC meetings.

— The Secretary of the Treasury normally will attend NSC meetings, except that on occasions when the subject matter so dictates, he will be asked not to attend.

— The Attorney General will be invited to attend meetings pertaining to his jurisdiction, including covert actions.

— Heads of other Executive departments and agencies, the special statutory advisors to the NSC, and other senior officials will be invited to attend meetings of the NSC where appropriate in light of the issues to be discussed.

The Assistant to the President for National Security Affairs shall be responsible, at the President's direction and in consultation with the Secretaries of State and Defense, for determining the agenda and ensuring that the necessary papers are prepared.

NSC Sub-Groups

Three NSC sub-groups are established by the Directive: The NSC Principals Committee (NSC/PC); The NSC Deputies Committee (NSC/DC); and, The NSC Policy Coordinating Committees (NSC/PCC's).

— The NSC/PC is the senior interagency forum for consideration of policy issues affecting national security.

It shall review, coordinate, and monitor the development and implementation of national security policy.

Members of the NSC/PC are the Secretaries of State and Defense, the Assistant to the President for National Security Affairs (Chairman), the Director of Central Intelligence, and the Chairman, Joint Chiefs of Staff, as well as the Chief of Staff to the President. Participation of the Secretary of the Treasury and the Attorney General will be governed by the guidelines outlined above. In consultation with the Secretaries of State and Defense, the NSC/PC Chairman may invite other participants as also outlined above to attend NSC/PC meetings as issues to be discussed dictate.

The NSC/PC Chairman is responsible, in consultation with the above Secretaries, for calling NSC/PC meetings, determining the agenda, and for ensuring that the necessary papers are prepared.

— The NSC/DC is the senior sub-Cabinet interagency forum for consideration of policy issues affecting national security. It shall review and monitor the work of the NSC interagency process (including the interagency groups outlined below) and make recommendations concerning the development and implementation of national security policy.

Members of the NSC/DC are the Deputy Assistant to the President for National Security Affairs (Chairman), the Under Secretary of Defense for Policy, the Under Secretary of State for Political Affairs, the Deputy Director of Central Intelligence, and the Vice Chairman, Joint Chiefs of Staff. At the direction of the Assistant to the President for National Security Affairs, and in consultation with the Secretaries of State and Defense, the NSC/DC may convene at the deputy secretary level for the Departments of State and Defense. The NSC/DC Chairman, in consultation with the representatives of the Departments of State and Defense, may invite other participants in accordance with the guidelines outlines under the NSC/PC. When meeting on covert actions, the attendees will include a representative of the Attorney General.

The NSC/DC Chairman is responsible, in consultation with the above named representatives, for calling NSC/DC meetings, for determining the agenda, and for ensuring the necessary papers are prepared.

The NSC/DC shall ensure that all papers to be discussed by the NSC or the NSC/PC fully analyze the issues, fairly and adequately set out the facts, consider a full range of views and options, and satisfactorily assess the prospects, risks, and implications of each. The NSC/DC may task the interagency groups (NSC/PCC's) described below.

— An NSC/PCC is established for each of the following: regional areas—Europe, the Soviet Union, Latin America, East Asia, Africa, and Near East/South Asia; functional areas—defense, international economics, intelligence, and arms control. Each NSC/PCC is the principal interagency forum for the development and implementation of national security policy for that regional or functional area. The NSC/PCC is responsible for identifying and developing policy issues for consideration by the NSC, including preparation of the necessary papers for NSC consideration.

Members of each NSC/PCC include a representative at the Assistant Secretary level from each of the Executive departments or agencies that have members on the NSC/DC. NSC/PCC's established pursuant to NSD-1 shall be chaired by a person of Assistant Secretary rank appointed as follows:

— each regional NSC/PCC, by the Secretary of State;
— defense NSC/PCC, by the Secretary of Defense;
— international economics NSC/PCC, by the Secretary of the Treasury;
— intelligence NSC/PCC, by the Director of Central Intelligence;
— arms control NSC/PCC, by the Assistant to the President for National Security Affairs.

Each NSC/PCC will have an NSC staff member appointed by the Assistant to the President for National Security Affairs who will serve as its Executive Secretary to assist the Chairman in scheduling NSC/PCC meetings, determining the agenda, preparing a brief statement of actions taken and tasks assigned, ensuring timely responses to decisions and taskings from more senior NSC interagency groups, and ensuring timely transmission of papers and recommendations for consideration by the NSC/DC, the NSC/PC, and the NSC. Each NSC/PCC Chairman, in consultation with the Executive Secretary, may invite others as provided for in the NSC section above.

The Assistant to the President for National Security Affairs, at my direction and in consultation with the Secretaries of State and Defense, may establish additional NSC/PCC's as appropriate.

Existing Presidential Guidance

NSD-1 shall take precedence over NSDD 266, NSDD 276, and all other existing presidential guidance on the organization of the National Security Council system. The Assistant to the President for National Security Affairs, in consultation with the Secretaries of State and Defense, shall review and revise such prior guidance as appropriate.

LIST OF ADDITIONAL POLICY COORDINATING COMMITTEES

The following Policy Coordinating Committees (PCCs) were approved by the President in NSD 10 and are in addition to those set forth in NSD 1.

— Counter-terrorism. Chairman: Ambassador-at-Large for Counter-terrorism, Department of State.

— Special Activities. Chairman: Senior Director for Intelligence Programs, National Security Council.

— Refugees. Chairman: Ambassador-at-Large and U.S. Coordinator for Refugee Affairs, Department of State.

— International Oceans, Environment, and Science Affairs. Chairman: Department of State.

— Resources for International Affairs Programs. Chairman: Department of State.

— Emergency Preparedness/Mobilization Planning. Chairman: Director, Federal Emergency Management Agency.

— Nonproliferation Policy. Chairman: Under Secretary of State for Security Assistance, Science and Technology, Department of State.

— Technology Transfer Policy. Chairman: Senior Director for International Economic Affairs, National Security Council.

— National Security Telecommunications. Chairman: Assistant Secretary of Defense for C3I, Department for C3I, Department of Defense.

Presidential Decision Directive 2

THE WHITE HOUSE
WASHINGTON

January 20, 1993

SUBJECT: Organization of the National Security Council

To assist me in carrying out my responsibilities in the area of national security, I hereby direct that the National Security Council system be organized as follows.

A. *The National Security Council (NSC)*

The National Security Council (NSC) shall be the principal forum for consideration of national security policy issues requiring responsibilities of the NSC shall be as set forth in the National Security Act of 1947, as amended, and this Presidential Decision Directive. The NSC shall advise and assist me in integrating all aspects of national security policy as it affects the United States—domestic, foreign, military, intelligence and economic (in conjunction with the National Economic Council). Along with its subordinate committees, the NSC shall be my principal means for coordinating Executive departments and agencies in the development and implementation of national security policy.

The NSC shall have as its members the President, Vice President, Secretary of State and Secretary of Defense, as prescribed by statute. The Director of Central Intelligence and the Chairman, Joint Chiefs of Staff, as statutory advisors to the NSC shall attend NSC meetings. In addition, the new membership of the NSC shall include the Secretary of the Treasury, the U.S. Representative to the United Nations, the Assistant to the President for National Security Affairs, the Assistant to the President for Economic Policy, and the Chief of Staff to the President. The Attorney General shall be invited to attend meetings pertaining to his jurisdiction, including covert actions. The heads of other Executive departments and agencies, the special statutory advisers to the NSC, and other senior officials shall be invited to attend meetings of the NSC where appropriate.

The NSC shall meet as required. The Assistant to the President for National Security Affairs, at my direction and in consultation with the Secretaries of State and Defense and, when appropriate, the Secretary of the Treasury and the Assistant to the President for Economic Policy, shall be responsible for determining the agenda and ensuring that the necessary papers are prepared. Other members of the NSC may propose items for inclusion on the agenda. The Assistant to the President shall be assisted by a National Security Council staff, as provided by law.

B. *The NSC Principals Committee (NSC/PC)*

An NSC Principals Committee (NSC/PC) is established as the senior interagency forum for consideration of policy issues affecting national security. The NSC/PC shall review, coordinate, and monitor the development and implementation of national security policy. The NSC/PC should be a flexible instrument—a forum available for Cabinet-level officials to meet to discuss and resolve issues not requiring the President's participation. The Assistant to the President for National Security Affairs shall serve as Chair. The Assistant to the President for Economic Policy shall be informed of meetings and be invited to attend all those with international economic considerations.

The NSC/PC shall have as its members the Secretary of State (if unavailable, the Deputy Secretary of State or the designee of the Secretary of State); the Secretary of Defense (if unavailable, the Deputy Secretary of Defense or the designee of the Secretary of Defense); the U.S. Representative to the United Nations; the Assistant to the President for National Security Affairs (Chair); the Director of Central Intelligence; the Chairman, Joint Chiefs of Staff; and the Assistant to the President for Economic Policy, as appropriate. The Secretary of the Treasury, the Attorney General or other heads of departments or agencies shall be invited as needed.

The Assistant to the President for National Security Affairs shall be responsible—in consultation with the Secretaries of State and Defense, and, when appropriate, the Assistant to the President for Economic Policy—for calling meetings of the NSC/PC, for determining the agenda, and for ensuring that the necessary papers are prepared.

C. *The NSC Deputies Committee (NSC/DC)*

An NSC Deputies Committee (NSC/DC) shall serve as the senior sub-Cabinet interagency forum for consideration of policy issues affecting national security. The NSC/DC shall review and monitor the work of the NSC interagency process (including Interagency Working Groups established pursuant to Section D below). The Deputies Committee also shall focus significant attention on policy implementation. Periodic reviews of the Administration's major foreign policy initiatives shall be scheduled to ensure that they are being implemented in a timely and effective manner. Also, these reviews should periodically consider whether existing policy directives should be revamped or rescinded.

The NSC/DC shall have as its members the Deputy Assistant to the President for National Security Affairs (who shall serve as the Chairman); the Under Secretary of Defense for Policy; the Under Secretary of State for Political Affairs; the Deputy Director of Central Intelligence; and the Vice Chairman, Joint Chiefs of Staff; the Assistant to the Vice President for National Security Affairs; and the Deputy Assistant to the President for Economic Policy, as needed. The Deputy Assistant to the President for National Security Affairs, in consultation with the representatives of the Departments of State and Defense, may invite representative of other Executive departments and agencies, and other senior officials, to attend meetings of the NSC/DC where appropriate in light of the issues to be discussed. When meeting on sensitive intelligence activities, including covert actions, the attendees shall include the appropriate senior representative of the Attorney General.

The Deputy Assistant to the President for National Security Affairs shall be responsible—in consultation with the representatives of the Departments of State and Defense, and the NEC, as appropriate—for calling meetings of the NSC/DC, for determining the agenda, and for ensuring that the necessary papers are prepared. The NSC/DC shall ensure that all papers to be discussed by the NSC or the NSC/PC fully analyze the issues, fairly and adequately set out the facts, consider a full range of views and options, and satisfactorily assess the prospects, risks, and implications of each. The NSC/DC may task the interagency groups established pursuant to Section D of this Presidential Decision Directive.

The NSC Deputies Committee shall also be responsible for day-to-day crisis management, reporting to the National Security Council. In this capacity, the group shall be designated the *Deputies Committee/CM* for Crisis Management. And NSC principal or deputy, as well as the Assistant to the President for National Security Affairs, may request a meeting of the Deputies Committee in its crisis management capacity. The Committee also shall focus on crisis prevention—including contingency planning for major areas of concern. While meeting as the Deputies Committee/CM, the group shall be assisted by a small support staff—to provide institutional memory, develop agendas and record decisions.

D. *Interagency Working Groups (NSC/IWGs)*

A system of Interagency Working Groups—some permanent, others *ad hoc*—is hereby authorized. The NSC/IWGs shall be established at the direction of the Deputies Committee, which shall also determine the chair of the NSC/IWG—either departmental or NSC or NEC. In general, foreign policy and defense issues should be chaired at the Assistant-Secretary level by the Departments of

State and Defense, respectively; international economic issues by the Department of the Treasury or the NEC, as appropriate; and intelligence, nonproliferation, arms control and crisis management by the NSC. The IWGs shall convene on a regular basis—to be determined by the Deputies Committee—to review and coordinate the implementation of Presidential decisions in their policy areas. Strict guidelines shall be established governing the operation of the Interagency Working Groups, including participants, decision-making path and time frame. The number of these working groups shall be kept to the minimum needed to promote an effective NSC system.

/s/ William J. Clinton

Appendix D

The National Security Act of 1947 — 26 July 1947

(Public Law 253 — 80th Congress)
(Chapter 343 — 1st Session)
(S. 758)

AN ACT

To promote the national security by providing for a Secretary of Defense; for a National Military Establishment; for a Department of the Army, a Department of the Navy, and a Department of the Air Force; and for the coordination of the activities of the National Military Establishment with other departments and agencies of the Government concerned with the national security.

BE IT ENACTED BY THE SENATE AND HOUSE OF REPRESENTATIVES OF THE UNITED STATES OF AMERICA IN CONGRESS ASSEMBLED,

Short Title

That this Act may be cited as the "National Security Act of 1947".

Table of Contents

Title II—The National Military Establishment

Title III—Miscellaneous

Declaration of Policy

Sec. 2. In enacting this legislation, it is the intent of Congress to provide a comprehensive program for the future security of the United States, to provide for the establishment of integrated policies and procedures for the departments, agencies, and functions of the Government relating to the national security; to provide three military departments for the operation and administration of the Army, the Navy (including naval aviation and the United States Marine Corps), and the Air Force, with their assigned combat and service components; to provide for their authoritative coordination and unified direction under civilian control but not to merge them; to provide for the effective strategic direction of the armed forces and for their operation under unified control and for their integration into an efficient team of land, naval, and air forces.

TITLE I—COORDINATION FOR NATIONAL SECURITY

National Security Council

Sec. 101. (a) There is hereby established a council to be known as the National Security Council (hereinafter in this section referred to as the "Council").

The President of the United States shall preside over meetings of the Council: Provided, That in his absence he may designate a member of the Council to preside in his place.

The function of the Council shall be to advise the President with respect to the integration of domestic, foreign, and military policies relating to the national security so as to enable the military services and the other departments and agencies of the Government to cooperate more effectively in matters involving the national security.

The Council shall be composed of the President; the Secretary of State, the Secretary of Defense, appointed under section 202; the Secretary of the Army, referred to in section 205; the Secretary of the Navy; the Secretary of the Air Force, appointed under section 207; the Chairman of the National Security Resources Board, appointed under section 103; and such of the following named officers as the President may designate from time to time: The Secretaries of the executive departments, the Chairman of the Munitions Board appointed under section 213, and the Chairman of the Research and Development Board appointed under section 214; but no such additional member shall be designated until the advice and consent of the Senate has been given to his appointment to the office the holding of which authorizes his designation as a member of the Council.

(b) In addition to performing such other functions as the President may direct, for the purpose of more effectively coordinating the policies and functions of the departments and agencies of the Government relating to the national security, it shall, subject to the direction of the President, be the duty of the Council—

(1) to assess and appraise the objectives, commitments, and risks of the United States in relation to our actual and potential military power, in the interest of national security; for the purpose of making recommendations to the President in connection therewith; and

(2) to consider policies on matters of common interest to the departments and agencies of the Government concerned with the national security, and to make recommendations to the President in connection therewith.

(c) The Council shall have a staff to be headed by a civilian executive secretary who shall be appointed by the President, and who shall receive compensation at the rate of $10,000 a year. The executive secretary, subject to the direction of the Council, is hereby authorized, subject to the civil service laws and the Classification Act of 1923, as amended, to appoint and fix the compensation of such personnel as may be necessary to perform such duties as may be prescribed by the Council in connection with the performance of its functions.

(d) The Council shall, from time to time, make such recommendations, and such other reports to the President as it deems appropriate or as the President may require.

Central Intelligence Agency

Sec. 102. (a) There is hereby established under the National Security Council a Central Intelligence Agency with a Director of Central Intelligence, who shall be the head thereof. The Director shall be appointed by the President, by and with the advice and consent of the Senate, from among the commissioned officers of the armed services or from among individuals in civilian life. The Director shall receive compensation at the rate of $14,000 a year.

(b) (1) If a commissioned officer of the armed services is appointed as Director then—

(A) in the performance of his duties as Director, he shall be subject to no supervision, control, restriction, or prohibition (military or otherwise) other than would be operative with respect to him if he were a civilian in no way connected with the Department of the Army, the Department of the Navy, the Department of the Air Force, or the armed services or any component thereof; and

(B) he shall not possess or exercise any supervision, control, powers, or functions (other than such as he possesses, or is authorized or directed to exercise, as Director) with respect to the armed services or any component thereof, the Department of the Army, the Department of the Navy, or the Department of the Air Force, or any branch, bureau, unit or division thereof, or with respect to any of the personnel (military or civilian) of any of the foregoing.

(2) Except as provided in paragraph (1), the appointment to the office of Director of a commissioned officer of the armed services, and his acceptance of and service in such office, shall in no way affect any status, office, rank, or grade he may occupy or hold in the armed services, or any emolument, perquisite, right, privilege, or benefit incident to or arising out of any such status, office, rank, or grade. Any such commissioned officer shall, while serving in the office of Director, receive the military pay and allowances (active or retired, as the case may be) payable to a commissioned officer of his grade and length of service and shall be paid, from any funds available to defray the expenses of the Agency, annual compensation at a rate equal to the amount by which $14,000 exceeds the amount of his annual military pay and allowances.

(c) Notwithstanding the provisions of section 6 of the Act of August 24, 1912 (37 Stat. 555), or the provisions of any other law, the Director of Central Intelligence may, in his discretion, terminate the employment of any officer or employee of the Agency whenever he shall deem such termination necessary or advisable in the interests of the United States, but such termination shall not affect the right of such officer or employee to seek or accept employment in any other department or agency of the Government if declared eligible for such employment by the United States Civil Service Commission.

(d) For the purpose of coordinating the intelligence activities of the several Government departments and agencies in the interest of national security, it shall be the duty of the Agency, under the direction of the National Security Council—

(1) to advise the National Security Council in matters concerning such intelligence activities of the Government departments and agencies as relate to national security;

(2) to make recommendations to the National Security Council for the coordination of such intelligence activities of the departments and agencies of the Government as relate to the national security;

(3) to correlate and evaluate intelligence relating to the national security, and provide for the appropriate dissemination of such intelligence within the Government using where appropriate existing agencies and facilities: PROVIDED, That the Agency shall have no police, subpena, law-enforcement powers, or internal-security functions: PROVIDED FURTHER, That the departments and other agencies of the Government shall continue to collect, evaluate, correlate, and disseminate departmental intelligence: AND PROVIDED FURTHER, That the Director of Central Intelligence shall be responsible for protecting intelligence sources and methods from unauthorized disclosure;

(4) to perform, for the benefit of the existing intelligence agencies, such additional services of common concern as the National Security Council determines can be more efficiently accomplished centrally;

(5) to perform such other functions and duties related to intelligence affecting the national security as the National Security Council may from time to time direct.

(e) To the extent recommended by the National Security Council and approved by the President, such intelligence of the departments and agencies of the Government, except as hereinafter provided, relating to the national security shall be open to the inspection of the Director of Central Intelligence, and such intelligence as relates to the national security and is possessed by such departments and other agencies of the Government, except as hereinafter provided, shall be made available to the Director of Central Intelligence for correlation, evaluation, and dissemination: PROVIDED HOWEVER, That upon the written request of the Director of Central Intelligence, the Director of the Federal Bureau of Investigation shall make available to the Director of Central Intelligence such information for correlation, evaluation, and dissemination as may be essential to the national security.

(f) Effective when the Director first appointed under subsection (a) has taken office—

(1) the National Intelligence Authority (11 Fed. Reg. 1337, 1339, February 5, 1946) shall cease to exist; and

(2) the personnel, property, and records of the Central Intelligence Group are transferred to the Central Intelligence Agency, and such Group shall cease to exist. Any unexpended balances of appropriations, allocations, or other funds available or authorized to be made available for such Group shall be available and shall be authorized to be made available in like manner for expenditure by the Agency.

National Security Resources Board

Sec. 103. (a) There is hereby established a National Security Resources Board (hereinafter in this section referred to as the "Board") to be composed of the Chairman of the Board and such heads or representatives of the various executive departments and independent agencies as may from time to time be designated by the President to be members of the Board. The Chairman of the Board shall be appointed from civilian life by the President, by and with the advice and consent of the Senate, and shall receive compensation at the rate of $14,000 a year.

(b) The Chairman of the Board, subject to the direction of the President, is authorized, subject to the civil-service laws and the Classification Act of 1923, as amended, to appoint and fix the compensation of such personnel as may be necessary to assist the Board in carrying out its functions.

(c) It shall be the function of the Board to advise the President concerning the coordination of military, industrial, and civilian mobilization, including—

(1) policies concerning industrial and civilian mobilization in order to assure the most effective mobilization and maximum utilization of the Nation's manpower in the event of war;

(2) programs for the effective use in time of war of the Nation's natural and industrial resources for military and civilian needs, for the maintenance and stabilization of the civilian economy in time of war, and for the adjustment of such economy to war needs and conditions;

(3) policies for unifying, in time of war, the activities of Federal agencies and departments engaged in or concerned with production, procurement, distribution, or transportation of military or civilian supplies, materials, and products;

(4) the relationship between potential supplies of, and potential requirements for, manpower, resources, and productive facilities in time of war;

(5) policies for establishing adequate reserves of strategic and critical material, and for the conservation of these reserves;

(6) the strategic relocation of industries, services, government, and economic activities, the continuous operation of which is essential to the Nation's security.

(d) In performing its functions, the Board shall utilize to the maximum extent the facilities and resources of the departments and agencies of the Government.

TITLE II—THE NATIONAL MILITARY ESTABLISHMENT

Establishment of the National Military Establishment

Sec. 201. (a) There is hereby established the National Military Establishment, and the Secretary of Defense shall be the head thereof.

(b) The National Military Establishment shall consist of the Department of the Army, the Department of the Navy, and the

Department of the Air Force, together with all other agencies created under title II of this Act.

Secretary of Defense

Sec. 202. (a) There shall be a Secretary of Defense, who shall be appointed from civilian life by the President, by and with the advice and consent of the Senate: PROVIDED, That a person who has within ten years been on active duty as a commissioned officer in a Regular component of the armed services shall not be eligible for appointment as Secretary of Defense. The Secretary of Defense shall be the principal assistant to the President in all matters relating to the national security. Under the direction of the President and subject to the provisions of this Act he shall perform the following duties:

(1) Establish general policies and programs for the National Military Establishment and for all of the departments and agencies therein;

(2) Exercise general direction, authority, and control over such departments and agencies;

(3) Take appropriate steps to eliminate unnecessary duplication or overlapping in the fields of procurement, supply, transportation, storage, health, and research;

(4) Supervise and coordinate the preparation of the budget estimates of the departments and agencies comprising the National Military Establishment; formulate and determine the budget estimates for submittal to the Bureau of the Budget; and supervise the budget programs of such departments and agencies under the applicable appropriation Act: PROVIDED, That nothing herein contained shall prevent the Secretary of the Army, the Secretary of the Navy, or the Secretary of the Air Force from presenting to the President or to the Director of the Budget, after first so informing the Secretary of Defense, any report or recommendation relating to his department which he may deem necessary: AND PROVIDED FURTHER, That the Department of the Army, the Department of the Navy, and the Department of the Air Force shall be administered as individual executive departments by their respective Secretaries and all powers and

duties relating to such departments not specifically conferred upon the Secretary of Defense by this Act shall be retained by each of their respective Secretaries.

(b) The Secretary of Defense shall submit annual written reports to the President and the Congress covering expenditures, work, and accomplishments of the National Military Establishment, together with such recommendations as he shall deem appropriate.

(c) The Secretary of Defense shall cause a seal of office to be made for the National Military Establishment, of such design as the President shall approve, and judicial notice shall be taken thereof.

Military Assistants to the Secretary

Sec. 203. Officers of the armed services may be detailed to duty as assistants and personal aides to the Secretary of Defense, but he shall not establish a military staff.

Civilian Personnel

Sec. 204. (a) The Secretary of Defense is authorized to appoint from civilian life not to exceed three special assistants to advise and assist him in the performance of his duties. Each such special assistant shall receive compensation at the rate of $10,000 a year.

(b) The Secretary of Defense is authorized, subject to the civil-service laws and the Classification Act of 1923, as amended, to appoint and fix the compensation of such other civilian personnel as may be necessary for the performance of the functions of the National Military Establishment other than those of the Departments of the Army, Navy, and Air Force.

Department of the Army

Sec. 205. (a) The Department of War shall hereafter be designated the Department of the Army, and the title of the Secretary of War shall be changed to Secretary of the Army. Changes shall be made in the titles of other officers and activities of the Department of the Army as the Secretary of the Army may determine.

(b) All laws, orders, regulations, and other actions relating to the Department of War or to any officer or activity whose title is changed under this section shall, insofar as they are not inconsistent with the provisions of this Act, be deemed to relate to the Department of the Army within the National Military Establishment or to such officer or activity designated by his or its new title.

(c) The term "Department of the Army" as used in this Act shall be construed to mean the Department of the Army at the seat of government and all field headquarters, forces, reserve components, installations, activities, and functions under the control or supervision of the Department of the Army.

(d) The Secretary of the Army shall cause a seal of office to be made for the Department of the Army, of such design as the President may approve, and judicial notice shall be taken thereof.

(e) In general the United States Army, within the Department of the Army, shall include land combat and service forces and such aviation and water transport as may be organic therein. It shall be organized, trained, and equipped primarily for prompt and sustained combat incident to operations on land. It shall be responsible for the preparation of land forces necessary for the effective prosecution of war except as otherwise assigned and, in accordance with integrated joint mobilization plans, for the expansion of peacetime components of the Army to meet the needs of war.

Department of the Navy

Sec. 206. (a) The term "Department of the Navy" as used in this Act shall be construed to mean the Department of the Navy at the seat of government; the headquarters, United States Marine Corps; the entire operating forces of the United States Navy, including naval aviation, and of the United States Marine Corps, including the reserve components of such forces; all field activities, headquarters, forces, bases, installations, activities, and functions under the control or supervision of the Department of the Navy; and the United States Coast Guard when operating as a part of the Navy pursuant to law.

(b) In general the United States Navy, within the Department of the Navy, shall include naval combat and services forces and such aviation as may be organic therein. It shall be organized, trained, and equipped primarily for prompt and sustained combat incident to operations at sea. It shall be responsible for the preparation of naval forces necessary for the effective prosecution of war except as otherwise assigned, and, in accordance with integrated joint mobilization plans, for the expansion of the peacetime components of the Navy to meet the needs of war.

All naval aviation shall be integrated with the naval service as part thereof within the Department of the Navy. Naval aviation shall consist of combat and service and training forces, and shall include land-based naval aviation, air transport essential for naval operations, all air weapons and air techniques involved in the operations and activities of the United States Navy, and the entire remainder of the aeronautical organization of the United States Navy, together with the personnel necessary therefor.

The Navy shall be generally responsible for naval reconnaissance, antisubmarine warfare, and protection of shipping.

The Navy shall develop aircraft, weapons, tactics, technique, organization and equipment of naval combat and service elements; matters of joint concern as to these functions shall be coordinated between the Army, the Air Force, and the Navy.

(c) The United States Marine Corps, within the Department of the Navy, shall include land combat and service forces and such aviation as may be organic therein. The Marine Corps shall be organized, trained, and equipped to provide fleet marine forces of combined arms, together with supporting air components, for service with the fleet in the seizure or defense of advanced naval bases and for the conduct of such land operations as may be essential to the prosecution of a naval campaign. It shall be the duty of the Marine Corps to develop, in coordination with the Army and the Air Force, those phases of amphibious operations which pertain to the tactics, technique, and equipment employed by landing forces. In addition, the Marine Corps shall provide detachments and organizations for service on armed vessels of the Navy, shall provide security detachments for the protection of naval property at naval stations and bases, and shall perform such other duties as the President may direct: PROVIDED, That such additional duties shall not detract from or interfere with the operations for which the Marine Corps is primarily organized. The Marine Corps shall be responsible, in accordance with integrated joint mobilization plans, for the expansion of peacetime components of the Marine Corps to meet the needs of war.

Department of the Air Force

Sec. 207. (a) Within the National Military Establishment there is hereby established an executive department to be known as the Department of the Air Force, and a Secretary of the Air Force, who shall be the head thereof. The Secretary of the Air Force shall be appointed from civilian life by the President, by and with the advice and consent of the Senate.

(b) Section 158 of the Revised Statutes is amended to include the Department of the Air Force and the provisions of so much of title IV of the Revised Statutes as now or hereafter amended as is not inconsistent with this Act shall be applicable to the Department of the Air Force.

(c) The term "Department of the Air Force" as used in this Act shall be construed to mean the Department of the Air Force at the seat of government and all field headquarters, forces, reserve components, installations, activities, and functions under the control or supervision of the Department of the Air Force.

(d) There shall be in the Department of the Air Force an Under Secretary of the Air Force and two Assistant Secretaries of the Air Force, who shall be appointed from civilian life by the President by and with the advice and consent of the Senate.

(e) The several officers of the Department of the Air Force shall perform such functions as the Secretary of the Air Force may prescribe.

(f) So much of the functions of the Secretary of the Army and of the Department of the Army, including those of any officer of such Department, as are assigned to or under the control of the Commanding General, Army Air Forces, or as are deemed by the Secretary of Defense to be necessary or desirable for the operations of the Department of the Air Force or the United States Air Force, shall be transferred to and vested in the Secretary of the Air Force and the Department of the Air Force: PROVIDED, That the National Guard Bureau shall, in addition to the functions and duties performed by it for the Department of the Army, be charged with similar functions and duties for the Department of the Air Force, and shall be the channel of communication between the Department of the Air Force and the several States on all matters pertaining to the Air National Guard: AND PROVIDED FURTHER, That, in order to permit an orderly transfer, the Secretary of Defense may, during the transfer period hereinafter prescribed, direct that the Department of the Army shall continue for appropriate periods to exercise any of such functions, insofar as they relate to the Department of the Air Force, or the United States Air Force or their property and personnel. Such of the property, personnel, and records of the Department of the Army used in the exercise of functions transferred under this subsection as the Secretary of Defense shall determine shall be transferred or assigned to the Department of the Air Force.

(g) The Secretary of the Air Force shall cause a seal of office to be made for the Department of the Air Force, of such device as the President shall approve, and judicial notice shall be taken thereof.

United States Air Force

Sec. 208. (a) The United States Air Force is hereby established under the Department of the Air Force. The Army Air Forces, the Air Corps, United States Army, and the General Headquarters Air Force (Air Force Combat Command), shall be transferred to the United States Air Force.

(b) There shall be a Chief of Staff, United States Air Force, who shall be appointed by the President, by and with the advice and consent of the Senate, for a term of four years from among the officers of general rank who are assigned to or commissioned in the United States Air Force. Under the direction of the Secretary of the Air Force, the Chief of Staff, United States Air Force, shall exercise command over the United States Air Force and shall be charged with the duty of carrying into execution all lawful orders and directions which may be transmitted to him. The functions of the Commanding General, General Headquarters Air Force (Air Force Combat

Command), and of the Chief of the Air Corps and of the Commanding General, Army Air Forces, shall be transferred to the Chief of Staff, United States Air Force. When such transfer becomes effective, the offices of the Chief of the Air Corps, United States Army, and Assistants to the Chief of the Air Corps, United States Army, provided for by the Act of June 4, 1920, as amended (41 Stat. 768), and Commanding General, General Headquarters Air Force, provided for by section 5 of the Act of June 16, 1936 (49 Stat. 1525), shall cease to exist. While holding office as Chief of Staff, United States Air Force, the incumbent shall hold a grade and receive allowances equivalent to those prescribed by law for the Chief of Staff, United States Army. The Chief of Staff, United States Army, the Chief of Naval Operations, and the Chief of Staff, United States Air Force, shall take rank among themselves according to their relative dates of appointment as such, and shall each take rank above all other officers on the active list of the Army, Navy, and Air Force: PROVIDED, That nothing in this Act shall have the effect of changing the relative rank of the present Chief of Staff, United States Army, and the present Chief of Naval Operations.

(c) All commissioned officers, warrant officers, and enlisted men, commissioned, holding warrants, or enlisted, in the Air Corps, United States Army, or the Army Air Forces, shall be transferred in branch to the United States Air Force. All other commissioned officers, warrant officers, and enlisted men, who are commissioned, hold warrants, or are enlisted, in any component of the Army of the United States and who are under the authority or command of the Commanding General, Army Air Forces, shall be continued under the authority or command of the Chief of Staff, United States Air Force, and under the jurisdiction of the Department of the Air Force. Personnel whose status is affected by this subsection shall retain their existing commissions, warrants, or enlisted status in existing components of the armed forces unless otherwise altered or terminated in accordance with existing law; and they shall not be deemed to have been appointed to a new or different office or grade, or to have vacated their permanent or temporary appointments in an existing component of the armed forces, solely by virtue of any change in status under this subsection. No such change in status shall alter or prejudice the status of any individual so assigned, so as to deprive him of any right, benefit, or privilege to which he may be entitled under existing law.

(d) Except as otherwise directed by the Secretary of the Air Force, all property, records, installations, agencies, activities, projects, and civilian personnel under the jurisdiction, control, authority, or command of the Commanding General, Army Air Forces, shall be continued to the same extent under the jurisdiction, control, authority, or command, respectively, of the Chief of Staff, United States Air Force, in the Department of the Air Force.

(e) For a period of two years from the date of enactment of this Act, personnel (both military and civilian), property, records, installations, agencies, activities, and projects may be transferred between the Department of the Army and the Department of the Air Force by direction of the Secretary of Defense.

(f) In general the United States Air Force shall include aviation forces both combat and service not otherwise assigned. It shall be organized, trained, and equipped primarily for prompt and sustained offensive and defensive air operations. The Air Force shall be responsible for the preparation of the air forces necessary for the effective prosecution of war except as otherwise assigned and, in accordance with integrated joint mobilization plans, for the expansion of the peacetime components of the Air Force to meet the needs of war.

Effective Date of Transfers

Sec. 209. Each transfer, assignment, or change in status under section 207 or section 208 shall take effect upon such date or dates as may be prescribed by the Secretary of Defense.

War Council

Sec. 210. There shall be within the National Military Establishment a War Council composed of the Secretary of Defense, as Chairman, who shall have power of decision; the Secretary of the Army; the Secretary of the Navy; the Secretary of the Air Force; the Chief of Staff, United States Army; the Chief of Naval Operations; and the Chief of Staff, United States Air Force. The War Council shall advise the Secretary of Defense on matters of broad policy relating to the armed forces, and shall consider and report on such other matters as the Secretary of Defense may direct.

Joint Chiefs of Staff

Sec. 211. (a) There is hereby established within the National Military Establishment the Joint Chiefs of Staff, which shall consist of the Chief of Staff, United States Army; the Chief of Naval Operations; the Chief of Staff, United States Air Force; and the Chief of Staff to the Commander in Chief, if there be one.

(b) Subject to the authority and direction of the President and the Secretary of Defense, it shall be the duty of the Joint Chiefs of Staff—

(1) to prepare strategic plans and to provide for the strategic direction of the military forces;

(2) to prepare joint logistic plans and to assign to the military services logistic responsibilities in accordance with such plans;

(3) to establish unified commands in strategic areas when such unified commands are in the interest of national security;

(4) to formulate policies for joint training of the military forces;

(5) to formulate policies for coordinating the education of members of the military forces;

(6) to review major material and personnel requirements of the military forces, in accordance with strategic and logistic plans; and

(7) to provide United States representation on the Military Staff Committee of the United Nations in accordance with the provisions of the Charter of the United Nations.

(c) The Joint Chiefs of Staff shall act as the principal military advisers to the President and the Secretary of Defense and shall perform such other duties as the President and the Secretary of Defense may direct or as may be prescribed by law.

Joint Staff

Sec. 212. There shall be, under the Joint Chiefs of Staff, a Joint Staff to consist of not to exceed one hundred officers and to be composed of approximately equal numbers of officers from each of the three armed services. The Joint Staff, operating under a Director thereof appointed by the Joint Chiefs of Staff, shall perform such duties as may be directed by the Joint Chiefs of Staff. The Director shall be an officer junior in grade to all members of the Joint Chiefs of Staff.

Munitions Board

Sec. 213. (a) There is hereby established in the National Military Establishment a Munitions Board (hereinafter in this section referred to as the "Board").

(b) The Board shall be composed of a Chairman, who shall be the head thereof, and an Under Secretary or Assistant Secretary from each of the three military departments, to be designated in each case by the Secretaries of their respective departments. The Chairman shall be appointed from civilian life by the President, by and with the advice and consent of the Senate, and shall receive compensation at the rate of $14,000 a year.

(c) It shall be the duty of the Board under the direction of the Secretary of Defense and in support of strategic and logistic plans prepared by the Joint Chiefs of Staff—

(1) to coordinate the appropriate activities within the National Military Establishment with regard to industrial matters, including the procurement, production, and distribution plans of the departments and agencies comprising the Establishment;

(2) to plan for the military aspects of industrial mobilization;

(3) to recommend assignment of procurement responsibilities among the several military services and to plan for standardization of specifications and for the greatest practicable allocation of purchase authority of technical equipment and common use items on the basis of single procurement;

(4) to prepare estimates of potential production, procurement, and personnel for use in evaluation of the logistic feasibility of strategic operations;

(5) to determine relative priorities of the various segments of the military procurement programs;

(6) to supervise such subordinate agencies as are or may be created to consider the subjects falling within the scope of the Board's responsibilities;

(7) to make recommendations to regroup, combine, or dissolve existing interservice agencies operating in the fields of procurement, production, and distribution in such manner as to promote efficiency and economy;

(8) to maintain liaison with other departments and agencies for the proper correlation of military requirements with the civilian economy, particularly in regard to the procurement or disposition of strategic and critical material and the maintenance of adequate reserves of such material, and to make recommendations as to policies in connection therewith;

(9) to assemble and review material and personnel requirements presented by the Joint Chiefs of Staff and those presented by the production, procurement, and distribution agencies assigned to meet military needs, and to make recommendations thereon to the Secretary of Defense; and

(10) to perform such other duties as the Secretary of Defense may direct.

(d) When the Chairman of the Board first appointed has taken office, the Joint Army and Navy Munitions Board shall cease to exist and all its records and personnel shall be transferred to the Munitions Board.

(e) The Secretary of Defense shall provide the Board with such personnel and facilities as the Secretary may determine to be required by the Board for the performance of its functions.

Research and Development Board

Sec. 214. (a) There is hereby established in the National Military Establishment a Research and Development Board (hereafter in this section referred to as the "Board"). The Board shall be composed of a Chairman, who shall be the head thereof, and two representatives from each of the Departments of the Army, Navy, and Air Force, to be designated by the Secretaries of their respective Departments. The Chairman shall be appointed from civilian life by the President, by and with the advice and consent of the Senate, and shall receive compensation at the rate of $14,000 a year. The purpose of the Board shall be to advise the Secretary of Defense as to the status of scientific research relative to the national security, and to assist him in assuring adequate provision for research and development on scientific problems relating to the national security.

(b) It shall be the duty of the Board, under the direction of the Secretary of Defense—

(1) to prepare a complete and integrated program of research and development for military purposes;

(2) to advise with regard to trends in scientific research relating to national security and the measures necessary to assure continued and increasing progress;

(3) to recommend measures of coordination of research and development among the military departments, and allocation among them of responsibilities for specific programs of joint interest;

(4) to formulate policy for the National Military Establishment in connection with research and development matters involving agencies outside the National Military Establishment;

(5) to consider the interaction of research and development and strategy, and to advise the Joint Chiefs of Staff in connection therewith; and

(6) to perform such other duties as the Secretary of Defense may direct.

(c) When the Chairman of the Board first appointed has taken office, the Joint Research and Development Board shall cease to exist and all its records and personnel shall be transferred to the Research and Development Board.

(d) The Secretary of Defense shall provide the Board with such personnel and facilities as the Secretary may determine to be required by the Board for the performance of its functions.

TITLE III—MISCELLANEOUS

Compensation of Secretaries

Sec. 301. (a) The Secretary of Defense shall receive the compensation prescribed by law for heads of executive departments.

(b) The Secretary of the Army, the Secretary of the Navy, and the Secretary of the Air Force shall each receive the compensation prescribed by law for heads of executive departments.

Under Secretaries and Assistant Secretaries

Sec. 302. The Under Secretaries and Assistant Secretaries of the Army, the Navy, and the Air Force shall each receive compensation at the rate of $10,000 a year and shall perform such duties as the Secretaries of their respective departments may prescribe.

Advisory Committees and Personnel

Sec. 303. (a) The Secretary of Defense, the Chairman of the National Security Resources Board, and the Director of Central Intelligence are authorized to appoint such advisory committees and to employ, consistent with other provisions of this Act, such part-time advisory personnel as they may deem necessary in carrying out their respective functions and the functions of agencies under their control. Persons holding other offices or positions under the United States for which they receive compensation while serving as members of such committees shall receive no additional compensation for such service. Other members of such committees and other part-time advisory personnel so employed may serve without compensation or may receive compensation at a rate not to exceed $35 for each day of service, as determined by the appointing authority.

(b) Service of an individual as a member of any such advisory committee, or in any other part-time capacity for a department or agency hereunder, shall not be considered as service bringing such individual within the provisions of section 109 or 113 of the Criminal Code (U.S.C., 1940 edition, title 18, secs. 198 and 203), or section 19 (e) of the Contract Settlement Act of 1944, unless the act of such individual, which by such section is made unlawful when performed by an individual referred to in such section, is with respect to any particular matter which directly involves a department or agency which such person is advising or in which such department or agency is directly interested.

Status of Transferred Civilian Personnel

Sec. 304. All transfers of civilian personnel under this Act shall be without change in classification or compensation, but the head of any department or agency to which such a transfer is made is authorized to make such changes in the titles and designations and prescribe such changes in the duties of such personnel commensurate with their classification as he may deem necessary and appropriate.

Saving Provisions

Sec. 305. (a) All laws, orders, regulations, and other actions applicable with respect to any function, activity, personnel, property, records, or other thing transferred under this Act, or with respect to any officer, department, or agency, from which such transfer is made, shall, except to the extent rescinded, modified, superseded, terminated, or made inapplicable by or under authority of law, have the same effect as if such transfer had not been made; but, after any such transfer, any such law, order, regulation, or other action which vested functions in or otherwise related to any officer, department, or agency from which such transfer was made shall, insofar as applicable with respect to the function, activity, personnel, property, records or other thing transferred and to the extent not inconsistent with other provisions of this Act, be deemed to have vested such function in or relate to the officer, department, or agency to which the transfer was made.

(b) No suit, action, or other proceeding lawfully commenced by or against the head of any department or agency or other officer of the United States, in his official capacity or in relation to the discharge of his official duties, shall abate by reason of the taking effect of any transfer or change in title under the provisions of this Act; and, in the case of any such transfer, such suit, action, or other proceeding may be maintained by or against the successor of such head or other officer under the transfer, but only if the court shall allow the same to be maintained on motion or supplemental petition filed within twelve months after such transfer takes effect, showing a necessity for the survival of such suit, action, or other proceeding to obtain settlement of the questions involved.

(c) Notwithstanding the provisions of the second paragraph of section 5 of title I of the First War Powers Act, 1941, the existing organization of the War Department under the provisions of Executive Order Numbered 9082 of February 28, 1942, as modified by Executive Order Numbered 9722 of May 13, 1946, and the existing organization of the Department of the Navy under the provisions of Executive Order Numbered 9635 of September 29, 1945, including the assignment of functions to organizational units within the War and Navy Departments, may, to the extent determined by the Secretary of Defense, continue in force for two years following the date of enactment of this Act except to the extent modified by the provisions of this Act or under the authority of law.

Transfer of Funds

Sec. 306. All unexpended balances of appropriations, allocations, nonappropriated funds, or other funds available or hereafter made available for use by or on behalf of the Army Air Forces or officers thereof, shall be transferred to the Department of the Air Force for use in connection with the exercise of its functions. Such other unexpended balances of appropriations, allocations, nonappropriated funds, or other funds available or hereafter made available for use by the Department of War or the Department of the Army in exercise of functions transferred to the Department of the Air Force under this Act, as the Secretary of Defense shall determine, shall be transferred to the Department of the Air Force for use in connection with the exercise of its functions. Unexpended balances transferred under this section may be used for the purposes for which the appropriations, allocations, or other funds were originally made available, or for new expenditures occasioned by the enactment of this Act. The transfers herein authorized may, be made with or without warrant action as may be appropriate from time to time from any appropriation covered by this section to any other such appropriation or to such new accounts established on the books of the Treasury as may be determined to be necessary to carry into effect provisions of this Act.

Authorization for Appropriations

Sec. 307. There are hereby authorized to be appropriated such sums as may be necessary and appropriate to carry out the provisions and purpose of this Act.

Definitions

Sec. 308. (a) As used in this Act, the term "function" includes functions, powers, and duties.

(b) As used in this Act, the term "budget program" refers to recommendations as to the apportionment, to the allocation and to the review of allotments of appropriated funds.

Separability

Sec. 309. If any provision of this Act or the application thereof to any person or circumstances is held invalid, the validity of the remainder of the Act and of the application of such provision to other persons and circumstances shall not be affected thereby.

Effective Date

Sec. 310. (a) The first sentence of section 202 (a) and sections 1, 2, 307, 308, 309, and 310 shall take effect immediately upon the enactment of this Act.

(b) Except as provided in subsection (a), the provisions of this Act shall take effect on whichever of the following days is the earlier: The day after the day upon which the Secretary of Defense first appointed takes office, or the sixtieth day after the date of the enactment of this Act.

Succession to the Presidency

Sec. 311. Paragraph (1) of subsection (d) of section 1 of the Act entitled "An Act to provide for the performance of the duties of the office of President in case of the removal, resignation, death, or inability both of the President and Vice President", approved July 18, 1947, is amended by striking out "Secretary of War" and inserting in lieu thereof "Secretary of Defense", and by striking out "Secretary of the Navy,".

Approved July 26, 1947.

Index

functions, 45; supporting staff
for, 168
Joint Requirements Oversight
Council (JROC), 53
Judis, John B., 103
Kagan, Robert, 128–129
Kaplan, Robert, 111–112, 115
Kennedy, John F., 149, 176
Kennedy, Paul, 92, 106, 115
King, Ernest J., 45, 168
Kissinger, Henry: on new and old
world orders, 18, 19, 27, 84–
85, 94–95, 152–153
Korean War, 45
Krauthammer, Charles, 95
Kristol, William, 128–129
Lake, Anthony, 108–109
Laqueur, Walter, 113
Law, international: as source of
individual rights, 14–15
League of Nations, 38
Leahy, William D., 45, 168
Legislative branch: struggle for
control with executive branch,
85–86
Lincoln, Abraham, 45
Lind, Michael, 103
Luttwak, Edward, 101–102
Madison, James, 2–3, 44
Manpower Act (1946), 173
Marshall, George C., 45, 168, 174
Marshall Plan, 45
Mathews, Jessica T., 105, 122, 126–
128, 134–135
Maynes, Charles William, 130
Military forces: interest-based view of
maintaining U.S., 22–23, 85;
issues-based view related to
U.S., 23; pre–World War I U.S.,
34; requirements in post–Cold
War era, 49; Weinberger-Powell
doctrine of overwhelming, 22
Military power: effect of information
revolution on use of, 120; role

in United States after World
War II, 40; U.S. post–World
War II, 39–40
Military power, U.S.: with other
forms of power, 40–41
Missiles (*see also* Nuclear weapons;
Weapons of mass destruction
[WMD]): ballistic, 110; cruise-
missile technology, 110
National Defense University (NDU):
INSS report on information
revolution (1996), 119, 125;
Institute for National Strategic
Studies (INSS), 108
National Intelligence Council (NIC),
184
Nationalism: economic, 103–105; as
fragmenting force, 104
National Security Act (1947):
amendments (1949), 147, 160,
169; amendments alter security
structure under, 43–44; creation
of Central Intelligence Agency
under, 43, 87, 181; Department
of Defense created under, 87,
157, 160–161; full text, 228–
252; JCS established under, 43,
169; National Military Establishment under, 159–160; NSC
created under, 43; origins and
radical character of, 86–87;
president's power under, 87;
security establishment organization under, 43; structure created
by, 159–160; study related to
revision of, 1–2
National security adviser, 46
National Security Council (NSC):
Ad Hoc Groups, 197, 193–194;
under Bush administration,
155–156; under Carter
administration, 152–153;
under Clinton administration,
156–157; creation under

About the Author and Contributors

Stephen A. Cambone is the director of research at the Institute for National Strategic Studies, National Defense University, in Washington, D.C. While in the Office of the Secretary of Defense as director of the strategic defense policy office, he contributed to the decision to refocus the Strategic Defense Initiative program. He spent from 1993 to 1998 at CSIS as a senior fellow and, most recently, has served as staff director of the congressionally mandated Commission to Assess the Ballistic Missile Threat to the United States.

Patrick J. Garrity is a senior policy analyst with the Los Alamos National Laboratory (based in Washington, D.C.). He has also taught at Catholic University of America and at the Naval Postgraduate School and has been a visiting fellow at the Foreign Policy Institute of the Johns Hopkins University School of Advanced International Studies. He recently coauthored *A Sacred Union of Citizens: George Washington's Farewell Address and the American Character* (1996).

Alistair J. K. Shepherd holds an M.A. degree in strategic studies from the University of Aberdeen (Scotland), where he is currently pursuing a Ph.D. degree. In addition to his work on security and defense issues in the CSIS Political-Military Studies program, he has been on the staff of Petrodata Ltd., where he specialized in energy forecasting and reporting.